Motorcycle Art

OTTO GRIZZI

MV AGUSTA F4

THE WORLD'S MOST BEAUTIFUL BIKE

- technology
- passion
- art
- speed

GIORGIO NADA EDITORE

As ever, and again,
for Rosa, my daughter

Graphic design: Yoshihito Furuya
Layout: Sansai Zappini
Editing: Francesco Milo
Picture research: Otto Grizzi and Cristina Reggioli
English translations: Neil Davenport
Editorial coordination: Davide Mazzanti

Particular thanks are due to the President and the Curator of the Agusta Foundation-Museum,
Gianluigi Marasi and Enrico Sironi, and to the Gruppo Lavoratori Agusta Seniores
(the Agusta Senior Workers Group).
The Publisher thanks the Instituto Ayrton Senna.

Distribution: Giunti Editore Spa, via Bolognese 165 I – 50139 Firenze   www.giunti.it

Printed by Giunti Industrie Grafiche S.p.A. – Stabilimento di Prato

MV AGUSTA F4 The world's most beautiful bike
Isbn 978-88-7911-512-4

Claudio Castiglioni

"THERE ARE PLENTY OF BEAUTIFUL BIKES, LOADS OF THEM.

MV AGUSTA IS SOMETHING ELSE..."

DREAM AND ENTERPRISE

Just as we were about to got to print with this book, Claudio Castiglioni passed away.

The man who in almost 35 years of impassioned entrepreneurial adventure succeeded

in realising the most beautiful "two-wheeled dreams" for himself and for bikers

all over the world.

The man who, during the course of 13 thrilling seasons, fearlessly challenged the four

Japanese majors in the blue ribbon Grand Prix class, succeeding in defeating them

on the track and just missing out on the world title.

Giacomo Agostini has revealed that only a couple of months ago he had spoken with him

about the reborn MV Agusta's possible return to racing: "To do something truly great."

Massimo Tamburini has confessed: "Now that he's gone, it's like a piece of me is missing."

I can still hear that voice on the telephone:

"As soon as I can we'll meet up to talk about our beloved MV Agusta."

Ciao Claudio, may the earth rest lightly.

(o.g.)

FOREWORD
by Giovanni Castiglioni

There are things in this world that have defined an era. Others continue to do so and one of these is the MV Agusta F4, unique and eternal, a two-wheeled symbol.

Before I even saw the F4 I actually rode it. It was back in 1995 and I was a boy of 15. One Sunday my father brought home a very special bike... It was a Cagiva GP 500, the bike raced by Kocinski, but it had been fitted with lights and had a sound very different to the GP two-strokes of the time.

Enthusiastic, I asked my father what it was and he replied: "This will be the new MV Agusta F4, with our new 750 cc four-cylinder engine." And he added, "It's going to be world's most beautiful bike, let's go and try it!"

At 15 years of age, I rode that prototype for 30 kilometres on the autostrada. The sensations? Unique. Thanks to the thrill of riding a "grown-up's" bike and because I was aboard what over the next two years was to become a "grown-up" bike.

One morning, 24 months later, my father told me we would be going to CRC, our research centre at San Marino where some of the world's most famous motorbikes were born. During the trip he added:
"Today you'll see the first MV Agusta F4, the real one!"

As soon as we entered CRC he told me to close my eyes: when I opened them I saw what was to become every biker's dream. It was there, alongside my father's Ferrari F40, the car that inspired details such as the famous organ pipe exhausts. Beautiful, futuristic, unlike any other bike I had ever seen. Shortly afterwards the bike was presented to the world's press and became an icon.

Over the course of the years the F4 has evolved, redefining with each new version perfection on two wheels. The new F4 was introduced in 2010, the result of an arduous challenge: creating an all-new bike, one that would be better in every respect but which would without doubt and without compromise be an F4. We succeeded, giving rise to the greatest road bike of all time.

What do I see in few years time? Another F4, better still, more beautiful and faster. But still an F4. Because our bikes last over time.

I would like to thank my father, who passed away as we were finishing this book, for his courage, his intuition and his astuteness in having created these works of art.

SUMMARY

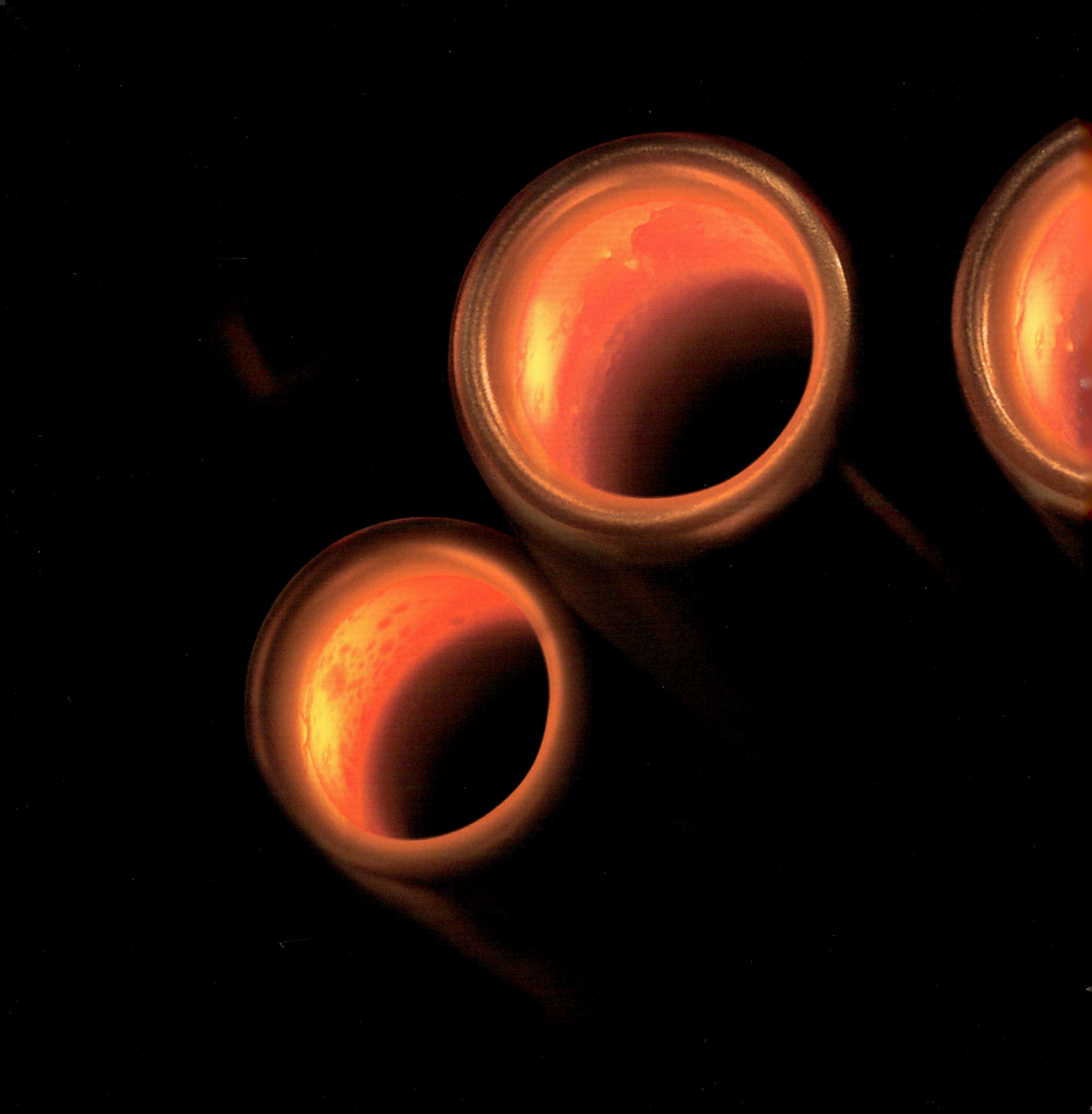

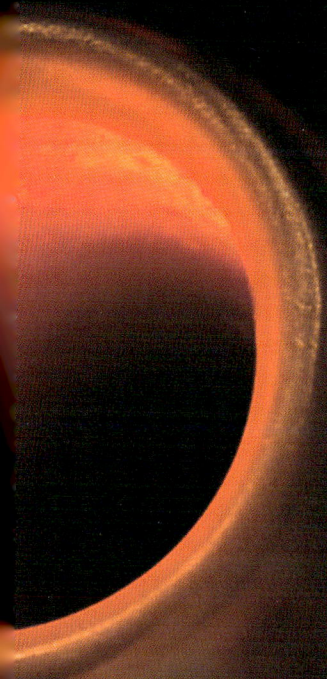

I

THE FLIGHT OF THE GLIDER
THE ROAR OF THE ENGINES

A long story (1907-1977) in short

38 world riders' titles, 37 world constructors' titles, 270 Grands Prix, 28 Italian Seniors' titles, 34 Tourist Trophy wins, 3,028 victories in total: such is the remarkable roll of honour of MV Agusta, the motorcycling marque that for over 30 years (1946-1977) dominated the sector. A legendary name, a global symbol of Italian ingenuity that, as if in a modern-day myth, rose from the ashes in 1997 to reclaim its rightful glory.

The great adventure of the Agusta family, Sicilians from Palermo for generations, began back in 1907, the year in which the 28-year-old Giovanni decided to leave his hardly unglamorous position as a representative for a Belgian diamond firm in Antwerp and follow his overwhelming passion for aviation, the epochal novelty that had heralded the 20th century and of which he was soon to become one of the Italian pioneers. It was perhaps no coincidence that this upheaval coincided with the birth on the 28th of February of Domenico the first of four sons borne by his wife Giuseppina and later followed by Vincenzo, Mario and Corrado. What sparked Giovanni Agusta's fatal attraction for "flying machines" (the enthralling "aeroplanes" that were to be the focus of a highly original and decidedly futuristic sporting and entrepreneurial career) was the enthusiasm aroused throughout the world by the brief flight achieved by the brothers Orville and Wilbur Wright on the beach of the American town of Kitty Hawk (1903), the subsequent experiments of Louis Blériot culminating in the first cross-channel flight (1909) and the glorious insanity of the Franco-Peruvian Geo Chavez's flight over the Alps (1910). It was in 1907 that our young hero decided to build his own aeroplane, designing and constructing an unpowered biplane, a glider in short, that triumphantly took to the air on Valentine's Day three years later: the novice aeronautical constructor's future had been plotted.

"NOTHING'S BORN OUT OF DIAMONDS…"

MV and Carlo Ubbiali, the symbolic pairing of the Varese firm's early years. The photo was taken on the 19th of May 1957: in pouring rain, the 28-year-old four-time World Champion (three titles with MV), speeds around the Hockenheim circuit during the German GP. With his 125 twin-cam, he was to win the race in a sprint finish (a classic tactic by the Bergamo-born "fox"), ahead of Tarquinio Provini on a Mondial.

The Società Anonima Meccanica Verghera, founded in February 1945 by Domenico Agusta at Cascina Costa, was on its way to becoming the world's most famous motorcycling marque. Its success was largely based on the experience in working with light alloys and other aviation materials gained between the two wars by Costruzioni Aeronautiche Giovanni Agusta, the company founded by Domenico's father and where he had worked as director from 1927.

In 1911, he enrolled as a volunteer for the war in Libya, attracted not so much by the late-imperialist rhetoric regarding the conquest of the "third shore" but rather by the opportunity of "making his bones" as an engineer, working for two years in the Gulf of Sidra on the first bombers of the nascent Italian air force. The original nucleus of the new military force with an airfield and flying school was taking shape on the moors of Malpensa on the borders of the provinces of Varese, Novara and Milan. It was there that Giovanni Agusta was to work through to the outbreak of the First World War, in the Officine Caproni workshops recently founded by another aviation pioneer, Gianni Caproni of Trento. It was also there that the Sicilian spent the war years as a technical inspector for the still thinly spread combat squadrons. And it was still there that, immediately after the war, he decided to settle, close to a farmhouse on a ridge or *costa*, hence the name Cascina Costa. Who would ever have said that in the three decades following the Second World War that minuscule toponym was destined to become the legendary centre of the world of racing motorcycles.

Having returned to work for Caproni, Agusta remained until 1921, accumulating invaluable experience in the aeronautical field that, two years later, was to encourage him to strike out on his own and found Costruzioni Aeronautiche Giovanni Agusta, with workshops at Cascina Costa. Initially lacking the resources to construct its own aircraft, the company specialised in the refurbishment, maintenance and repair of the aircraft of the newly reformed Italian air force, before building its first two aeroplanes in 1926-1927. Towards the end of 1927, Giovanni died and his energetic wife Giuseppina took over the running of the company with her eldest son Domenico acting as factory manager. Business boomed, the number of employees increased and new factories were built at Samarate and Verghera, both in the province of Varese, while the Agusta family received the noble title of count, not through any ancient lineage but by Mussolinian decree. The terrible Second World War then arrived with its endless tragedies, but also its lucrative military commissions.

Top left, Giovanni Agusta, the businessman of Sicilian origins who in 1907 became one of the founding fathers of Italian aviation.

Top right, a drawing of the famous biplane glider, Agusta's first creation: on the 14th of February 1910 it successfully flew from Capua's Piazza d'Armi, towed into the air by a car. Its development proceeded through to 1911: the last version featured a tube-like container housing a "safety device", a large parachute designed to save the aircraft itself and also the fruit of a design by the Palermo-born aviator.

Bottom, the AG2, the light sports aircraft equipped with a 12 hp engine built by Agusta in 1926; the photo was taken on the Cascina Costa airfield, the site that was eventually to become known among aviation insiders as "the cradle of rotating wing flight."

Towards the end of the war, allied bombing meant that production in the factories of northern Italy (including those of Agusta, Siai Marchetti, Macchi, Caproni and other smaller aeronautical firms) had all but ceased. When peace was eventually established the situation if anything worsened. All those companies prevalently linked to the munitions industry were thrown into crisis, both in terms of the obsolete technology they employed compared with that available to the winners of the conflict and the difficulty in getting hold of raw materials with which to restart production. For obvious strategic motives, the Paris Peace Treaty imposed restrictions on the expansion of the aeronautical sector severely compromised by the two decades of Fascism. Partial or total reconversion of the industrial plants was required, with Agusta identifying utilitarian motorcycles as an ideal product and one of the fundamental factors in the motorization of the masses that was to underpin national reconstruction: reliable and economical light motorcycles were the only means of motorized transport that the Italian people could afford at the time. As early as the 12th of February 1945, a new company, Società Anonima Meccanica Verghera, later known to all as MV, was formed. Its chairman, Domenico Agusta, had always been a motorcycling enthusiast and had even raced on two wheels. Furthermore, as has been rightly observed, the constructor could hardly have failed to be attracted by that "way of life, that atmosphere full of the unknown, of risk, of adventurous appeal with which the motorcycling world was still impregnated."

However, Count Agusta was not only a sporting enthusiast, he was first and foremost a hands-on businessman, at one with his company that he was to lead through to 1971 (the year of his death), in person and with an iron grip. He was also a talented engineer with knowledge of precision mechanics and the working of metals thanks to the experience gained in his father's business and he was a man with clear ideas regarding the future of the factory.

MV, FINALLY

Reconversion of production (playing a part through the supply of goods and services in the reconstruction of a nation largely reduced to rubble) would allow workers and engineers to be kept on (especially the skilled and highly qualified members of staff), with the tooling being updated in view of a return to the aeronautical sector. This was not to come about until 1949, while 1952 saw the company begin producing helicopters following the agreement signed with the American company Bell Helicopter. With admirable foresight, as early as 1943 plans had been drawn up and foundry models made for a light motorcycle equipped with a 98 cc two-stroke engine. Following the events of the 8th of September, in order to avoid this precious material falling into the hands of the German troops occupying the factory, the models were hidden in the house of a factory foreman, Mario Gernetti, while the drawings were kept by a clerk, Mario Rossi, who was later to become the head of the MV technical office through to the closure of the firm.

It was hardly going to be easy for the new company to find room on an already crowded market featuring "sacred cows" such as Moto Guzzi, Gilera, Sertum and Bianchi as well as thoroughbred newcomers like Ducati, Garelli, Parilla, Rumi, not to mention the Piaggio and Innocenti phenomena; however, MV itself had an ace up its sleeve in the form of its experience in the sophisticated field of aeronautical engineering. In effect, when the company began to use components in Avional, Ergal or titanium (materials unknown to other marques that at best used less sophisticated and less expensive aluminium alloys) it was more than a match for any rival.

In the large photo, taken in the May of 1954, the Costruzioni Aeronautiche Giovanni Agusta factory on the Malpensa moors. It was in that period that the AB-47G helicopter, the first to be built entirely in Italy, emerged ready to make its maiden flight.
It was the fruit of a commercial agreement signed two years earlier between the Varese company and the American firm Bell Helicopter, the first stage in a process that led to Agusta enjoying a position of supremacy in the sector fifty years later.

In the small photo, Domenico Agusta (left) with a colleague. The entrepreneur, who died in 1971 at the age of 64, had a decisive personality backed up by a notable understanding of engine design and manufacture.

The first motorcycle to be produced was the Model 98 powered by the above mentioned 98 cc single cylinder engine producing 3.5 hp at 3500 rpm. Boasting a top speed of 65 kph, the 98 was constructed between 1946 and 1949. Robust and economical, it was an ideal vehicle for the straitened Italian economy of the time. The new product was initially known as the Vespa 98, but this name (clearly visible on the front mudguard fin) soon had to be withdrawn as it had already been registered by Piaggio for its universally successful scooter. The 98 failed to achieve significant commercial success (around fifty examples of the pre-series were sold at L.98,000), but what was important was that it was the first MV to go on sale, the forebear of a vast range of models of between 48 and 800 cc. It was no coincidence that the prototype (completed in the face of myriad problems caused by a chronic lack of components, tyres included) was presented on Christmas Eve in 1945, in the Necchi shop at No. 2, Piazza Cordusio, Milan, the Pavia-based sewing machine manufacturer's historic showroom. On either side of the tank was the new company badge featuring a winged gear wheel (recalling the firm's aeronautical origins); modified two years later, it was soon to become a well-known sight on race tracks.

In the meantime, in fact, in parallel with the firm's standard production models, Domenico Agusta had decided to launch a racing programme (a sure way of reinforcing the marque image), the first victory being achieved as early as 1946, albeit in a minor event. For the record, Vincenzo Nencioni was the first rider (one of the new marque's first dealers) to take the chequered flag aboard an MV in the Coppa del Golfo regularity trial at La Spezia. Thus it was that on the 6th of October the inseparable combination of industrial production and sport characterising the Varese marque was born. However, it was in 1948, with the reintroduction after a 20-year gap of an Italian Motorcycling Federation championship for light motorcycles, that an MV specifically designed for racing was entered for an official series: the Competizione model with a 125 cc, single-cylinder, two-stroke engine featuring three ports, a three-speed gearbox, a tubular cradle frame, a parallelogram front fork and a swinging rear fork controlled by telescopic friction dampers. Initially capable of reaching 110 kph, it was updated in 1949 to become "the world's fastest 125 two-stroke" with its 10.5 hp at 6700 rpm providing a top speed of over 130 kph. From this model, the marque's racing machinery systematically mirrored the production models through to the mid-Fifties before breaking away completely from then onwards. In any case, the racing bikes were always designed and produced specifically for competition, with no budget or marketing restrictions to slow them down. The legendary Racing Department was also created around the finest MV mechanics and entrusted to Guido Cella who was to manage it (dealing above all with the Grand Prix 125s and 250s) through to 1958 when he was replaced by the former Ducati man Ruggero Mazza. From 1950, the four-cylinder 500 GP machines were run by Arturo Magni before he went on to become the entire department's technical manager.

Then there was the man himself, the Count, who through to the end was present at every track, foreign circuits included, alongside his machines and his riders.

In the photos on the left, from the top: the racing 125 three-speed two-stroke (Faenza model) that won the GP of Nations with Franco Bertoni in 1948, MV's first triumph in a Grand Prix; the 125 TEL, a light road-going four-speed two-stroke produced from 1949 to 1954 in Turismo and Sport versions, producing maximum power outputs of 5 and 6 hp respectively; the 125 four-speed two-stroke built between 1949 and 1950 was considered to be "the fastest two-stroke in circulation" thanks to its 130 kph top speed and was sold to private buyers at L.400,000.

In the large photo, Arturo Magni holds a fuel tank for a racing bike, complete with a sponge on which the rider could rest his chin when tucking in along the straights. Alongside him, the riders Carlo Ubbiali (first left) and Carlo Bandirola (last on the right), the famous "Lion of the Oltrepò."

FIRST BIKES, FIRST VICTORIES

To take a step backwards, it should be emphasised that from the outset in order to diversify production to satisfy a market crying out for virtually everything, in 1946 the first light motorcycle had already been flanked by a three-wheeled truck (powered by the same engine) with a wooden loading bed, the first in a series of goods vehicles (comprising trucks, vans and… a lawn mower) built through to 1969. In the meantime, the development of MV motorcycles proceeded apace. Displacements and performance increased in line with the nation's standard of living. 1948 therefore saw the adoption of the larger, albeit still utilitarian, 125 cc capacity (4.5 hp at 4500 rpm and over 80 kph) which led to numerous successful variants, while a year earlier the company had presented two models that might be described as "nice, but out of the question." One was a two-stroke 125 cc twin, while the second was a four-stroke 250 single, both unattractive in commercial terms at that time as they were considered to be unsuited to the times; that is to say, too expensive to purchase, run and maintain.

The first MV scooter arrived in 1949: a two-stroke 125 with a monocoque frame – one of the numerous but ill-fated attempts to break up the consolidated Vespa and Lambretta duopoly in the sector. 1950 was instead the year in which MV Agusta turned to four-stroke technology: the inauguration of this new direction could hardly have been more sensational as it came in the form of the four-cylinder 500 model in racing and touring forms (see pages 62, 66 and 70 for the 600, 750 and 800 cc variants), the mechanical jewel designed by the engineer Piero Remor. Still in 1950, Franco Bertoni won the Italian 125 cc Championship on an MV, the marque's first national title; while that same year, again in the 125 category, Renato Magi triumphed in the famous Milan-Taranto long distance race.

With the reconstruction of the nation and economic recovery well underway, thanks in part to the five years of the Marshall Plan, the early Fifties offered Italian industry new opportunities for development in all areas, naturally including mechanical engineering. It was in this particularly favourable economic climate that in 1952 MV became a publicly traded company, MV-Meccanica Verghera SpA, the capital of which was held in its entirety by the Agusta family, with Giuseppina as Chairperson and Domenico Managing Director. The company statute stated that its business consisted of "mechanical engineering and in particular the fabrication of light motorcycles and motor vehicles in general, internal combustion and jet engines, three-wheeled trucks, marine engines, refrigerators, pumps, conditioners, technical systems, tooling, gas producers and accessories for motorcycles, motor cars and aircraft and mechanical equipment and components." At the same time, on the crest of the growing wave of economic recovery, the displacement of the standard production models was increased to 150 cc in 1953 (by which time MV had in just a few short years become one of the major Italian manufacturers in the sector). Two years later, the 175 cc threshold was reached (with the company's products now almost exclusively being four-stroke models). The flagship for this displacement was to be the famous Disco Volante or Flying Saucer, sold successfully through to 1958. It was also used in endurance and long distance racing and owed its name to the unusual shape of the fuel tank that allowed the rider to rest his forearms on the straights, providing a minimum of additional comfort.

In the meantime, in the field of racing the GP version of the 500 four made a positive debut in the sec-

FLYING SAUCERS AND CHAMPIONSHIP TITLES

ond World Championship in Belgium on the 2nd of July 1950 with Arciso Artesiani in the saddle. At the end of the following year, development of the 500 cc machine was entrusted to the expert English rider Leslie Graham, a former RAF ace, who rode it to its first World Championship victories at Monza and Barcelona in 1952. That same year, in the 125 cc class, another Englishman, Cecil Sandford, won the World Championship title, MV taking the constructors' championship, a feat repeated in 1953. These were the first titles in a peerless roll of honour that was to number no less than 75.

FROM BOOM TO CRISIS

The reduction in list prices decided in 1953 by the MV board of directors (in effect, Count Domenico) was designed to take full advantage of the expanding market (a situation that was to last until 1957), a strategy adopted by many other Italian motorcycle manufacturers. That year, the Varese-based manufacturer's output exceeded 20,000 units that were distributed by no less than 250 concessionaires.

On the crest of the wave of enthusiasm generated by the first World Championship titles conquered in the 125 cc class, as well as the results obtained in the same class in the highly popular MSDS races for production sports bikes, MV turned its attention to this displacement for its standard production bikes too. The 125 Turismo Rapido was sold for four years and in seven different versions from 1954 (the base model four-stroke engine producing 6.5 hp at 6000 rpm was good for 90 kph).

1954 also saw the presentation of the prototype Vetturetta, a clever microcar powered by a 350 cc horizontal twin, four-stroke boxer engine producing 34 hp at 8000 rpm. Designed entirely by the aforementioned Remor, it featured a monocoque body and four-wheel drum brakes. It never went into production but could have represented an ideal opportunity for MV to join the Iso Isetta, Piaggio Vespa 400, MI-Val Mivalino, Benelli BBC and Ducati D-4 in attempting to counter Fiat's imminent monopoly of the small car sector.

With a market now characterised by a motorization of the masses extended to women and young people, MV ventured into the field of mopeds, launching a 48 cc two-stroke model in 1955 with a three-speed handlebar-shift gearbox, a pressed steel girder frame, a front fork with leading links and rear suspension boasting telescopic dampers. Inevitably, the new MV moped faced tough opposition in the form of classics such as the Cucciolo and the Motom, both with four-stroke engines...

In racing, from 1955 MV turned its attention to the 250 class too, claiming its first victories in the Tourist Trophy (the fabulous Isle of Man TT) with the Englishman Bill Lomas on a quarter-litre bike, while in the 125 class Carlo Ubbiali also triumphed and went on to claim the first of his eight World Championship titles with MV at the end of the season. The following year the diminutive Bergamo-born champion repeated the feat in both the 125 and 250 cc classes, while John Surtees, having recently arrived from England, conquered the marque's first 500 cc world title. With regard to the Constructors' Championship, MV took the 125 and 250 class titles in 1955-1956 and the 500 class title in 1956.

Again in 1956, the displacement of the production models was increased in the case of the single-cylinder, single camshaft Raid to 250 cc, reaching 300 cc three years later.

In the photos on the left, from the top: during a winter test at the Monza autodrome, Carlo Ubbiali (right) together with Tarquinio Provini, the rider born in Piacenza in 1933 who won the World Championship title with MV in 1957 (125 class) and 1958 (250 class); the famous Vetturetta from 1954 (right, a view of the cockpit), the prototype ultra-utility vehicle designed by Pietro Remor – according to an accredited urban legend, it was realised in a period in which the great designer had been placed in a form of quarantine by Domenico Agusta due to the divergent opinions of the pair regarding certain technical decisions within the MV racing department directed by the engineer from Rome.

In the photos on the right, from the top: the 125 single-cam producing 16 hp and capable of 150 kph, sold to privateers from 1953 to 1956 for Formula Sport races; a 250 racing single produced between 1954 and 1959, here with a front dustbin rather than a full-length fairing; the rider Fortunato Libanori racing a Squalo 175, a modified production model (complete with lights and silencer) built in 1954 for the Formula Sport road races and characterised by magneto rather than flywheel ignition and an Earles fork.

1957 was the year the Nuova 500 arrived in the FIAT dealers' showrooms, a masterpiece of small-car design able to offer the majority of Italians hitherto restricted to motorcycles the chance to own a four-wheeled car. The result was that after a five-year period in which MV had achieved remarkable industrial expansion, the first signs of the terrible crisis about to hit the sector and to last for over eight years began to appear. It was up to Domenico Agusta, chairman of the company since the death of his mother Giuseppina in the November of 1955, to attempt to carry the marque forwards.

To avoid being overwhelmed by the depression affecting the motorcycle sector (a fate suffered by numerous marques, including prestigious names such as Parilla), MV initially adopted measures taken by most of the other constructors and thinned out its range and reduced costs in order to be able to lower its list prices as it had done four years earlier. Fundamentally, this meant building only small capacity motorcycles that were cheap to buy and economical to run and maintain. In view of this marketing strategy, between 1958 and 1960 the MV catalogue featured the Ottantatrè, a utilitarian machine with, as the name would suggest, a displacement of 83 cc with highly unusual origins. The capacity was, in fact, the result of a series of tests and calculations designed to guarantee a power output of 3,7 hp at 6000, a value considered to be sufficient to travel two-up at 75 kph. The model was never particularly popular and neither was the contemporary 175 AB, a robust machine producing 7.5 hp at 7500 rpm (good for almost 100 kph) that, despite being presented in a number of different versions, was dropped the following year. These poor results confirmed a theory that was well known to those working in the sector: even in the hardest of times, the Italian motorcycle (and car) market turned its back on overtly modest products, preferring to wait for the depression to ease to acquire more expensive and better quality vehicles.

In 1959, the MV Agusta concessionaires began to take delivery of the Centomila, a 125 producing 7.5 hp at 6200 rpm, whose name derived from the number of kilometres covered by its guarantee. It was partnered by the 150 RS (with a five-speed gearbox), the displacement of which just exceeded 150 cc, the minimum for autostrada use on the basis of the new Highway Code introduced that year. The Bik, presented late in 1959, was an interesting 165 cc, twin-cylinder, four-stroke scooter that never made it past the prototype stage. 1960 instead saw the launch of the Chicco scooter (a 155 cc two-stroke producing 5.8 hp at 5200 rpm) that could be ridden on the autostradas, had a top speed of 75 kph and was produced through to 1964 and the popular Checca light motorcycle with two displacements, 83 cc producing 4 hp at 6000 rpm and 99 cc with 5.1 hp at 6000 rpm. Prices? For example, the Sport GT version of the 99 cc Checca cost L.162,000.

It should come as no surprise that MV's range was so diversified in terms of models and displacements at a time in which the crisis in the sector had become so serious as to oblige many factories to close. It was clearly a strategy adopted by the marque to corner the biggest possible share of a market that while depressed had become more demanding and Domenico Agusta, on the strength of the economic success achieved in the aeronautical field, was not a man to give way to any one, neither in the field of production nor on the track.

POOR BUT POSH

In the photos on the left, from the top: the 99 Checca Turismo, introduced early in 1960 as the replacement for the earlier model 83 – the engine was a four-stroke single mated to a four-speed 'box; the 99 Checca Sport, slightly more powerful than the Turismo version (5.1 hp against 4) and was also on sale between 1960 and 1969; the 150 RS (Rapido Sport), sold between 1959 and 1970 – the 150 cc displacement came back into fashion in 1959 with the introduction of the new Highway Code that set it as the minimum engine size for vehicles used on the autostrada. Note the Abarth silencer and the rear shocks with exposed springs.

Top right, the engine from a Centomila Turismo 125 from 1959 – a four-stroke single with pushrods and rockers, it was characterised by an oil circuit with a centrifugal filter system that was responsible for the greater durability that gave it its name.

Bottom right, the Chicco scooter had a displacement of 155 cc (and could therefore be driven on the autostrada) and was produced between 1960 and 1964. The two-stroke, single-silencer engine was designed ex novo for this model with a horizontal cylinder, forced cooling and a duplex chain primary drive. Prices started at L.157,500.

NOT JUST MOTORCYCLES:
THE AGUSTA AVIATION DIVISION

With regard to Agusta's aviation division, after Count Domenico had conducted his first experiments with rotors in the early Thirties, in 1952 the company signed an agreement with the American firm Bell Helicopter to produce the 47G helicopter under licence. Two years later, in May, the AB-47G, the first of these aircraft built entirely in Italy, took off over Cascina Costa. In 1956, 100 examples were constructed: a sign that, little more than 10 years after the end of the war, the advanced technology of rotary wings was a prerogative of the Varese-based company. That same year, thanks to Filippo Zappata, one of the greats of Italian aeronautical design, work began on the development of the four-engined AZ.8 that made its maiden flight in 1958. It was to be the last transport aircraft designed and built in Italy. There followed an uninterrupted sequence of helicopters that enjoyed significant commercial success at home and abroad, the most significant of which are cited below: the Agusta 103, prototype single-seater from 1959, the 10-seater 102 from 1960, the AB 204B, the first turbine helicopter from 1961, the 32-seater Agusta 101G tri-turbine from 1962, the 204 anti-submarine helicopter from 1964, the twin-engined Agusta 212 from 1970. After Domenico Agusta's death in 1971, production has continued through to the present day. Mention should also be made of the celebrated A109 series, launched in 1971, the most recent variants of which have helped consolidate Agusta's peerless reputation for high quality products.

Top left, Domenico Agusta (right) with the engineer Filippo Zappata, designer of the famous AZ.8 (Agusta-Zappata 8) transport aircraft, built at Cascina Costa between 1957 and 1958. The great Ancona-born engineer had "made his bones" as a young man in France, in the workshops of the aviation pioneer Louis Blériot before joining Breda in Milan and then Agusta (1951), where he was to pass from designing fixed wing craft to those with rotating blades.
Above right, the AB 47-G1 helicopter and the more modern AW109 Power, two examples of the highly successful range of models licensed from Bell Helicopter from 1952.
Facing page, a hanger at Cascina Costa in the April of 1957: the Agusta AZ.8 aircraft (in construction) looms over the MV motorcycles ready for delivery to the dealers. In the foreground, on the left, examples of the 125 TRL (Turismo Rapido Lusso).

In racing, 1958 saw World Championship titles conquered by Carlo Ubbiali and Tarquinio Provini in the 125 and 250 classes respectively, and by John Surtees in the 350 ad 500 classes, repeated in 1959 and 1960. It is worth pointing out that while the 500 was the same constantly updated machine from 1952 (the year in which its shaft drive was abandoned in favour of a chain), the four-cylinder 350 was born in 1953 as a derivation of the 500 cc model, put to one side for a number of years and then taken up again, totally revised and finally made to perform. For his part, Ubbiali went on to repeat his title triumphs in 1959 and 1960 in both the 125 and 250 classes, before retiring unbeaten at the end of the season for family reasons.

A few extra words regarding the retirement of this remarkable rider (when a nine-time world champion and at the height of his powers) are appropriate here. The motive (as he told us in one of our many meetings) was the death due to natural causes of his elder brother Maurizio, Carlo's trusted manager and track adviser since his very first races. Some one else might have reacted to the loss differently, but not Ubbiali, a champion who was truly different to any other, even when racing. He was a rider who was able to provide the MV mechanics preparing his bikes with the support of his infinite mechanical knowledge and peerless attention to detail. He calculated everything and was capable of winning a race at the death, beating his adversaries by just a few centimetres, perhaps at the end of the race on the old Nürburgring, where every one of the dozens of laps was over 20 kilometres long.

Following the 1957 project for a prototype six-cylinder 500 cc GP bike (as short-lived as the similar design for a 350 GP six in 1969), the years from 1958 to 1960 saw MV conquer the Constructors' Championship titles in the 125, 250, 350 and 500 classes, as well as repeated TT wins: in 1959, the Cascina Costa riders actually won every World Championship class.

1961 represented something of a racing sabbatical for MV as the great Ubbiali had retired, contributing to the marque's definitive withdrawal from the minor classes, while Surtees had decided to prove himself on four wheels too (moving to Ferrari and Formula 1, winning the World Championship in 1964). Only Gary Hocking, promoted to the larger classes the year before, was entrusted with a four-cylinder 350 GP and a 500 GP four, both carrying a conspicuous MV-Privat logo on the fuel tank: the manufacturer's contribution was restricted to providing a mechanic and spare parts. The Rhodesian, who along with Ubbiali had probably been the fastest rider of all in dry conditions, comfortably won the championship titles in both classes, but at the end of the season he was joined by the young phenomenon Mike Hailwood. Between 1962 and 1965, the Englishman was to record four straight championships aboard the Cascina Costa half-litre, MV collecting the World Constructors' Championship titles in the 350 and 500 classes in 1961 and in the 500 in 1962, '63, '64 and '65.

CARLETTO UBBIALI TRIUMPHANT

In the large photo, Ubbiali on the celebrated Solitude circuit (Stuttgart) riding an MV with a full fairing. This aerodynamic feature was to be banned in 1957 due to the perilous turbulence it provoked, with the result that in competition the front wheel and part of the rear remained free of any type of "bodywork."

Bottom, from the left: John Surtees, the British rider who joined the "court" of Domenico Agusta in 1956 and immediately won the 500 cc World Championship title: he was 22 yeas old and, uniquely, he later moved into Formula 1 and won the World Championship with Ferrari in 1964; the legendary concentration of Ubbiali at the start of a race; the tank of a multi-cylinder MV with the Privat script that characterised the GP bikes entrusted to privateers in 1961.

Returning to the production side, late in 1963 (and therefore still in the middle of the depression: this was now the sixth year of suffering for the entire sector), the company turnover had fallen by 40% with little more than 3,500 motorcycles produced in the previous 12 months against the 20,000 units of 10 years earlier, while the number of employees was also plummeting to its lowest ever level. In the final months of 1965, the 557 employees of 1965 dropped to just 115, with the MV Agusta workers fortunately being transferred to helicopter division. It would only be right to say that this last division escaped the recession thanks to the fact that it was a privileged supplier to certain governments of the time from that of France to that of Portugal, who were using the aircraft to repress the guerrilla movements in the African colonies struggling for independence such as Algeria, Angola and Mozambique.

As well as in politics (1968 was on the horizon), the first timid signs of a changing economic wind were appearing too and finally a general recovery began to be felt that the motorcycle market immediately picked up on. Late in 1964, the MV catalogue was extended with the direct descendents of 1959's Centomila, the 125 GT and GTL producing 9.5 hp at 8000 rpm (and boasting a five-speed gearbox from November 1965 when the scrambler version was also presented), followed by the 125 Regolarità, again with the four-stroke single and five speeds, but a power output of 10 hp at 8000 rpm (which rose to no less than 13 hp at 8500 rpm with the second series, the list price also rising from L.310,000 to L.380,000).

The 125 Regolarità was the manufacturer's first production bike providing a response to young Italian motorcyclists' growing interest in off-road riding and competition: it went on sale after exhaustive testing (including competitive events) and was to enjoy commercial success from 1965 through to 1970. However, 1965 was above all the year of the presentation of MV's first four-cylinder production bike: the all-black 600 model, a descendant of the 500 of 15 years earlier. The so-called "black queen" made a dramatic debut, a stunning machine powered by an engine deriving from its Grand Prix-winning sister bikes (with the highly sophisticated gear-driven twin overhead camshafts) that offered its flank to numerous criticisms that compromised its commercial success, the same fate awaiting the larger-engined 750 and 800 cc models.

1965 also saw Giacomo Agostini joining the MV racing team from Moto Morini: just a few figures are sufficient to paint a telling portrait of one of the greatest motorcycle racers of all time. He was to win the 500 cc World Championship title from 1966 to 1972 and the 350 cc title from 1968 to 1973. With MV alone, his career-end statistics featured 13 world titles, with 125 wins out the total of 311 he obtained, including triumphs in the Tourist trophy with the 350 in 1966, with the 500 in 1971 and with the 350 and 500 in 1968, '69, '70 and '72. His bike of choice was to be the 500 GP triple, a true symbol of an era and an unbeatable combination used by Mino from 1966, the year in which he still alternated it with the 500 four, through to 1972. He instead won his 350 GP races with the smaller version of the triple that made its debut in 1965, replacing the earlier four-cylinder machine on which Surtees and Hocking had starred. As an example of our personal opinion of this great champion (for further facts and figures regarding Agostini see

ALONG CAME A CERTAIN AGOSTINI

Top left, an AB 47J-5 helicopter. The aviation department has always represented Agusta's core business, despite being among the motives for the definitive end to Meccanica Verghera production in the autumn of 1977.

The protagonist in the other photos is Giacomo Agostini. The great Bergamo-born champion's naturally photogenic looks favoured an acting career that saw him appear in four films. The first was *Continental Circus*, directed in 1969 by Jerôme Laperrousaz, followed in 1970 by no fewer than three movies: *Amore Formula 2* directed by Mario Amendola, *Bolidi sull'asfalto – A tutta birra* by Bruno Corbucci and *Formula 1 – Nell'inferno del Grand Prix*, by James Reed (in reality the very Italian Guido Malatesta).

the interview with him on page 46) we would mention only the remarkable impression created by watching and rewatching archive footage of his wins in the Tourist Trophy on the Isle of Man: his breathtaking leaps at 200 kph at Ballaugh Bridge will remain in our memory as ineffable examples of ability and courage. In the meantime, the Constructors' title was conquered in 1967, '68, '69, '70, '71, '72 and '73 in the 500 class and in 1968, '69, '70, '71, '72 and 1973 in the 350. 1967 was the year that provided clear signs that something in the sector had changed for the better and for MV the time had come to try again with the medium-large displacements, given the now stable economic conditions of the Italian middle class who now saw the motorcycle not merely as a means of transport but also as a status symbol. 1968 saw the launch of the 350 Sport twin (with 29 hp at 7600 rpm and a top speed of 170 kph), heir to the 250 that had entered production the previous year (19 hp at 7800 for 135 kph); a scrambler version was also offered for soft-road use.

In 1969, the 350 range was extended to include Sport and GT versions equipped with electronic ignition. In that same year, the 750 Sport was introduced as the heir to the 600 four (with further versions being presented later), while in 1975 it was the turn of the 800 America. These are all models, like the earlier 500 from 1950, the daring forebear of the entire series, and its less successful 600 cc heir from 1965, that we shall discuss in more detail later in this book. The last edition of the 350 was the Ipotesi (34 hp at 8500 rpm) styled by Giorgio Giugiaro, presented as a show prototype at the end of 1973 and put on sale two years later in the usual Sport and GT versions. Finally, it was the 125 Sport single of 1975 that sadly brought the MV production history to a close: a pushrod four-stroke producing 12 hp at 8500 rpm and good for 115 kph, it boasted a five-speed gearbox and a single front disc brake.

In the meantime, Count Domenico Agusta had died on the 2nd of February 1971. With him died a remarkable kind of entrepreneur, one so competitive as to sacrifice significant resources to the demands of his beloved racing department rather than direct them to the production side of the business. He was succeeded by his brother Corrado, but as early as 1972, the Agusta Group, in search of indispensable capital, above all for the development of the helicopter division, joined forces with a public partner. This took place when Breda Ferroviaria Partecipazioni e Finaziamenti Costruzioni Ferroviarie of the EFIM group (Ente Finanziamento Industria Manifatturiera) acquired a 51% holding of the share capital of Costruzioni Aeronautiche Giovanni Agusta, a further 30% being acquired in 1979 and the remaining 19% in 1992. From this point on, it was to be an uphill struggle for MV, with a succession of spurious attempts to revive the firm, including a phantomatic agreement with Ducati (another EFIM company; that is to say, the classic second cockerel in the state financed "motorcycling chicken run"), which the public power that be within the group had shamefully decided to ditch in favour of the more profitable albeit less exciting corporate core business: the production of helicopters. A final, unrealistic attempt to relaunch production was made in 1975 with the aforementioned presentation of the prestigious four-cylinder 800 America,

THE COUNT DIES AND...

In the photos on the left, from the top: Angelo Bergamonti racing in 1971 aboard the MV 350 triple – the unfortunate Cremona-born rider had joined MV the previous year, at 31 years of age, finishing third in the 350 World Championship and sixth in the 500 class; he suffered a fatal accident in the rain on 4 April 1971 at the Riccione circuit during a classic stage of the Temporada Romagnola; Domenico Agusta in one of his innumerable racing circuit visits alongside his riders.

Right, from the top: a second series 750 Sport (1973), an evolution of the "Lady in Red" presented at the Milan Motorcycle show in November 1969, now with dual Scarab front disc brakes in place of the original Grimeca four-shoe central drum; a 125 Sport from 1975 (with a single front disc brake) and a 350 Ipotesi from 1976 (designed by Giorgio Giugiaro), which represent Meccanica Verghera's swan song before the closure in late 1977.

but then the curtains finally closed for Meccanica Verghera, despite the occasional story in the press about the "beginning of a new era for MV." 1976 saw the final retirement from competition after the last World Championship titles had been conquered in 1973-1974, with Agostini's victory in the 350 class in '73 and those of Phil Read in the 500 in both seasons, the Englishman having taken the popular Mino's place when he moved to Yamaha. The 500 cc bike of these triumphs debuted in 1972 and was to win its last GP in Germany (on the legendary Nürburgring) on the 29th of August 1976, again with Agostini, who had returned to the saddle of an MV, albeit a privately entered machine. The 350 was instead a four-cylinder model deriving from the Bergamo-born rider's highly successful triple and debuted with Alberto Pagani in the GP of Nations in 1971.

In the April of 1977, withdrawal from competition with immediate effect was announced via an official statement from the company that somewhat ambiguously read: "Following recent articles that have appeared in the national and foreign press regarding MV Agusta and in order to eliminate misunderstandings particularly detrimental to the company, the Board of Directors declares: that competitive activities have been suspended for the 1977 season until the International Motorcycling Federation takes such steps as to permit the constructors of "four-strokes" to participate on an equal footing rather than being severely penalised by absurd regulations, not least the famous 110 decibels limit. Research shall continue within the Agusta Group, of which MV is a part, in order not to lose that technological heritage expressed by the Grand Prix engines. Production activities: MV's motorcycle business shall proceed independently and on the basis of market conditions. The fusion with Ducati, ventilated by the press, was impractical, at least in the short term, due to the diversities of the two companies. Approval has been given to the existing projects for new machines that in time shall replace the current models, with designs that should concretize early in the new year and on which rests our faith in the future of the company."

With respect to these events, Fredmano Spairani of Pavia, one of the state managers most closely involved in the episode declared that: "I joined the Agusta Group from Ducati in 1973 and stayed until 1985. In 1976, I was charged with supervision of the MV racing department (Magni remaining the director) and at the end of the season I wrote the famous wholly negative "report" on the competition future of our motorcycles that had been overtaken by the mighty Japanese two-strokes. Count Corrado thanked me for my work and stated that if this was the case then he had decided that for his bikes it was no longer a question of either two or four stokes, simply that the 'era of MV triumphs had ended.' As painful as it was I then realised that I had been involuntarily responsible for the final fading of a legend."

Early in the autumn of 1977, production also ceased, while the final, spectacular chapter was recorded at the end of the year when the stand that had been reserved at the Milan Cycle and Motorcycle Show remained empty. There was a final, emotional attempt by the exhibition organizers (the manufacturers under the ANCMA umbrella) to convince MV to reverse its decision, but it was

... MV DIES TOO

Top left, a moment from the first race of the 1975 500 cc World Championship, the French GP on the Paul Ricard circuit at Le Castellet. Phil Read, the reigning champion since 1973 (with the number 0), and Armando Toracca, both on MVs, are leading the field, but the race was to be won by Giacomo Agostini (followed by his teammate Kanaya) who the previous year had switched to Yamaha and conquered the title with Read second. The following year the great British rider was to leave the Cascina Costa team in favour of Suzuki, but was never to forget the marque with the winged cogwheel of which, the proud owner of one of the first F4 750 Oros, he frequently attends the rallies.

Top, right, the Englishman Stanley Michael Bailey Hailwood, universally known as "Mike the Bike", one of the greatest riders of all time, joined the Cascina Costa racing team at the end of 1961 — in each of the following four years he was to win the 500 cc World Championship with the Varese marque and in 1964 aboard a 500 four (Privat) at Daytona he was to beat the hour and the 100 km records with an average speed of over 233 kph.

Bottom, the 33-year-old Alberto Pagani (son of Nello) after his 1971 triumph aboard an MV 500 triple in the GP of Nations at Monza — in the same class he was to finish the following season in second place behind Agostini.

all in vain. The following February saw the sad moment of the dismantling of the factory, with only the sales department remaining operational for a couple of years, after which just spare parts were available. Finally, the company was placed in liquidation (1982) and consequently almost all of the remaining effects of the racing department were to be sold off. Thanks to the intervention of an enthusiastic collector, Ubaldo Elli of Varese, the piecemeal dispersal of the material, possibly abroad, was initially avoided. Subsequently, a scandalous public auction (July 1986) was to permit all that remained (13 bikes, 6 engines, 2 frames) to cross the ocean and end up in the Team Obsolete collection of the Brooklyn lawyer Robert Iannucci. The whole episode was accompanied by judicial vicissitudes that dragged on for years. What was saved from the sales, added to the original material in old MV Agusta Museum of Technology and Labour at Gallarate (Province of Varese), founded in 1977 and closed in 1992, is proudly displayed in the Agusta Museum at Cascina Costa, opened in the December of 2002 thanks to the intervention of the Agusta management (today AgustaWestland) but also strongly supported by the GLA (The Agusta Senior Workers' Group).

This was the least that could be done for such a peerless heritage of experience and success for men and machines lasting over 30 years.

Top, four images of the fabulous collection of Ubaldo Elli who can be seen in the first from the left. The entire collection may be viewed on appointment at Busto Arsizio.

Centre left, the infamous auction that in the summer of 1986 allowed much of the material from the MV racing department to be transferred abroad, including the extremely rare four-cylinder boxer that in 1975 might have represented the marque's last chance to counter the all-conquering two-strokes in the GP class.

Centre right, a view of a number of bikes exhibited in the old MV Agusta Museum of Technology and Labour at Gallarate.

Bottom, three rooms of the unique Agusta Museum at Cascina Costa, opened in 2002 and directed by Gian Luigi Marasi. It contains a varied overview of Meccanica Verghera's racing and production bikes (1945-1977), as well as comprehensive documentation of the aviation side of the Agusta company, from its origins to the present day.

GIACOMO AGOSTINI:
THE MAN, THE CHAMPION, HIS LEGEND

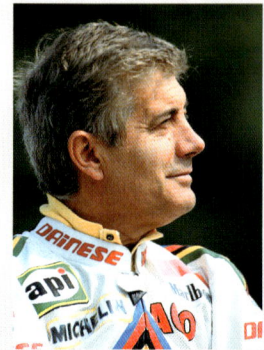

The great racing champion Giacomo Agostini (Ago to everyone, Mino to his friends) was born on the 16th of June 1942 in a clinic at Brescia, while his family lived at Lovere, an attractive town on Lake Iseo. After debuting with a Parilla in motocross, Ago's first great racing exploit came in 1961 when he finished 2nd in the Trento-Bondone aboard a Morini Settebello. Following a series of fine results with the same famous pushrod 175, Alfonso Morini engaged him as a works rider. After his debut at the Cesanatico circuit, he won his first Italian national titles in the Juniores championship and the 2nd Category of the Mountain Championship. Subsequently, Mino was "promoted" to ride the legendary Bolognese 250 cc twin-cam single, aboard which, the following year, he won the Italian Seniores title. At the end of 1964, our man rolled up at the court of Domenico Agusta, the head of Mecccanica Verghera (MV) of Cascina Costa. It was the beginning of a golden era that lasted no fewer than 12 years and resulted in an incredible sequence of victories alongside and against riders of the calibre of Mike Hailwood, Jim Redman, Phil Read, Renzo Pasolini, Jarno Saarinen, Johnny Cecotto, Angelo Bergamonti, Gianfranco Bonera, Alberto Pagani, Barry Sheene and Kenny Roberts... The inimitable series began on the 25th of April 1965 at the Nurbürgring when, on the terrible Eifel mountain circuit, the 23-year-old Bergamasco rider scored a debut win in the 350 class with the GP triple, the bike he came to be identified with: through to 1973 he was to win six World Championship titles in the 350 class and seven in the 500. After moving to Yamaha in 1974, what was for him the all-new experience of the Japanese two-stroke philosophy caused no particular problems as the ever-popular champion immediately conquered 350 (1974) and 500 cc (1975) titles. We can

hardly ignore his last great masterpiece before MV withdrew from racing in late 1977; that is to say, the victory on the 29th of August 1976, once again aboard an MV Agusta 500 GP and once again on the legendary German Ring, 11 years after his first triumph with a red and silver bolide. Later there were roles as the sporting manager for Yamaha and Cagiva and then, finally, as a testimonial for the ineffable MV Agusta F4.
We caught up with Mino to ask him both about MV Agusta in the Golden Age and the marque's current (and future) fortunes.

A memory of the MV Agusta of the past?

"When the end of MV Agusta's two-wheeled adventure was pronounced in 1977, I remember feeling that it was a crazy decision. A wealth of hard work, culture and sport risked being lost because of a decision taken from on high to privilege the construction of helicopters rather than motorcycles, when the two products could have happily co-existed. We're talking about a name and a marque that were without equals in the world, as subsequently I have had the opportunity to confirm at the hundreds of rallies in which I have participated.
I've seen tens of thousands of people out to watch my historic GP bike demonstrations, numbers even greater than when I was actually racing. All of them enthusiastic, happy just to hear the familiar roar of my bikes' engines... In the ovations that uninterruptedly accompanied (and accompany) my demonstrations I could feel all the love of an entire generation inseparably bound up with the aching memory of times and feats that seemed unrepeatable".

How did you feel when MV was reborn?

"If you think that no fewer than 13 of my 15 world titles were conquered in the saddles of bikes carrying the MV Agusta logo, you can well imagine the depth of the emotion I felt on seeing, 20 years down the line, that old badge once again on the tanks of the red and silver motorcycle, the F4.
I saw, like in a film, the whole sequence of the world

On this page, a recent close-up of the great man.
On the facing page, Ago in the boardroom of the MV Agusta factory at Schiranna, surrounded by a group of F4s ready to be delivered to the store from which they will sent out to the dealers.
From the presentation of the first model (1997), the former rider has acted as the "face" for the fabulous Varese four, a role that is his by right thanks to his glorious past aboard the marque's bikes that has also given rise to the production of a version dedicated to him, the F4 1000 Ago.

titles won, defending those colours on the world's circuits and competing under the banner of that golden cogwheel. Golden like the period that had appeared to be finished forever and instead was about to start over thanks to a model such as the F4, the fruit of highly advanced technological research and with technical and aesthetic characteristics second to none of the products of any other motorcycle constructor."

What has impressed you the most about this resurrection?

"In Claudio Castiglioni's truly epochal decision to revive the glories of the legendary MV marque I have found the same love and competitive passion that were once displayed by the unforgettable Agusta family."

Looking at the F4 2010, what can you tell us about this model that is projected towards the future, the fruit of important design decisions under the banner of the "evolution without revolution" strategy.

"After many years it's still a very up-to-date model."

It's inevitable that you ask yourself about a return to racing for MV.

"It would be fantastic, but first they've got to get the company on an even keel, after which a return to racing by such a prestigious marque would reflect well on the nation too".

What do you hope lies in the future for "your" marque?

"I just hope that someone believes in the marque enough to carry it to the heights it reached during my era."

On this page, three photos of Ago riding old and new multi-cylinder bikes with the winged cogwheel. While the class remains the same, the helmet has certainly changed, from the classic Cromwell "pudding basin" to the full-face type adopted from 1971.
On the facing page, the incredible sequence of race wins by Giacomo Agostini aboard the all-conquering MV GP bikes.

GIACOMO AGOSTINI'S VICTORIES WITH MV AGUSTA

1965
German GP, 350 class

1966
Belgian GP, 500 class
German GP, 350 class
GP of Finland, 500 class
British GP, 350 class
Italian GP, 350 class
Italian GP, 500 class

1967
German GP, 500 class
Belgian GP, 500 class
East German GP, 500 class
GP of Finland, 500 class
Gp of Ireland, 350 class
Italian GP, 500 class

1968
German GP, 350 class
German GP, 500 class
Spanish GP, 500 class
British GP, 350 class
British GP, 500 class
Dutch GP, 350 class
Dutch GP, 500 class
Belgian GP, 500 class
East German GP, 350 class
East German GP, 500 class
Czech GP, 350 class
Czech GP, 500 class
GP of Finland, 500 class
Gp of Ireland, 350 class
Gp of Ireland, 500 class
Italian GP, 350 class
Italian GP, 500 class

1969
Spanish GP, 350 class
Spanish GP, 500 class
German GP, 350 class
German GP, 500 class
French GP, 500 class
British GP, 350 class

British GP, 500 class
Dutch GP, 350 class
Dutch GP, 500 class
Belgian GP, 500 class
East German GP, 350 class
East German GP, 500 class
Czech GP, 350 class
Czech GP, 500 class
GP of Finland, 350 class
GP of Finland, 500 class
Gp of Ireland, 350 class
Gp of Ireland, 350 class

1970
German GP, 350 class
German GP, 500 class
French GP, 500 class
GP of Yugoslavia, 350 class
GP of Yugoslavia, 350 class
British GP, 350 class
British GP, 500 class
Dutch GP, 350 class
Dutch GP, 500 class
Belgian GP, 500 class
East German GP, 350 class
East German GP, 500 class
Czech GP, 350 class
GP of Finland, 350 class
GP of Finland, 500 class
Gp of Ireland, 350 class
Gp of Ireland, 500 class
Italian GP, 350 class
Italian GP, 500 class

1971
Austrian GP, 350 class
Austrian GP, 500 class
German GP, 350 class
German GP, 500 class
British GP, 500 class
Dutch GP, 350 class
Dutch GP, 500 class
Belgian GP, 500 class
East German GP, 350 class
East German GP, 500 class
Swedish GP, 350 class
Swedish GP, 500 class
GP of Finland, 350 class
GP of Finland, 500 class

1972
German GP, 500 class
French GP, 500 class
Austrian GP, 350 class
Austrian GP, 500 class
Italian GP, 350 class
Italian GP, 500 class
British GP, 350 class
British GP, 500 class
Dutch GP, 350 class
Dutch GP, 500 class
Belgian GP, 500 class
East German GP, 500 class
Czech GP, 500 class
Swedish GP, 350 class
Swedish GP, 500 class
GP of Finland, 350 class
GP of Finland, 500 class

1973
French GP, 350 class
Italian GP, 350 class
Dutch GP, 350 class
Belgian GP, 500 class
Czech GP, 500 class
GP of Finland, 350 class
GP of Finland, 500 class

1974
French GP, 350 class
Austrian GP, 350 class
Austrian GP, 500 class
Italian GP, 350 class
Dutch GP, 350 class
Dutch GP, 500 class
GP of Yugoslavia, 350 class

1975
French GP, 500 class
Spanish GP, 350 class
German GP, 500 class
Italian GP, 500 class
GP of Finland, 500 class

1976
Dutch GP, 350 class
German GP, 500 class

Engine Architecture: the "Italian School"

His name is Piero Remor: the high priest behind the irresistible rise of the MV marque. A design engineer, he was the founder of the "Italian School" of transverse four-cylinder in-line engines that was to hold sway among motorcycle manufacturers from Italy to Japan through to the present day. Because everything started with a multi-cylinder engine he designed together with a friend in 1924…

Remor first saw the light of day in Portovenere (La Spezia) on the 11th of December 1896, but the young Piero moved to Rome in 1919 to graduate in mechanical engineering and it was there that his only son Carlo was to be born and it was also there that he was to die on the 18th of July 1964.

In 1923, together with the young Roman engineer Carlo Gianini, in a small workshop near the Baths of Deocletian, Remor signed off the design of a revolutionary 500 cc front-facing four-cylinder engine. The explicit scope of the project was to combine the lightness of a motorcycle frame with the "nobility" of a multi-cylinder car-type engine. All this with an added touch of genius: rotating the cylinder block through 90° and locating it transversally in the frame was the key to resolving the old problem of the overheating of the longitudinal air-cooled multi-cylinder engines (for example the famous four designed by the Englishman Charles Binks).

In 1924, the Remor-Gianini duo became a trio with the arrival of Count Giovanni Bonmartini of Rome, an enthusiastic aircraft pilot and racing driver who, with along other aviators, had in 1920 founded CNA, the Cooperativa Nazionale Aeronautica, shrewdly transformed in 1922, the year of the march on Rome, into the less subversive Compagnia Nazionale Aeronautica. Bonmartini financed Remor and Gianini's project through a new company, GRB (from the initials of the three musketeers' surnames) and the engine was finally built: it produced a maximum power output of 28 hp at 6000

PIERO REMOR, THE HIGH PRIEST OF FOUR-CYLINDER ENGINES

The engineer Piero Remor and the 500 GP shaft-drive four from 1950-1953. The great designer was "poached" from Gilera in the autumn of 1949, after a race on the Ospedaletti circuit (San Remo) thanks to an offer made by Domenico Agusta in person.
On that occasion, along with Remor, the rider Arciso Artesiani and the mechanic Arturo Magni, the Roman engineer's right-hand man were also co-opted by MV.
The bike, prepared for the Milan Trade Fair in the April of 1950, was finished in metallic silver with light blue "flashes" and adopted torsion bar suspension front and rear. Only with the 1951 version was a telescopic fork fitted, while the rear end continued to feature the torsion bars that represented Remor's design "signature."

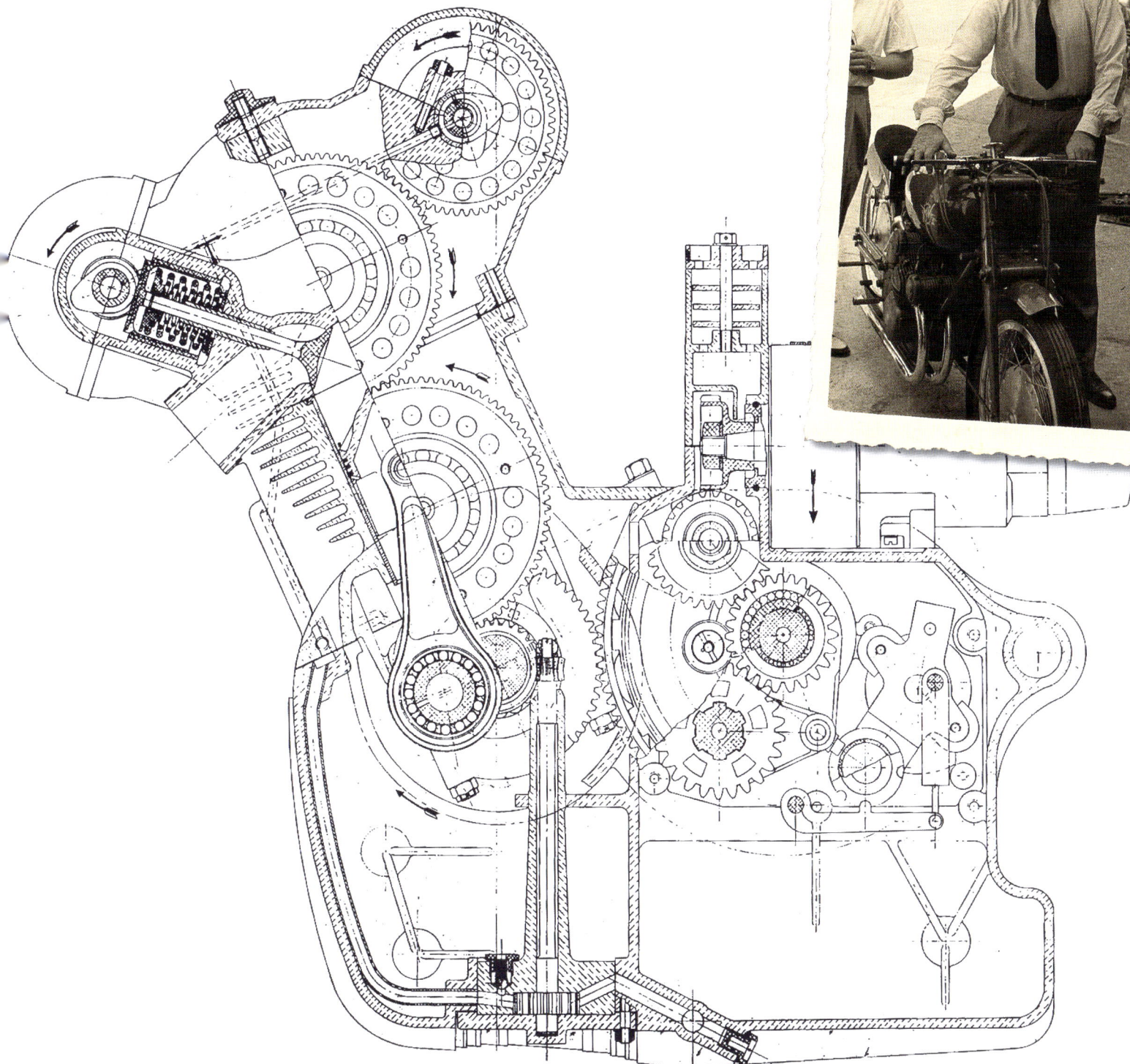

rpm. The architecture of the GRB 500, as the engineer Sandro Colombo rightly underlines in his fundamental *Gilera quattro* "anticipated engineering patterns that were to constitute the basis for the development of diverse families of racing engines over the following years and, from the late Sixties, the Japanese mass produced four-cylinder engines."

In order to develop and market the project, OPRA (Officine Precisione Romane Automobilistiche) was founded in Via Francesco Neri, Rome, adjacent to Via Ostiense. Here, the two designers created a new engine (30 hp at 6200 rpm, subsequently 30.6 hp at 6400 rpm) that was immediately mounted in a frame designed by the talented Remor who thus began to display his ability as an "all-round designer" taking care of the cycle side and the styling of his creations. It was no coincidence that 15 years later he was to design the definitive frame for the Gilera GP 500 "four" (supercharged) and then that of the post-war 500 GP "four" (naturally aspirated).

The OPRA 500 engine boasted significant new features compared to the GRB 500. For example, the crankshaft was fitted with two flywheels set between the central bearings. Between them, a cylindrical gear actuated the single overhead camshaft via an intermediate gear driving the cog keyed to the camshaft: thus was born the highly sophisticated geared camshaft drive that became the proud boast of the "Italian school." Furthermore, the primary drive (that series of components linking the crankshaft to the clutch) consisted of a pair of gears, one of which (the upstream one of the pair) was keyed to the crankshaft between the first and second cylinder. The resulting extreme transverse compactness of the engine-gearbox assembly is just another of the model's particularly important design features. In short, this was engine architecture that was to make history in racing and beyond.

After various vicissitudes, OPRA ceased all activity and Gianini moved (1929) to CAN (and subsequently to the Caproni Group) where the OPRA 500 was subjected to major modifications (that included a new name), becoming the CNA Rondine 500 (producing no less than 75 hp at 7200 rpm and boasting a top speed of over 240 kph thanks to supercharging), before being sold (after six examples had been constructed) to Gilera in 1936. Remor did not follow his friend: he was about to enter a "lost" decade (regarding which the author has tried to research but only found evidence of a consultancy for the production of a 1500 cc eight-cylinder car engine for OM of Brescia) that terminated with his joining Gilera in 1939. Our man remained at Arcore for over a decade (excluding the war years spent in Rome), through to the autumn of 1949 when he entered the court of Domenico Agusta, at the explicit request of the count, anxious to obtain the services of the best designer on the market.

In the meantime, on behalf of Giuseppe Gilera, Remor set to work on a new four-cylinder racing engine intended as a replacement for the Gilera GP derived from the Rondine. By 1940 the engine was already bench testing. A propos of this, in a true scoop from Arcore, *Motociclismo* of the 26th of September 1940 spoke of "a marvel, an authentic prodigy of transcendental engine mechan-

Top, a chain-drive 500 four from 1952-1966 (now conserved in the Agusta Museum at Cascina Costa) with, below right, a 500 MV Privat from 1964 with Hailwood riding on the Daytona circuit.

Bottom right, a Gilera 500 GP from 1953 with, left, a cutaway drawing of the 1955 version. The family feeling between the two models, from the architecture of the mechanical components is remarkable but inevitable as both the prestigious Lombard multi-cylinder bikes were the offspring of the same "father": Piero Remor.
It was to be no coincidence that the championship triumphs of the Arcore 500 (the 500 cc World Championship title in 1950 with Umberto Masetti, repeated in 1952, with Geoffrey Duke in 1953, 1954 and 1955 and with Libero Liberati in 1957) were to be followed by the 20-year sequence of Meccanica Verghera's world titles, starting with John Surtees successes in 1956, 1958, 1959 and 1960.

"TRANSCENDENTAL MECHANICAL ENGINEERING"

GILERA 500 4C.

ics". All that needs to be said is that thanks to the development of Remor's engine, destined to lose its supercharging in the post-war period due to the changing international race regulations, the Corse Gilera works team was to win (through to 1957, the year of the famous "abstention pact", with the firm's withdrawal from racing together with Moto Guzzi and Mondial) no less than six Riders' and five Constructors' titles in the 500 class, the blue ribbon category of the newborn (1949) World Championship.

With his arrival at Cascina Costa, the designer's biography became inextricably linked with the history of the original, exclusive MV four-cylinder power units. Remor was to remain on the moors of Varese through to 1953 when, after having designed a last racing four (a 350 cc unit derived from his previously mentioned first 500 cc design from 1950), only leaving after his relationship with the count deteriorated irreparably. The reasons for the divorce? Basically, the fact that the designer believed his technical decisions to be undisputable and inevitably clashed with the strong-willed Domenico Agusta to the point where the differences became irreparable and Remor was placed in a form of quarantine and asked to work on the design of the famous 350 cc Veturetta. Those working in the sector well remember how the imposing Piero Remor, in his double-breasted suits, an ever-present cigarette between his fingers, would respond to those who criticised him for certain original technical features, both on the engine and chassis sides (first and foremost, his beloved torsion bars of aeronautical origins), by coolly asking: "Where did you study?" His own three decades of brilliant ideas applied to motorcycles and cars spoke volumes. With regard to his MV period, it remains to be said that his 500 GP, albeit with myriad modifications, concluded its triumphant career as late as 1967 (in May, with Agostini's victory in Salzburg), no fewer than 17 years after its debut.
From 1954, Remor worked for Motom at Baranzate di Bollate in the Milanese hinterland and in late 1954 completed the 98 TS, a model housed in New York's MOMA after having been presented in the Industrial Design section of the XI Triennale in Milan in 1957. This light motorcycle was in effect the summation of the designer's theories, of his exploration of original and sophisticated solutions in a kind of never-ending search for the most advanced technology, and also his spiritual testimony in that after three years at Motom, from 1957 Remor took on only consultancy work before dying in 1957.
Looking back at his professional relationship with Piero Remor, Arturo Magni, the legendary engineer who the designer had "brought with him" from Gilera to the MV racing department and the irreplaceable eye-witness to the era (as well as our own personal Virgil, *si parva licet*... through the pages of this history through to the miracle of the MV Agusta F4) remembers him thus: "The engineer had the ability to do complicated sums as if he were an electronic calculator: this and other talents made him become what I define as the greatest of the designers of his era, the inventor of features that in various ways have made their mark."

The engineer Remor, wearing a jacket and tie even in the pits, in the company of the three Meccanica Verghera riders: from the right, Reginald "Reg" Armstrong, Renato Magi and Arciso Artesiani.
The first, an Irishman, was to be runner-up in the 250 cc World Championship with NSU, while the second was to be killed on the 17th of April 1951 during an attempt to break a number of speed records on the Terracina "strip" with a fully-faired MV 125.
After Renato Magi's death, Domenico Agusta prohibited any further world record attempts with his bikes, except in the case of the hour and 100 km records successfully broken by Mike "The Bike" Hailwood on a 500 GP at Daytona in 1964.
Lastly, wearing a helmet, Artesiani, who had the merit of riding the newborn 500 from Varese to an honourable debut result in the Belgian GP of July 1950 on the extremely fast Spa-Francorchamps circuit.

"EXCUSE ME, WHERE DID YOU STUDY?"

BAR CODE

Deriving directly from futuristic and intriguing aeronautical technology, torsion bars (which were to find applications on cars, motorcycles, aircraft and... tanks) were to become the "signature" of that connoisseur of fine mechanical design, the engineer Piero Remor. Made from the same steel normally used for coil springs, these "magic wands" work with one end fixed to a structure and the other free to be subjected to torsion, calibrated via classic splines.

Their first widespread use by the Roman designer exploited the self-damping effect deriving from the fact that the torsion angle, that is to say the amplitude of the springing movement, is directly proportional to the length of the bar itself. Thus we see them in the suspension configuration of the naturally aspirated Gilera GP 500 "four" in the immediate post-war period: at the front is a girder fork with four small torsion bars in correspondence with the four joints of the deformable parallelogram, while at the rear there was a swinging arm, the pivot of which took the form of a large torsion bar. While we again find the bars in the rear suspension of the British Douglas 350 twin of 1946 and later in that of the Lambretta D from 1951 (and the Lambrate-based firm's Motolambretta 125 and 250 racing scooters), in 1948 Remor designed the utilitarian Gilera 125, the first Italian four-stroke quarter-litre bike and a best-seller (along with its 150 cc sister model) for the Arcore marque. The design featured a torsion bar that, housed within the right-hand journal rotates the primary gear, acting as a flexible coupling between the crankshaft and the primary drive itself.

Two years later it was the turn of the four-cylinder MV Agusta 500 GP, where the Remor trademark can be found in both the front girder fork with torsion bars and the dual swinging arm with a jointed parallelogram action (thanks to 6 mm diameter bars) permitting the oscillation of the wheel (with a travel of 100 mm) along a straight trajectory, this overcoming the problems (the infamous torque "rebound" where the wheel itself judders when changing gear) deriving from the cardan shaft final drive. While the great rider Leslie Graham defined the torsion bar system as "the best possible springing", Arturo Magni recalls: "Our patented 'Parallelogram' for cardan shaft final drive motorcycles, reprises the Remorian doctrine on the subject. In fact, I hope that this is only the start of a future project of ours for a motorcycle with torsion bars used extensively, from the engine to the suspension: it would be the best possible tribute to my peerless maestro."

However, the true *summa* of the Remorian theories on torsion bars is the Motom 98TS from the April of 1955 on which the "magic wand" played a crucial role. We find it, in fact, as a flexible coupling between crankshaft and primary drive: transmission was effected via a pair of straight-cut gears with the crown wheel on the crankshaft rotated by a torsion bar acting as a flexible coupling "protecting" the crankshaft itself in the case of overly severe acceleration or deceleration. Torsion bars were also used in the engine's valvegear, acting as pivots for the rockers: here, the aim was to complete to best effect the return of the two valve springs (cylindrical coils that clearly worked on the torsion principle themselves).

Many years later, Honda was to use the valve return system on the twin-cylinder CB 450 twin-cam from 1965 and the successive CB 500 T from 1975. It does not end here though: on the cycle side of the 98 TS, torsion bars were used in the swinging arm suspension (front and rear) with rubber discs acting under torsion and providing springing through the effect of elastic hysteresis.

On this page, Arciso Artesiani aboard a shaft-drive MV 500 GP from 1950. On the facing page, on the left from the top: the twin-cam Honda CB 450 (1965), one of the first Japanese bikes to reach Italy, used a classic feature made famous by Remor: torsion bars as valve springs; the Motom 98 TS from 1955, a Remorian thesis on the application of torsion bars in both the power unit and the chassis of a motorcycle, on permanent display in the Museum of Modern Art of New York, alongside the Cisitalia 202. In the large photo, a close-up of the rear suspension of the 500 R19 from 1950, naturally suspended with torsion bars, a chassis refinement appreciated at the time by riders and engineers, especially when combined with a secondary drive featuring a cardan shaft and constant velocity joints.

First, in the June of 1950, came the press release. Then, from the 2nd to the 12th of December, the brand new road-going MV 500 Gran Sport (later the 500 R19) could be seen in the flesh, presented by the young Varese-based marque at the Triennale building in Milan's Parco Sempione: an all light alloy, four-cylinder, transverse engine, 40 hp (estimated) at 8500 rpm and 170 kph (estimated), twin overhead camshafts actuated by a gear train, dual rear swinging arms, shaft drive and twin headlights.

Even though the mechanical data were somewhat vague as at the time the engine's beautiful casings contained no mechanical components, the new bike (painted in extremely elegant metallic silvers, painstakingly finished and featuring abundant use of ultra-light aeronautical alloys) was breathtakingly innovative. There was plenty to *épater les bourgeois*, to the point where the British magazine The Motorcycle on the 7th of December 1950 spoke with an admiring tone of the "Vincent HRD of Italy", in reference to the marque from Stevenage (located in Her Majesty's verdant Hertfordshire), famous from the mid-Twenties for the exclusive appeal of its twin-cylinder models. The effect was enhanced because that multi-cylinder engine had already been seen in April at the Milan Trade Fair, mounted in the first example (proudly displayed despite being unfinished given taste for surprises typical of Count Domenico) of the MV 500 GP that also featured shaft drive and which the engineer Piero Remor was building with all haste to allow the Lombard marque to compete in the 500 class of the soon to be revived World Championship. In short, it was inevitable that faced with the R19 powered by an engine mirroring the Grand Prix unit already seen that spring, the well-to-do clientele of the era would be thinking: "With this bike, I too could be a motorcycling champion!"

500 R19 (1950): THE BIRTH OF THE LEGEND

Almost a "Doni Tondo"... Curiously, the first project entrusted to Remor a few months after joining Domenico Agusta's court, had not been a racing bike (perhaps ready for the TT that was to have inaugurated on the 5th of June 1950 the second World Championship), but a road-going 500 cc model. By November 1949, under the designer's direction, the draughtsman Luigi Canziani had already pencilled in the first lines. Regarding this order of events, requested by Count Domenico for obvious motives of commercial image, Magni's testimony leaves no room for doubt, even though, incredibly, just a few weeks after work began word came down from above that all efforts should be focussed on a racing bike. This led to the MV 500 GP that was to be exhibited at the classic Milan Trade Fair in the spring and was then ready (its 50 hp at 9000 rpm being good for 190 kph) on the 2nd of July 1950 when Artesiani rode it on its debut in the Belgian GP on the extremely fast Spa-Francorchamps circuit. It finished with a fine fifth place overall and also recorded the highest speed on the straight in front of the pits.

Returning to the R19, it has to be said that due to an inexplicable order from the Count, the model never went into production despite everything being ready, with displays in the major dealerships and the possibility of ordering an example via "special forms". A price of L.950,000

Top, from the left: the road-going 500 four from 1950 and its racing "sister" from 1953, with an Earles fork and torsion bar rear suspension. In both, the final drive was via a cardan shaft with constant velocity joints, a system that on the Cascina Costa marque's racing half-litre had been considered a makeshift solution since the previous season when the racing department had adopted a classic chain drive.

Bottom, the 350 four from 1953-1965 (now conserved in the Agusta Museum), a model that debuted in the Tourist Trophy; the 350 cc displacement had been obtained by "sleeving" the bores of a half-litre engine, while later the power unit was completely redesigned. Bikes like this one were raced by the Rhodesian "meteor" Ray Amm and the Englishman John Surtees.

had been established, an astronomical sum for the era and sufficient to purchase a nice apartment in a city such as Milan. In this way the company policy of chasing an elite target had been established and the motorcycling world began to realise that the top of the range MV bikes were never going to be for all.

For obvious reasons (there were no mechanical components) any technical analysis inevitably had to wait for the successive 600 cc version (the first four-cylinder MV to be built in series and its larger 750 and 800 cc sister models: as far as the 500 is concerned, the information is decidedly patchy and summarized in a very brief official table (see the appendix). The R19's engine naturally had numerous features in common with Remor's earlier multi-cylinder creations (for example, the naturally aspirated Gilera "four" of some years earlier), but to those who underlined the fact, the designer replied: "What can I do, they're daughters of the same father." A father who, it is only right to point out, reprised concepts seen in the engines of historic racing cars from the 1920s such as the Miller 91 and the Bugatti 35B, from the gear-driven camshafts to the horizontally split crankcase.

In line with a tradition fairly well established in Italy from the 1930s, the fuel tank carried the two circular speedometer-milometer and rev-counter dials, in the classic left and right configuration. Further curiosities: the show prototype of the R19 featured provisional components such as the dual headlamp and telescopic rear dampers, while the ignition was taken care of by a British-made Lucas magneto (in place of an Italian unit by Magneti Marelli). Lastly, the secondary transmission unit (cardan shaft with constant velocity joints) was located on the left, in contrast with the definitive right-hand configuration on the larger 600, 750 and 800 cc models. It is worth underlining that the shaft drive (rather than a chain, which needed more maintenance and… created dirt) was adopted not only as a result of Count Domenico Agusta's famous anti-racing dictate (for privateers), but also as a selling point as with prestigious marques such as BMW.

If you look carefully, on both side of the engine block of the MV 500 Gran Sport on display in the Agusta Museum at Cascina Costa there is an enamelled "rondo" or medallion with the gilded script "Agusta R19". That R stands for Remor and is overlooked on both sides of the fuel tank by the gilded cogwheel and the two blue wings of the marque's traditional badge. The combination is evidence that the distant dream of an enthusiastic Sicilian lover of flight had found an heir in the great engineer who loved racing, the man known to the British as the Wizard.

Top left, a Bugatti 35B, the legendary French car that together with the American Miller 91 was the source of inspiration for a number of mechanical features of the original Italian fours, including the gear train actuating the camshafts, a refinement normally reserved for racing machinery.

Right, Domenico Agusta with Nello Pagani aboard an MV 500 four at a Rome GP. The popular rider (born in Milan in 1911), a world champion in 1949 with the Mondial 125 and later a flag-bearer for Gilera, had arrived at Cascina Costa in 1953: following his last GP in 1955 he was to conclude his career as director of the racing team.

Bottom, the drawing of the longitudinal section of the final drive of the 600: it was now on the right while on the 500 from 1950 it had been on the left.

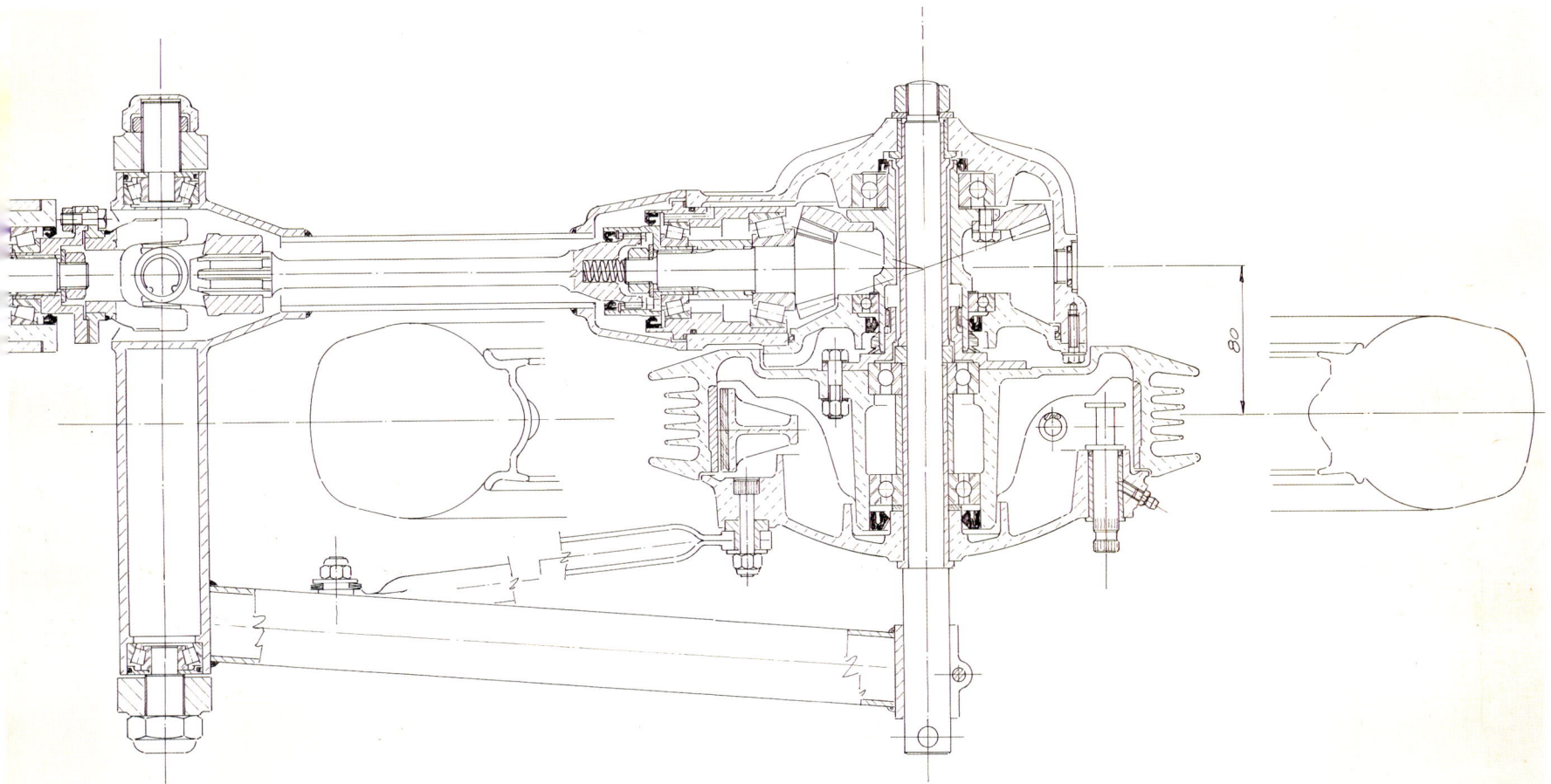

MOD. 199	199-15-051-0-00
ASSIEME MOZZO POSTERIORE E TRASMISSIONE	1:1
	14-12-56

After eight years of depression, 1965 saw clear evidence of a revival in the sector, with the market even demonstrating an appetite for new "heavy" motorcycles (later known as "maximotos"), this being an era in which the highest aspirations of an Italian biker would have been a Moto Guzzi Falcone, a Gilera 300B or, *rara avis*, a British or German twin. Three Italian marques (Italjet, Moto Guzzi and MV) were the first to take up the challenge, proposing models with displacements of over 500 cc: while the first two presented respectively the Grifon and V7 twins, the third daringly launched a four-cylinder...

It was hot, perhaps even too hot on that Saturday the 4th of November 1965 in the pavilions of the Milan Trade Fair at the inauguration of the 309th Cycle and Motorcycle Show. A number of incongruous pots of cyclamens embellished the crowded Meccanica Verghera stand, overlooked by a proud illuminated sign reading "59 World Championships Won in the Service of Serial Production" and featuring two empty, oval podiums on which, curiously a card with a large question mark was hung. Those in the know soon realised that this was another of Domenico Agusta's coups de theatre: the Count had, in fact, decided that only on the following Thursday the 9th would motorcycle enthusiasts be able to admire the Cascina Costa marque's most exciting new product. Finally, fifteen years after the prototype half-litre came the first Italian road-going four-cylinder built in (limited) series: the MV 600 4C6 (workshop code 199).

Presented in a severe black and chrome livery, it was hardly helped by an improbable headlight-tank-saddle line but transmitted the beauty of hand-made high craftsmanship, still leagues away from the assembly line, with assembly specifications more akin to those of the racing department than a normal production shop. Above all, that aluminium alloy engine (that, at first sight, appears to be a photocopy of that of the 500 GP recently ridden triumphantly by John Surtees and Mike Hailwood) displayed Meccanica Verghera's sophisticated technology. The enthusiastic comment in *Motociclismo* read: "It is with great pleasure that we salute the advent of this motorcycle that finally places on a practical level features long confined, as ends in themselves, to the field of competition", a phrase that summarized the expectations of all enthusiasts, given that the multi-cylinder engine could be the first four with a racing heritage for everyday use, the "ultimate weapon" with which to conquer the nascent and hugely attractive "superbike" market. Yet it was not to be.

Provocation on a grand scale. There were to be too many factors that weighed against commercial distribution of a model as exclusive as it was penalised by technical and other incongruities. And to think that the promise was there, from the twin overhead camshaft engine to the five-speed gearbox and the electric starting via an exclusive dynamotor. In that late Milanese autumn, in fact, the first road-going superbike of the modern era truly had seen the light of day, the machine that was to provoke the motorcycle industry of the Land of the Rising Sun into swamping the market with its own fours some time later...

600 4C6 (1965): THE "BLACK QUEEN"

Top, the 600 four from 1965. On its presentation, the model was came in for severe criticism because it appeared to be so different to the marque's successful contemporary racing bikes. As is well known, on the basis of precise indications from Domenico Agusta, certain features of the bike (from the cardan shaft to the unusual displacement, from the mechanically actuated rather than hydraulic dual Campagnolo front discs to the excessive weight) were intended to discourage privateers from using it for racing.

Bottom, from the left: Count Domenico riding pillion on a 600 piloted by an executive from Bell Helicopter, a division of the American Bell Aircraft Corporation and partner of Agusta from 1952; Corrado Agusta, the successor to Domenico in 1971 at the head of the company, also seen aboard a 600.

Unfortunately, when in the April of 1967 the first clients finally received the object of their desires (52 hp at 8000 rpm, 160 kph... rather than the declared 185 kph), it was to be clear to all that the 600 4C6 was by no means a "replica" of the racing models, but rather that MV's idea (or rather that of Count Domenico) was that of presenting the world with a motorcycle like no other (it featured no less that 30 cogs and not a single chain!), a machine the advertising of the era was to define as the "two-wheeled Rolls Royce." Certainly, it had the inebriating music of the four cylinder and the submerged song of the famous and oh-so-sporting gear train, but it also had that rather less sporting shaft drive and the two mechanically rather than hydraulically actuated Campagnolo front brake discs, inherited directly from the Maserati 250 GTL quarter-litre bike from over ten years earlier (patented by the engineer Guerrieri Gonzaga).

And then that 600 was heavy (221 kg dry) and devastatingly expensive (quality costs!), with the list price rising from L.1,060,000 to L.1,360,000. As a consequence, just 310 examples were sold (starting from frame number 199.001) through to the June of 1971: the purchasers were wealthy enthusiasts scattered around the world (one bike went to the Shah of Persia, another to Geneva and the garage of Vittorio Emanuele di Savoia who still owns it, others landed in the United States and a few in Japan. A single-seater prototype with simpler pushrod valvegear was prepared for tests in view of a commission from the Italian police, but it never went into production.

Then again, there were rumours that potential purchasers were required to provide a written declaration that they would not race the bike and that they would not sell it on to anyone intending to race it, that the Count would, as apparently Ettore Bugatti was accustomed to doing before letting one of his Type 35s go, "filter" them one by one on the basis of the census, only giving his consent to those prepared to swear on their honour (almost certainly placing their right hand on a Cascina Costa workshop manual autographed by Count Domenico...) never to use the "Black Queen" for racing. It has to be said that anyone thinking of racing that weighty 600 with its shaft drive and unusual displacement would have had their work cut out... As Magni recalls: "When Count Agusta ordered us to get the project up and running, he actually told us that the machine should have a specification that would prevent it being raced in the future."

It remains to be said that the machine featured wet sump lubrication, car-type ignition with a distributor and a multiple-plate oil-bath clutch, that the standard coil was soon replaced by the more astute riders with the famous Bosch "red" and that the frame (duplex closed cradle, hydraulic front fork and a rear swinging arm with hydraulic dampers) guaranteed good handling for such a heavy bike.

Lastly, having said that the engine was robust and flexible, that the two Dell'Orto MB twin-choke 245 mm carburettors were particularly attractive with their sporty filter-less intake trumpets and that the 600 as the first experimental design (see page 74) of a certain Massimo Tamburini, there remains the regret for what the "Black Queen" might have been but instead was not...

Vittorio Emanuele di Savoia on his 600, recently the object of a complete restoration.
Following its presentation, crowned heads and captains of industry were among the ultra-elite target group for sales of the "Black Queen". Even though Count Domenico Agusta, in certain cases, actually made a gift of one to the purchasers of his helicopters, ever the core business of the Agusta firm. This was the case with the Shah of Persia.
In effect, rather than a source of commercial profits, the Meccanica Verghera's road-going fours, so obviously closely related in mechanical terms to the racing bikes, always represented a prestigious "calling card" for MV's productive capacities, in parallel with its peerless sporting record.

Following the semi-flop of the 600 4C6 of 1965, no less than four years passed before colleagues and enthusiasts managed to persuade Domenico Agusta to present a new four-cylinder road bike more in tune with the spirit (if not the substance) of the rampant multi-cylinder GP machines that were sweeping the board on the world's circuits (this was in the middle of the Agostini era).

Count Domenico had continued to avoid the issue due to his old fears that mediocre results from a production bike with improved performance, perhaps raced by privateers, might tarnish the immense prestige conquered by the works racing team. This is why we had to wait until the Milan Motorcycle Show in the November of 1969 in order to admire the MV 750 4C75 (workshop code 214, frame numbering from 214.001); that is to say, the 750 Sport (or S).

This is the one, thought the die-hard MV fans. At first sight, in fact, the new model, whose precise displacement was 743 cc, was a complete contrast to the 600 thanks to styling mid-way between aggressive and elegant, combined with superior finishing, from the fire red frame to the beautiful leather saddle (also red!), the pretty round chrome headlight and the dramatic quadruple trumpet exhausts providing a sound nudging the legal limits. Not to speak of the declared performance: 69 hp at 7900 rpm (in later press releases this dropped to 65 hp at the same engine speed) with a top speed of 225 kph.

As usual, the Cascina Costa commercial department was not lacking in optimism. A maximum speed of this order would in fact have placed the 750 Sport at the pinnacle of world motorcycle production, yet as we shall see, this was not the case.

Beautiful but damned. However, a sporty appearance, emphasised by a dramatic red-blue-white livery was early evidence of the overall brio characterising the new bike, testimony to the successful resolution of many of the problems regarding the styling and substance of the staid 600 model.

The bike did though retain shaft drive and had a dry weight of over 230 kg, both factors serving to dissuade any gentleman riders from taking it to the track in anger.

The road testing of MV's latest "jewel" was entrusted to Angelo Bergamonti and Alberto Pagani, as well as the firm's usual in-house testers. Production of the model began almost a year after its presentation and it immediately went on sale, remaining available in various forms through to the launch of the America model in 1975. Late in 1970, the list price was L.1,970,000, neatly matching the sum required to purchase a pair of beautiful BSA Rocket 3s. An ultra-elite price, therefore, that went hand-in-hand with biblical delivery times, the usual more or less binding requests that purchasers should not use the bike for any form of racing and running and regular maintenance costs better suited to the budget of sheiks than those of ordinary motorcycling enthusiasts. All this created serious problems when it came to marketing the model and sales struggled to reach a total of 583 comprising all the versions: a number of examples ending up in North America, Great Britain, Australia and Germany.

Nonetheless, the 750 Sport boasted qualities and features that should have brought success on the

From the right, the rider Gianfranco Bonera (second in the 1974 World Championship aboard an MV 500) alongside Corrado Agusta while track testing with a 750 Sport. The tests highlighted poor roadholding in fast corners caused, above all, by the classic duplex cradle frame's lack of flexional and torsional rigidity and the bike's excessive weight.
This provoked dangerous snaking, especially under sudden braking. While, in spite of the prejudices in this regard, in normal conditions the bike never suffered from the feared shaft effect or other anomalous reactions (for example, juddering of the driven wheel with consequent loss of traction) due to the secondary transmission using a cardan shaft and constant velocity joints.

750 4C75 SPORT (1969): THE "LADY IN RED"

market, from the customary twin overhead camshafts and the gear train actuating them to the light alloy crankcase cast in one piece this time (and beautifully finished on the Genevoise, a legendary Swiss precision machine tool, then owned only by MV and Parilla) and the individually cast light alloy cylinders (this was the only four-cylinder engine in the world not to have a monoblock), from the sophisticated Magneti Marelli dynamotor for electric starting and ancillaries to the four filter-less carburettors fitted with extremely long, sports-style intake trumpets. Those 24 mm Dell'Orto UB's tended to go out of tune all too frequently (as the author, a fortunate long-term rider of the model, can confirm).

Completing this mechanical analysis, the engine featured wet-sump lubrication, coil and distributor ignition (and an enormous, car-style 12 volt battery) and the transmission system comprised an oil bath (or "oil mist" according to the manufacturer's picturesque description) multiplate clutch and a five-speed gearbox. The chassis configuration was based on the usual tubular duplex closed cradle frame that lacked a little rigidity when dealing with the revised engine. The front fork was an hydraulic Ceriani unit with 36 mm stems, while the hydraulic dampers fitted to the rear swinging arm (pivoting on sophisticated adjustable conical roller bearings, as did the steering) were also made by Arturo Ceriani of Samarate (a former valued member of the MV racing department) with the preloading of the (now exposed) springs being easily adjusted by hand. At the front, a purposeful Grimeca four-cam brake certainly looked the part. Apparently a little brusque, it instead proved to be progressive and resistant to prolonged heavy use. Only in the summer of 1974 was it to be definitively replaced by equally efficient Scarab discs (produced by a "satellite" company of the group and naturally hydraulic rather than mechanically actuated like the Campagnolo discs fitted to the 600).

Despite its significant weight, the 750 Sport (which in reality had a top speed approaching 200 kph) was a pleasant ride and its general manoeuvrability was an improvement on the 600. Vibration was virtually absent and a symphonic "sound track" was provided by engine and exhaust. The British press were to speak of a "an elegant flash of colour and sound" and "perforating clouds of sounds", adding that travelling on such a machine, "the sensual diffusion of sound from the engine is the best sound trip in the motorcycling world."

As mentioned, this model was to remain in the MV catalogue through to 1975 in diverse versions. The second, the 750 GT, produced in just 48 examples and mainly destined for Spain, dates from the November of 1971 and according to those in the know was the most well balanced, its 69 hp at 7000 rpm being good for over 190 kph. The fabulous 750 SS of the December of 1971 instead remained at the prototype stage (78 hp at 9000 rpm, 260 kph), as did its faired variant from 1974 with a displacement of 860 cc. The "second series" 750 Sport was sold in 110 examples between 1972 and 1973 and followed by the "third series" boasting 69 hp at 7,900 rpm and good for 214 kph thanks in part to 27 mm carburettors with integral float chambers.

Top, from the left, a photo of the 1973 version of the 750 Sport and a brochure for the first series. Among the most obvious modifications, the dual Scarab front discs replacing the original bulky Grimeca drum.

Bottom, from the left: A BSA Rocket 3, the fabulous British triple that was a contemporary of the MV 750 GT presented in November 1971 and featuring, according to a Meccanica Verghera press release, "very personal styling features." Among the most obvious: the sober ivory-metallic light bronze livery and the saddle (offering a seat and a half) in black leather. The list price rose from the L.1,95,000 of 1972 to L.2,336,000 in 1974, with delivery "three months after ordering."

Officially named the 750 S America (workshop code 221, frame numbering from 221.001), the new model's engine had a displacement of over 789 cc and consequently was universally known as the 800 America. Destined for the rich American market, the last road-going MV four was launched in 1975 as a final attempt to revive the fortunes of a marque that had already achieved legendary status but was now struggling. A model eagerly awaited by the US importer (COC of New York, with offices on Wall Street) who rather optimistically intended to sell 500 examples a year in the States, the 800 America found an enthusiastic internal sponsor in Fredmano Spairani, the aforementioned state manager of EFIM and it was realised under the supervision of the engineer Giuseppe Bocchi of Parma, the (former Lamborghini, Ferrari and Tecno) designer of the contemporary 500 GP four-cylinder boxer engine (Cascina Costa's never-developed "ultimate weapon" against the domination of the Japanese two-strokes in the second half of the 1970s).

The red livery of the 800 flattered its aggressive styling with more square-cut (GP-style) forms inline with most recent the aesthetic canons in the sector. Most importantly, a revised, thoroughbred engine matched the aggressive new exterior: 75 hp at 8500 rpm for a realistic maximum speed of 210 kph. Its wonderful architecture continued to remain in full view with plenty of race-style sandblasting establishing its place in the genealogy of Meccanica Verghera's GP machines. As with the previous four-cylinder units, the engine proved to be perfectly developed, with a British specialist magazine writing that the rule at MV would appear to be "assemble and forget."

The crankcase was in aluminium, like the cylinder heads and barrels, while the pressed in sleeves were in cast iron. The camshafts were still driven via a gear train, housed in the casing set in the well running from the cylinder head to the crankcase. Wet sump lubrication was retained, as was ignition via a distributor, coil and battery (the usual car-style 12 volt unit typical of almost all heavy Italian motorcycles of the period) all produced by Bosch. As with the previous models, there was no kick-start, the customary dynamotor (now also made by Bosch) acting as a classic starter motor. Four Dell'Orto VHB 26 mm carburettors with air filters were fitted: how the open trumpets of the past were missed! The gearbox continued to feature five speeds, while the shaft drive was perhaps "the most enjoyable we have ever tested" according to the *Motociclismo* testers who wrote the first road test.

Oh so dear MV! The new model could have been the "ultimate weapon" challenging the entire range of sports bikes with displacements of over 500 cc, but once again it was not to be. To start with, in late 1975, the list price of the America was L.4,112,590 ($6,000), far too expensive when you consider that a contemporary and highly desirable BMW R90S cost a good million less. In this respect, the head of the MV technical department, Mario Rossi, recalled the "struggle to sell the last 42 examples of a total production batch of 350 bikes." The road tests then brought to light a number of other negative issues, starting with the claim that in fast corners, the usual inadequacies of the frame and dampers were revealed and caused "conspicuous snaking that began at around 150 kph." In short, the old and never resolved torsional and flexional problems of a

800 AMERICA (1975): THE SWAN SONG

Top, the 800 America (the official name being the 750 S America) from 1975 and, below, its homologation sheet from the following year. The photo highlights the design efforts made to offer a bike that was fashionably stylish, especially the generally slim lines obtained despite the presence of the bulky twin overhead cam, four-cylinder engine. As an alternative to the aggressive racing-style black exhaust terminals (matching the black leather saddle and the matte black headlamp) four classic chrome silencers could subsequently be ordered.

Bottom right, the BMW R90S, the Bavarian marque's fantastic boxer twin that was a well-respected rival to Cascina Costa's latest road-going four on the market.

ECCANICA
ERGHERA
GALLARATE

MOTOCICLO
MV 221 (750 AMERICA)

Omologato dal Ministero dei Trasporti
Direzione Generale M.C.T.C. - Certificato n. 15510 OM in data 9-3-1976
E' autorizzato il rilascio della dichiarazione di conformità (art. 53 del T.U. 15-6-360)

ANNO
1976

Mod. D.G.M. 495

PUNZONATURA
(Caratteri e grandezza
dei veri)

AVVISATORE ACUSTICO

MV 221 ☆ 0123456789 ☆
DGM 15510 OM
Stampigliato sul telaio

* TIPO DELLA STRUTTURA telaio tubolare
- Posti .... n   2

DIMENSIONI
- Lunghezza max .... m   2,15
- Larghezza max .... m   0,72
- Passo (a carico) .... m   1,39

PESI
Peso a vuoto Kg. 230 + conducente
Kg. 70 .... Kg.   328
- Peso complessivo (2 posti) .. Kg.   398

SOSPENSIONI (tipo e descrizione) Anteriore forcella
telescopica. Posteriore forcellone oscillante.

| RUOTE con cerchio | anteriore | 2,15 x 18" |
| | posteriore | 2,50 x 18" |

| Pneumatici | anteriore | 3,50 V x 18" |
| | posteriore | 4,00 V x 18" |

* FRENI: v. retro

IMPIANTO ELETTRICO
Dinamotore .... Volt. 12 - Watt 130
Batteria .... Volt. 12 - Ah   32

Dispositivi illuminazione e segnalamento di tipo appro-
vato, proiettore anteriore con incorporata la luce di posizione. luce posizione posteriore con incorporata la luce di
arresto, luce targa e catadiottro, avvisatore acustico.

* Caratteristiche essenziali, la cui modifica comporta la necessità di una nuova omologazione (art. 226 del D.P.R. 30-6-1959 n. 420)

MOTORE
- Denominazione e modello   221
- Tempi .... n   4
- Cilindri .... n   4
- Diametro .... mm   65
- Corsa .... mm   56
- Cilindrata totale .... cm³   790
- Potenza fiscale Cv   11
Rapporto di compressione   9,3

- Potenza max effettiva Cv   78
                          a giri/1' 8000

Raffreddamento ....   aria
FRIZIONE: a dischi multipli in bagno di olio con comando
a mano sul manubrio a sinistra

CAMBIO DI VELOCITA'
N. 5 marce con comando selettore a pedale x destra
Trasmissione primaria: motore-cambio = 1 : 1,75

Cambio velocità	prima (15/30x21/25) = 1 : 2,38
	seconda (19/27x21/25) = 1 : 1,692
	terza (22/24x21/25) = 1 : 1,296
	quarta (24/22x21/25) = 1 : 1,09
	quinta (1 x 1) = 1 : 1

Trasmissione intermedia (rinvio)   (15/16) = 1 : 1,066
Trasmissione secondaria   (12/32) = 1 : 2,668

Velocità massima calcolata a n. giri di massima potenza
(rapporto totale motore-ruota 1 : 4,98 = Km/h 193

PRESTAZIONI: 1 Km	Partenza da fermo .. sec. 25,4
	Lanciato .... sec. 17,3
	Velocità max effettiva Km/h 208

Consumo (norme CUNA) lt/m/100 Km. 12,5
SERBATOIO: Capacità totale litri 19 circa di benzina
SILENZIATORE (v. retro)

chassis that was never the equal of its power unit. And to think that the 800 featured significant innovations. One, finally, was the inverted positioning of the gearshift and rear brake controls, unified with the Anglo Saxon system (also adopted by the Japanese manufacturers), with the pedal of the first on the left and the second on the right. Furthermore, the model was fully up-to-date with the strict US pollution legislation that, unfortunately albeit inevitably also concerned acoustic performance, hence the decision to limit the noise levels produced by the engine to the 80 decibel limit prescribed in the States. This was achieved, as mentioned, by fitting an air filter and virtually closed Lafranconi silencers (fake trombones). In this way, as *Motociclismo* underlined, the exhaust note of the four-cylinder MV "was no longer the wild scream of before, but emerged suffocated like that of an engine in poor health" and, what is more, the famous camshaft gear train "made itself heard with a loud and unpleasant noise that may confuse the non-experts with regard to the integrity of the internal mechanical parts." In recompense, the engine proved to be incredibly docile thanks to cooler cam profiles.

On the chassis side, there was the usual tubular duplex closed cradle frame, with a Ceriani fork and swinging arm controlled by Sebac hydraulic dampers adjustable via 5 spring preload positions. The aforementioned and efficient Scarab front disc brakes were retained. The standard Borrani wire wheels or the optional EPM cast aluminium alloys were shod with the Metzeler tyres highly recommended by the manufacturer and developed specifically for bikes with shaft drive (in other words, BMWs): some owners, willing to try any means of improving the bike's handling, did fit the more high performance Dunlop TT100s.

Dangerous curves. Let's take a seat aboard the America 800, on a saddle in black suede leather and equipped with a lockable hatch covering a storage compartment designed to house a tool kit and the bike's handbook and registration documents. Unfortunately, there were actually too many tools, no less than 14, to fit in: while nicely made by Beta in chrome vanadium, they were not of the same quality as the forged Stahlwille or Bahco tools that the enthusiasts soon replaced them with. The ignition key is no longer positioned in the usual starting-lighting unit on the instrument panel, but under the tank, on the left: it is tricky to reach from the saddle and uncomfortable to use. The switchgear on the handlebars is no longer the unpopular CEV units of the previous models, but more modern Aprilia equipment with clear Japanese influences. Nuts and screws are all thick chrome plated.

Manouevrability of the bike when stationary is limited in terms of steering response, because it is even heavier than the 750: a dry weight of 240 kg, with 104 on the front wheel, 136 at the rear. It is instead remarkably wieldy once on the move, on both straight and twisting roads even though, as mentioned previously, a degree of snaking always tends to set in through long, fast curves. And heaven help you if in the middle of that curve you have to brake hard...

Top, from an original Meccanica Verghera brochure, the 750 S (known to all as the 800) America, presented in Milan late in 1975: the front three quarters view showed to best effect the model's race-bred styling.

Bottom, from the left: the slim front end and the riding position of the last road-going MV four prior to the "resurrection" with the F4 in 1997; the engine and transmission assembly that was described by *Motociclismo* in the April of 1976 as "a great piece of engineering with a willingness to rev and the most enjoyable shaft drive we have ever tested"; the two-piece handlebars (by Menani rather than Tommaselli as on the 750 Sport) feature the new Aprilia switchgear in place of the antiquated (and uncomfortable to operate) CEV units.

750ˢ AMERICA

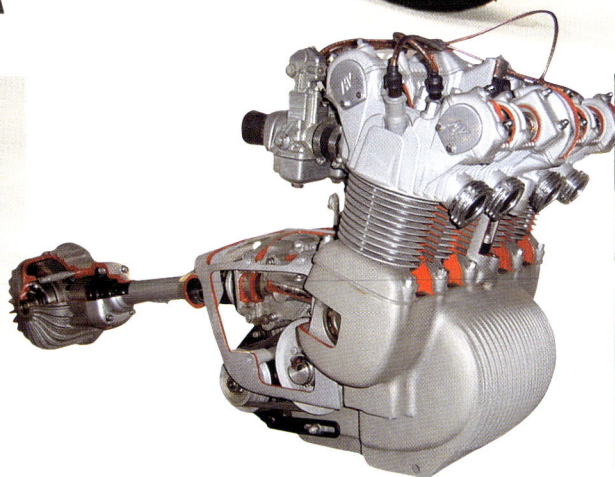

The 800 America model represents MV's swansong, after which the baton was taken up by the private tuners, craftsmen with boundless expertise who inherited a fabulous marque and accepted the challenge of developing the road-going fours with improvements to the mechanicals, the chassis and the styling which the manufacturer, for well known motives, was never willing to develop. In chronological order, the various episodes in this story are as follows:

Menani

In the beginning, it was Angelo Menani of Milan, the mechanic known as "Golden Hands": In 1969, he worked on a 600, starting with the front end (revised using components from a contemporary Honda 750 Four). Then it was the turn of the carburettors and a general revision that included an attractive sports tank in fibreglass.

Tamburini

Again on the basis of a 600 (this was in the winter of 1970-1971), Massimo Tamburini had fun developing his *opera prima*. The Rimini-born designer began by drawing up a brand new frame in chromium-molybdenum tubes, with Fontana drum brakes (four cams at the front) and a "long" Ceriani fork. After painstaking development of the cylinder head, the engine was fitted with the cylinders from the 750 Sport, with particular attention being paid to the fuel system: in place of the orginal twin Dell'Orto MB 24 carburettors, two SS 32 mm units revised by Malossi were fitted, with a remote float chamber between the two. The gearbox became a close-ratio unit, while above all the final drive employed a chain rather than a cardan shaft. After many vicissitudes, this historic bike is now owned by the Bologna-based collector Piero Parmeggiani.

Bimota

It was in 1976 that Bimota suggested to MV Agusta that a road-going model focussing on power and lightness might be developed from Agostini's German GP winning machine. A feasibility study was signed off by Morri and Tamburini (two of the three founders, together with Bianchi, of the new marque from Rimini): a four-cylinder, 16-valve engine was conceived with a displacment of between 750 and 1200 cc, a sump extended forwards as on the legendary triple the great Ago rode to so many triumphs, twin overhead camshafts actuated by a chain or a toothed belt situated on the left, either shaft or chain final drive and both electric and pedal starting. The revolutionary model might have been exhibited at the Milan Motorcycle Show in the late autumn of 1977 had, as we have seen, the Varese firm not deserted the event completely.

Top, the first masterpiece (winter 1970-1971) by Massimo Tamburini, the transformation of shaft-drive 600 into a chain-drive 750, with a new chrome-molybdenum steel frame and a fuel tank and saddle in thin aluminium hand-crafted by a Bolognese panel-beater.

Bottom left, the decidedly sporty configuration of the 600 special developed in 1969 by Angelo Menani (the popular Milan mechanic from the Porta Ticinese quarter), showing the aggressive new carburettors with no air filter and open trumpets and the race-style tank in fibreglass; right, road testing of the MV-Bimota "feasibility study" proposed to the Varese marque by the Bianchi, Morri (standing, next to the bike) and Tamburini's new company that never went into production.

FINAL FLOURISHES: TUNERS AND REPLICATORS

Magni

In 1977, one of the pillars of MV Agusta, the aforementioned head of the racing department and sporting director Arturo Magni, retired and founded together with his second son Giovanni, a mechanical engineer, Elaborazioni Magni, while two years earlier he had already created EPM (Elaborazioni Progettazioni Motociclistiche) with his eldest son Carlo, also a mechanical engineer. Both companies were located at Samarate (Varese) a stone's throw from Cascina Costa. Even though in the following years Arturo also worked on BMW, Guzzi and Honda bikes (succeeding in this last case in keeping even the Bol d'Or 900 on the road in a straight line as well in corners), from the outset he paid closest attention to the four-cylinder unit he had seen born.

As early as 1977, a series of mechanical and chassis transformations were proposed along with aerodynamic and styling modifications, starting with the kits increasing displacement firstly to 837 and then to 861 cc. The "packet" comprised paired cylinders in sand-cast aluminium alloy with pressed-in cast-iron sleeves, an ignition system initially featuring duplex platinum coated points and then Magneti Marelli electronics, PHF 30 or 32 mm carburettors with a pump to increase acceleration, a racing clutch and a chain rather than cardan shaft final drive. The four beautiful black exhaust pipes exhibited classic racing-style curves. The frame was fabricated entirely in Cr-Mo steel tubes with TIG (Tungsten Inert Gas) welding, the box-section swinging arm also being TIG welded. Suspension elements were by Ceriani. Over the years, there were countless production up-dates, still available on request. Among these, of particular note is the Parallelogramma, a patented swinging arm capable of eliminating the infamous torque twist that plagues cardan shaft secondary drive systems.

Segoni

From late 1977, Segoni Corse of Florence began producing a small series of a dozen or so "special" MV fours around a tubular beam frame of its own design. The project was inspired by the brothers Giuliano and Robert Segoni's passion for sports bikes: in 1978 the elder brother was tragically killed during the road-testing of one of his "creatures", while the second, an architect, spoke to us of their projects in an interview a few years ago: "The MV engine presented certain peculiarities that by no means facilitated its installation in our frame. However, with suitable 'gussets' and in virtue of the frame's great simplicity the problem was resolved."

Rossi

Again in Florence (Brozzi to be precise), between 1980 and 1985 another two brothers, Franco and Mario Rossi, worked on the development of a number of MV fours for both road and competition use. Once again the point of departure was the "classic" Magni recipe (861 cc engine, paired cylinders, racing clutch and, of course, chain drive) along with Bosch electronic ignition on the crankshaft.

Top, from the left: Giovanni and Arturo Magni (on the right), alongside one of their recent creations based on Suzuki mechanicals and a frame and superstructures that display the graphics (clearly it was no coincidence) of a classic MV 750 Sport, of which in the background can be seen an example that had arrived at Samarate for restoration; two modified versions of the Cascina Costa fours carrying the Magni "signature", with on the right a copy of Agostini's MV 750 from the Imola 200 Miles of 1972 ready for delivery to an enthusiastic Japanese collector.

Bottom left, the "badge" certifying the inscription of a bike in the MV Historic Register; right, from the top: a 1977 creation by the Florentine brothers Giuliano and Roberto Segoni, based on the famous girder frame they designed; the mechanical heart of an 850 (in reality 861 cc) version of the 800 America developed by the brothers Franco and Mario Rossi of Brozzi (Florence).

Hansen

In the December of 1982, a small series of 11 MV Agustas was put on sale in Germany and Great Britain equipped with an 1100 cc engine entirely built in Germany, albeit inspired by the usual Magni 861 cc power unit. The model was known as the Grand Prix and was built at the behest of the former German MV importer Michael Hansen (Lichtentalerstrasse 83, Baden Baden) in collaboration with with his chief mechanic Roland Schneider. They were bikes producing almost 100 hp and good for over 230 kph that were never distributed in Italy.

In this chapter devoted to what were effectively posthumous variations on the MV four-cylinder road bike theme, we have left to last those by firms we believe it is more correct to define as replicators rather than tuners. That is to say; while the latter are to be placed within the manufacturer's original "canon" (including the one-off Target, the fine styling exercise realised in the early Seventies by the German, Hans Muth, future designer of the BMW R65LS and the Suzuki Katana), the former represent a later and external factor, distracting when not actually misleading with respect to the subject of this book.
Here we are referring to the "replicas" that, while not while not wishing to tar them all with the same brush, are often spurious when not fanciful or inspired by purely commercial motives. We shall take a brief look at a couple of representatives of the phenomenon.

Kay

The first is the Briton David Kay, a great fan of the Cascina Costa marque. He has fabricated *ex novo*, parts, engines and even entire four-cylinder road-going and race bikes, starting in 1989 with a first four-cylinder MV 500 GP known as the Eiger SS.

Bold

The second replicator is Albert Bold, an American from Pennsylvania whose intense passion for the MV Agusta fours reaches the extreme heights of a true labour of love: he has, in fact, built *ex novo* a series of replicas starting with a racing "four" that required around 2,000 hours of work.

In the 20 years that passed between the end of the Meccanica Verghera production (1977) and the presentation of the F4 750 Oro (1997), alongside the private variations of the road-going MV four theme, there were also those who simply tried putting down on paper what might have been (but never was) the multi-cylinder with the winged cogwheel on the tank to be launched on the market to counter the all-powerful Japanese and British competition.
Seen here is the most attractive of the sketches of this kind, the work of an anonymous designer: the model proposed features sleek modern styling with an up-to-date integrated tank-saddle-tail configuration, swooping exhaust pipes reminiscent of the MV racers, while we can only imagine the most mechanical improvement; that is, the transformation from a shaft to chain final drive.

II

THE F4 MASTERPIECE AND THE FOUR
SEASONS OF THE RENAISSANCE

Genesis, reality and fortunes of the F4 legend

CLAUDIO CASTIGLIONI, BIKES IN THE BLOOD

Twenty years later, the day of the great return arrived. Like the phoenix, a myth that refused to die and was reborn from its own ashes, in 1997 the winged cogwheel returned to ignite the passion of the world of biking enthusiasts. While it is true that Piero Remor was the creative force behind the rise of MV, without doubt Claudio Castiglioni has been the artificer of its resurrection.

Castiglioni was born at Carnago (Varese) on the 23rd of November 1946. Having completed his studies, he began working alongside his elder brother Gianfranco in the family business producing small metal components founded by his father Giovanni in 1950. The name of the firm Ca.Gi.Va was derived from the initial letters of the founder's surname and name and followed by those of the city of Varese. The Castiglionis' great passion was motorcycles and it was no coincidence that in 1978 the two brothers bought the 8000 m² AMF-Harley-Davidson Aermacchi premises on Lake Varese. This was the first step in the creation of the Cagiva Group that in the 1990s, following the acquisition of Ducati (1985) and then Husqvarna and Moto Morini, was to achieve a consolidated turnover of over L.1,000 billion. The Centro Operativo Rimini (the Rimini Operations Centre or COR) was also founded and in 1987, under the guidance of Massimo Tamburini, became the renowned Cagiva Research Centre at San Marino (CRC). Subsequently, the Ducati and Moto Morini marques were sold off in 1996 and the MV Agusta F4 era was inaugurated in 1997.

Five years earlier, in the spring of 1992, in an act of motorcycling passion we can hardly praise enough, the Castiglionis had decided to acquire the old Meccanica Verghera marque from the Agusta heirs. The F4 750 Oro was thus to be the first of a series of models (born under the glorious emblems of a past that had been brought back to life) that were to bring the Varese-based firm numerous international bike-of-the-year-type awards as well as the honour of being included in the touring exhibition *The Art of the Motorcycle* organized by the Guggenheim Museum of New York, within the ambit of which the F4 was defined as "the ultimate technological expression".

1 Claudio Castiglioni, Eddie Lawson and Giacomo Agostini celebrating the American's victory in the 1992 Hungarian GP aboard a Cagiva 500 C592. The previous year, the four-time world champion had already rode the finally competitive Varese half-litre to victory in the Italian GP at Misano and the French GP at Paul Ricard.

2 Castiglioni and the Cagiva logo derived from the initial letters of Castiglioni Giovanni Varese.

3 The Cagiva Elefant 750 from 1994 with the alternative graphics (also adopted on the contemporary 900 cc model) to those of the new Lucky Explorer version (the first was from 1987).

4 The Elefant entered by the Cagiva-Lucky Explorer team, ridden by Edi Orioli of Friuli, heading towards victory in the Rally of the Pharaohs in 1993; the marque had first approached the "African marathons" in 1985 with Humbert Auriol's 8th place in the Paris-Dakar.

RACING, AN OVERWHELMING PASSION

In 1999, Claudio, married with a son (Giovanni) who was to follow him into the business, founded the group known as MV Agusta Motor Spa that concentrated all the know how and the premises of the previous motorcycle businesses. Production reached 30,000 units thanks to around 500 employees in the Schiranna, Morazzone and Cassinetta di Biandronno factories, all in the province of Varese, as well as the Crimson Styling Centre at Morazzone and the CRC in San Marino.

Special mention has to be made of Cagiva's participation in racing, the family's all-consuming passion: apart from the prestigious world championship motocross titles won in 1985 and 1986, the victories in the Paris-Dakar in 1989 and 1994 and other African marathons such as the Rally of the Pharaohs in 1987, 1989 and 1993, and the Husqvarna triumphs in motocross and the enduro category, the Castiglioni's sporting pride ensured that for 14 years the bikes with the elephant badge competed in the road-racing World Championship. Following the debut on the 24th of August at the German Grand Prix on the old Nürburgring circuit, with Virgion Ferrari aboard the first 500 built entirely at Schiranna, three victories (Eddie Lawson in the Hungarian GP in 1992, John Kocinski in the US GP in 1993 and the Australian GP in 1994), six pole positions and three fastest laps were achieved. The marque finally withdrew following the GP of Europe at Barcelona on the 9th of October 1994 that saw Kocinski finish 3rd on the Cagiva 500 C594 behind the giants Yamaha and Honda. As we shall see, the retirement from racing came about because the Varese firm had decided to dedicate all its human and financial resources to the development of the epochal F4 project.

The truth is that, for years Claudio had caressed the idea of an all but impossible enterprise, a project that kept him awake at night: guiding MV Agusta back to global heights, or rather, as has been well said, making of that brand "a stunning product, projected rocket-like into the future", in short, the "masterpiece of the entire MV epic." This was a "mad leap" to be made with the greatest of caution because the market sector requires steely nerves and an eagle-eyed business

1

2

3

4

1 The virtually unknown Cagiva-Ferrari 900 four built at Modena by Ferrari Engineering, the firm directed by the engineer Ferdinando Cassese (first left, half-hidden by Claudio Castiglioni), for Piero Ferrari (third left), son of the legendary Enzo and great friend of the Varese manufacturer.

2 and 3 The first Ferrari Engineering sketches of the F4 drawn in 1990 by Marco Ricci and Guido Campoli and presented to Castiglioni and Tamburini by Piero Ferrari to lay down the initial styling parameters but then completely abandoned (for example the box-section carbonfibre swinging arm).

4 1995: one of the two prototypes with reversed heads and the exhausts passing between the engine and the saddle before emerging at the rear from within the tail, as on the Cagiva 500 GP, the bodywork of which was used as camouflage for the road testing.

acumen. Our man was to make that leap and to succeed. As Claudio Castiglioni himself recalls, "Massimo Tamburini's and my own objective was always that of making a bike that was different to any other, a four-cylinder made entirely in Italy for the first time in decades. We were tired of seeing our enthusiasts turning to Japan because they couldn't find the bike they wanted here. In short, it was time to say enough of the "barges" of the past and privilege fast bikes that were also easy on the eye. With the MV Agusta F4 we can say that we succeeded. The debate with Massimo on this and other issues has been thorough, enhancing my respect and admiration first and foremost for the man himself and then as in my opinion the best designer around."

THE DNA OF THE PRANCING HORSE

It all began on Monday the 28th of July 1997, when a press release from the Cagiva Group announced the return to the market of a motorcycle carrying the historic MV Agusta marque: it was to be known as the F4. For the record, the MV legend rose from ashes exactly five days earlier, because on Wednesday the 23rd of July page one of the *Gazzetta dello Sport* featured a colour sketch depicting with reasonable approximation the new prototype. The title accompanying it, referring to the article by Enrico Minazzi found on page 16 ran: "MV rises. A legendary marque to take its bolides back to the tracks." Beneath the drawing, a brief caption stated that it represented "the supersport F4, with a four-cylinder, four-stroke, 750 cc engine (125 hp). The main article was furnished with two illustrations: one was the aforementioned sketch, defined simply as the work of "our artist", but clearly originating from the CRC styling centre in San Marino; the second was a photograph from 1995 of a Cagiva-badged prototype fitted with a 750 cc engine flatly described

1 and 2 Claudio Castiglioni and Massimo Tamburini. The artificers of the relaunch of the legendary MV Agusta marque, both motorcycling and racing "addicts", they have seen their professional destinies united since 1985, when the Varese businessman offered the Rimini designer the direction of the COR (Rimini Operations Centre), technological offshoot of Cagiva and the predecessor of the CRC (Cagiva Research Centre) founded at San Marino eight years ago.
In these 23 years together, the pair's passion and professionalism has produced masterpieces such as the Ducati Paso 750 (1986), the Cagiva Mito 125 (1990), the Ducati 916 (1994) and the MV Agusta F4 (1997) and Brutale (2000) series.

3 The MV Agusta factory at Schiranna on Lake Varese, that previously housed the Aermacchi and Cagiva production facilities.

as "built in Maranello by Ferrari Engineering". The text emphasised how over the previous month there had been even more insistent rumours than usual about a dramatic events in the offing for the Varese company. For example, the journalist had been able to identify Ferrari Engineering as the source of the design and realisation of the engine. There were hints for the first time about the probable principal mechanical and chassis characteristics, from radial valves to the extractable gearbox, from the frame in round Cr-Mo steel tubes to the magnesium swinging arm and the article concluded with a reference to a presumed list price of between 25 and L.30 million, defined with a bland euphemism as for "true enthusiasts."

Such was the scoop published by the *Gazzetta* on the 23rd of July 1997. But how did we actually arrive at the true miracle of the resurrection of a symbol of Italian sport and industry we had thought lost for ever? How at the end of a particularly tortuous path did the story finally achieve the happy ending represented by the magical MV Agusta F4?

ONE SEPTEMBER EVENING IN RIMINI

Castiglioni himself recounts the backstory to the birth of the F4 concept: "In the summer of 1989 I went to dinner with Massimo Tamburini in a restaurant in Rimini [Lo Squero]. We naturally ended up talking motorbikes and after a series of valuations of the state of the market at a certain point we started playing with the idea of building a new model ourselves with a brand new four-cylinder (all-Italian), high performance engine with a displacement of around 750 cc. The ultimate aim of the project was to have been the production of something capable of raising the profile of Cagiva whose catalogue at the time comprised bikes with small or medium displacements." Tamburini adds in this

1 and 2 1994 and the first chassis designs developed by Ferrari engineering are ready: on the left with a conventional cylinder head, on the right with the reversed head. The frame is a Deltabox-type with the structure conceived in box-section carbonfibre with bolted anchorage plates, a concept underlying the definitive mixed F4 frame with a tubular trellis and bolted plates.

3 Part of the Cagiva-Ducati staff charged with engine development. First on the left, the engineer Massimo Bordi, last on the right, the engineer Fausto Taglioni. Astride the bike is the former Morini engineer Luciano Negroni.

4 The heart of the F4 power unit with reversed heads developed in 1995. The exhausts passing beneath the rider caused problems of overheating that were never solved and led to the abandonment of the project.

respect: "We were thinking of a bike that was different to all the rest: Claudio above all insisted that the engine should be neither a Ducati nor an Aprilia, nor a Japanese, but something much more sophisticated that would make a clean break with the configurations of the past."

After that evening by the sea, the diverse commitments of both parties meant that the matter was taken no further until a few months later when the time was ripe and the decision was taken to entrust the realization of the prototype's engine to Ferrari Engineering of Modena, counting on Castiglioni's friendship with Piero Ferrari, a great motorcycle enthusiast.

Work began under the direction of the engineer Ferdinando Cassese, a former pupil of Ingenere Mauro Foghieri at Ferrari who had been appointed director of Ferrari Engineering in 1986.

1

2

3

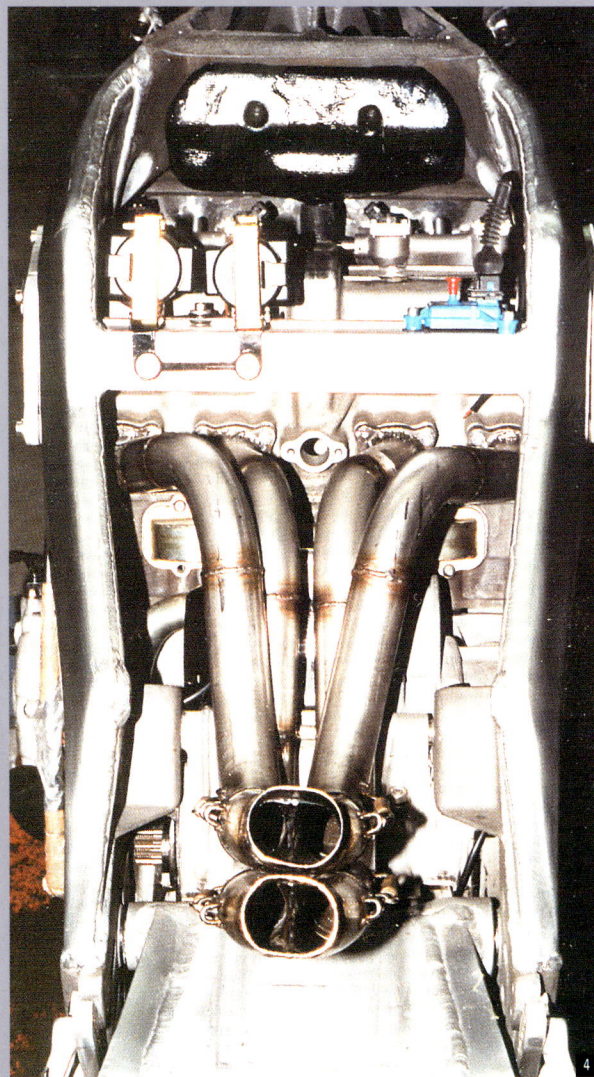

4

MY NAME IS F4, MV AGUSTA F4

As Cassese tells us: "I personally took care of the general configuration of the project, due in part to my great interest in the two-wheeled world. With me were Andrea Malagoli, Fulvio Sogliero and Gianni Sighinolfi, a famous former Ferrari engineer, here project chief for the Schiranna marque's power unit. In the end, it proved to be, and it was hardly a coincidence, a Ferrari engine in miniature: for example, the first of the two units realised had back-to-front heads (that is to say, with the intake at the front of the cylinder and the exhaust behind), and it became known as the "hammerhead." Our automotive roots could be found here, given that with that configuration we had tried to obtain the greatest possible intake charging, a search for a kind of turbo effect: we wanted plenty of power, given that our reference engine in this case was the highly potent four of the Suzuki GSX R 750. The choice of radial valves actuated by cams with a truncated cone profile drew on our experience in Formula 1."

The frame was instead entrusted to Luigi Botta, expert frame builder from the Cagiva Competition Department and son of Francesco Botta who had worked on the same site as a draughtsman since days of Aeronautica Macchi. Early in 1991, two 750 cc engines (bore and stroke 73.8x43.8 mm) arrived from Ferrari Engineering, assembled and complete with spare parts: one with conventional cylinder heads, the other with reversed heads (the aforementioned "hammerhead" architecture). In Ferrari's honour and in the wake of the stunning F40 model, the newborn four-cylinder was baptised as the F4, a name jointly chosen when work started on the project by Claudio Castiglioni and Piero Ferrari. Furthermore, inspired by the latter's passion for touring bikes, two prototypes (one of them functioning) of a sports tourer using the same power unit design were built at Modena and named as the "Cagiva-Ferrari GT 900", with a displacement increased to 846.5 cc (bore and stroke: 73.8x49.5 mm) and a frame again built by Ferrari engineering.

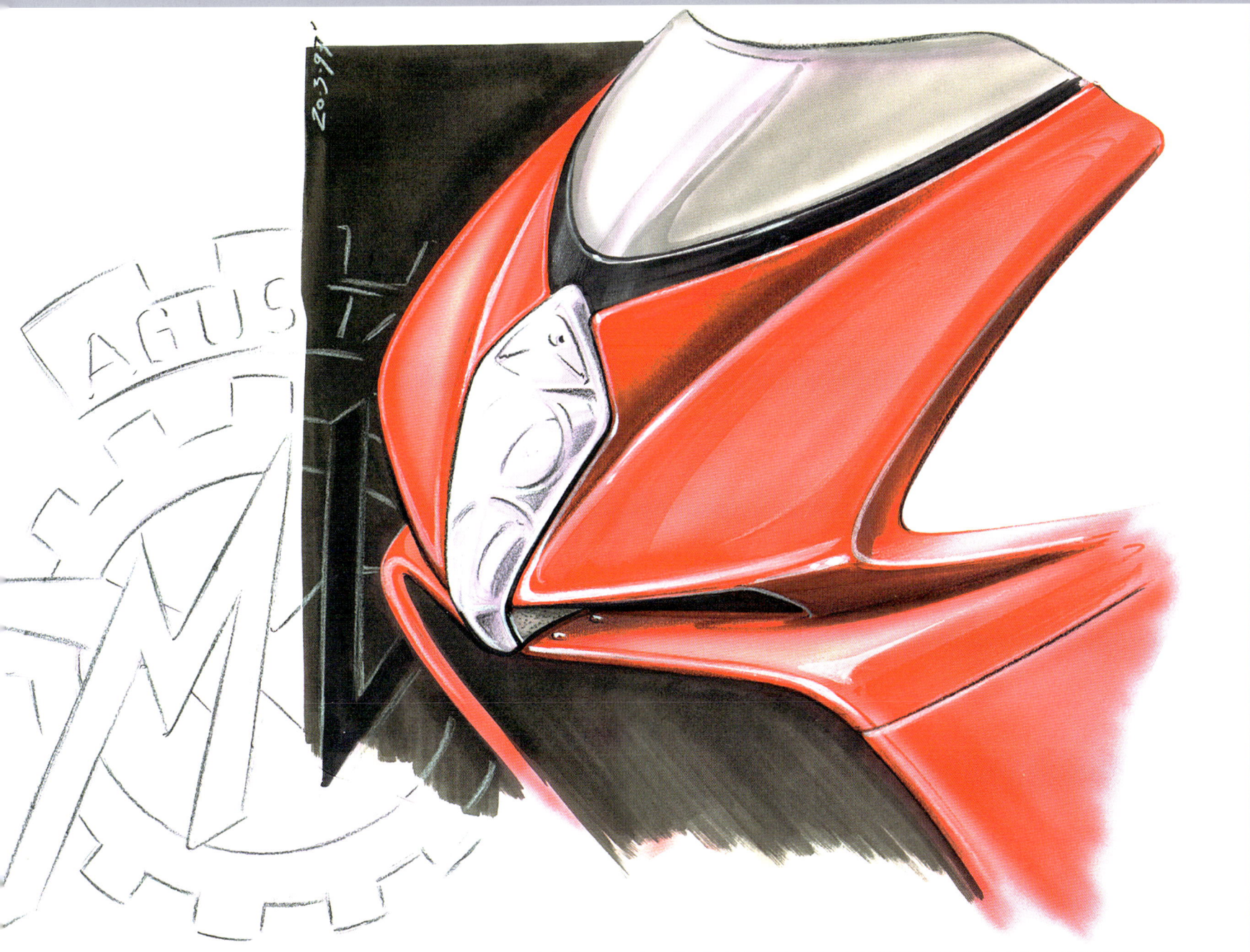

A DRAWING BOARD IN THE GARAGE

The chassis components all came from Cagiva and Cagiva Corse, the firm's competition department: the definitive frame design had been ready since the March of 1991 and was fabricated in July of that year; a classic Deltabox-type design in pressed aluminium that was very compact and widely adjustable.

It was based on the configuration plotted by Tamburini in mid-1990 in his home garage where, twenty or so years earlier he had developed his own version of the MV Agusta 600. As Botta recalls: "At that time, I often visited Tamburini in Rimini and one day he showed me a drawing board installed in the garage where in the evenings 'he would draw a few lines' outlining the new bike. The Deltabox-type frame was realised in a couple of examples, one of which was non-functioning and used only to verify the engine dimensions."

Late in the summer of 1991, all the chassis material left Schiranna for Borgo Panigale, including the fairings borrowed from the former Cagiva GP 500 bikes. The move was organized by the engineer Stefano Zacché.

From here on in, thanks in part to extensive road testing, the increase in performance and reliability was constant, development peaking in 1992 with the engine producing 136.5 hp.

1-4 Drawings and sketches (from details to the whole bike) of the F4 worked up by the CRC styling centres. The San Marino structure, created for the development and realisation of prototypes of new models for the Varese-based marque, was directed through to December 2008 by Massimo Tamburini and became famous for the imprinting it immediately received from the designer: extreme attention to detail, both in the creative and the development phases when the search for functionality is never divorced from aesthetic research. All this obtained with a highly original blend of craftsmanship and high technology.

5 Initial interpretation of the F4 as a sports bike: the chassis is already in part defined with a mixed structure with a structure in metal tubes and side plates and a single-sided swinging arm. The Cagiva group had yet to acquire the MV marque and has already sold Ducati, hence the bike was still being thought of as a Cagiva, of which a number of typical styling motifs can be seen.

6 With the same chassis as the previous image, a rear three quarters view of an alternative aesthetic to the definitive model.
This sketch was published by *Motociclismo* in the September of 1997, with a caption announcing an "even more attractive and aggressive" definitive version.

7 In the side view, the chassis has already achieved a precise definition and the CRC team began to concentrate on the details of the air intakes and the bodywork.
The air vents in the fairing and the side panel below the tanks are close to the configuration chosen for the final model.

1

2

3

4

5

6

7

TESTING AND YET MORE TESTING

At this point, however, orders arrived to stop development on the 750 cc engine because of the perceived urgency of moving on to a larger displacement that would be more competitive in terms of performance with the successful contemporary Japanese 900 cc units. Nonetheless, after yet another lengthy meeting to decide on the definitive displacement, the proposal for a 750 cc unit won the day and was to be produced in very short order.

In 1993 everything that concerned the new four-cylinder was moved to Schiranna where the engineer Riccardo Rosa, then head of the Cagiva Competition Department, also took over as technical director and development chief for the F4 engine.

Bench-testing and further project analysis followed, systematically and scrupulously compared with the Japanese competitors of the period. The results could hardly have been convincing as in the end the drastic decision was taken to completely redesign the entire engine, retaining only the radial valves, the central cam chain and little else from the old Ferrari Engineering configuration.

The "philosophy" of the Cagiva research centre ensured that there was a continuous relationship with the design courses of the faculty of Engineering of the University of Bologna and the Industrial Design course in the architecture faculty of La Sapienza University in Rome, contributing to the students' professional development. Further proof of the CRC's interest in new mechanical-stylistic solutions came in late 2003 when it launched a competition searching for new talent in motorcycle and other branches of design. The theme selected was the "Restyling of the MV Agusta F4. Evolution, but not revolution, of a legend: technical-stylistic proposal for the heir to the vehicle that re-vived the glorious MV marque."

1 Solutions proposed for the number plate holder and the rear indicators.

2 In the front three quarters view, a CRC proposal for the fairing air vents: two instead of three. The nose features two "NACA" ducts and its lines are becoming more refined while still maintaining the concept, later abandoned, of the two half shells embracing the headlamp. The design of the wheels is also beginning to take shape.

3-5 The creative development of the "tandem" front headlamp and its position in the fairing.

6 and 7 The non-circular section of the "organ pipe" terminals was not a prerogative of the F4 2010, but a solution proposed as early as 1996.

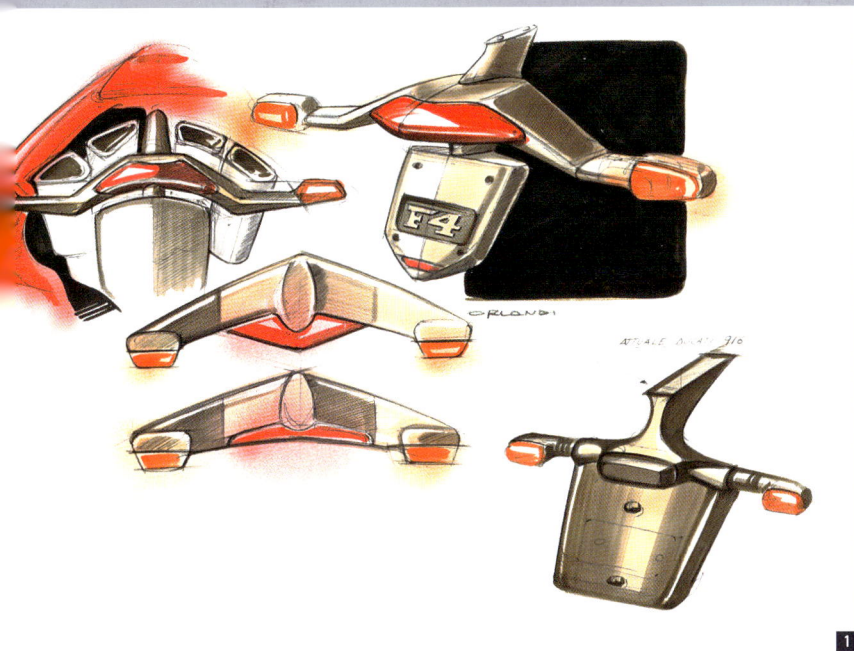

ORLANDI

F4

ATTUALE DUCATI 310

1

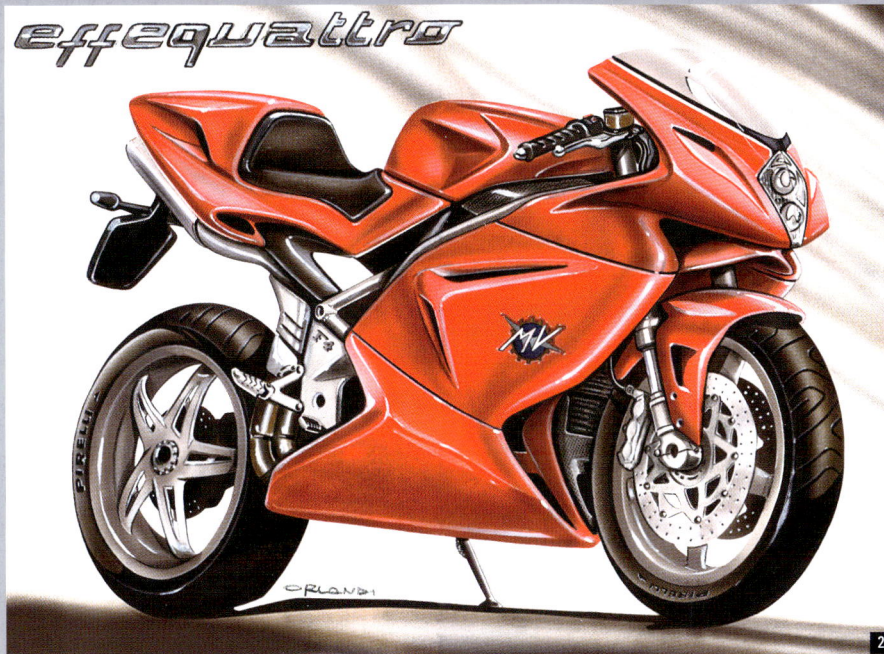

effequattro

MV

ORLANDI

2

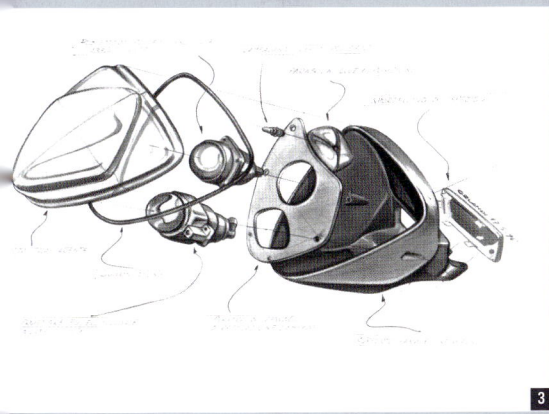

3

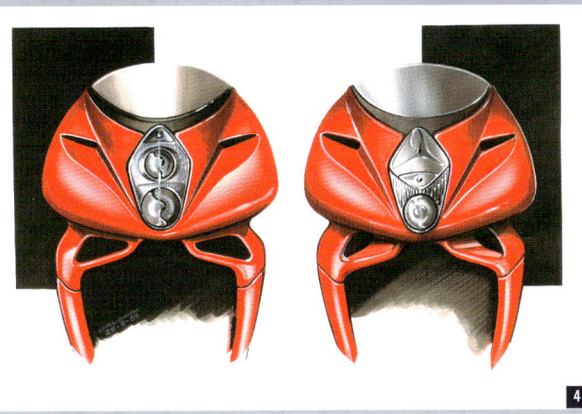

4

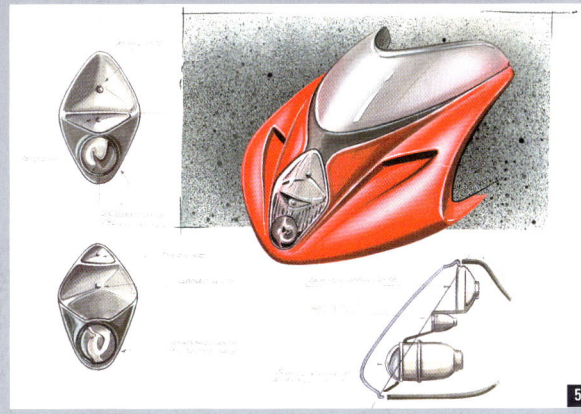

5

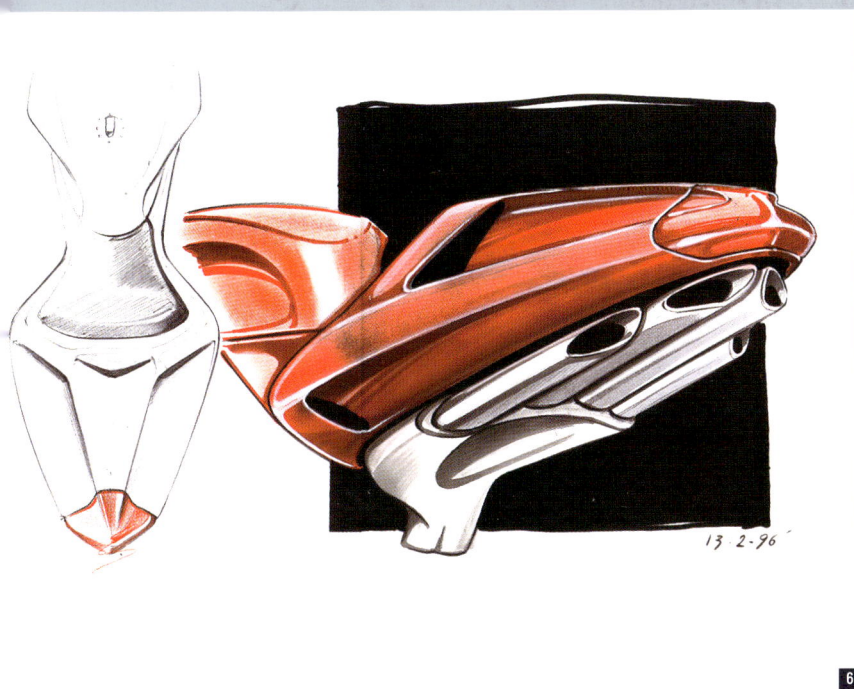

13-2-96

6

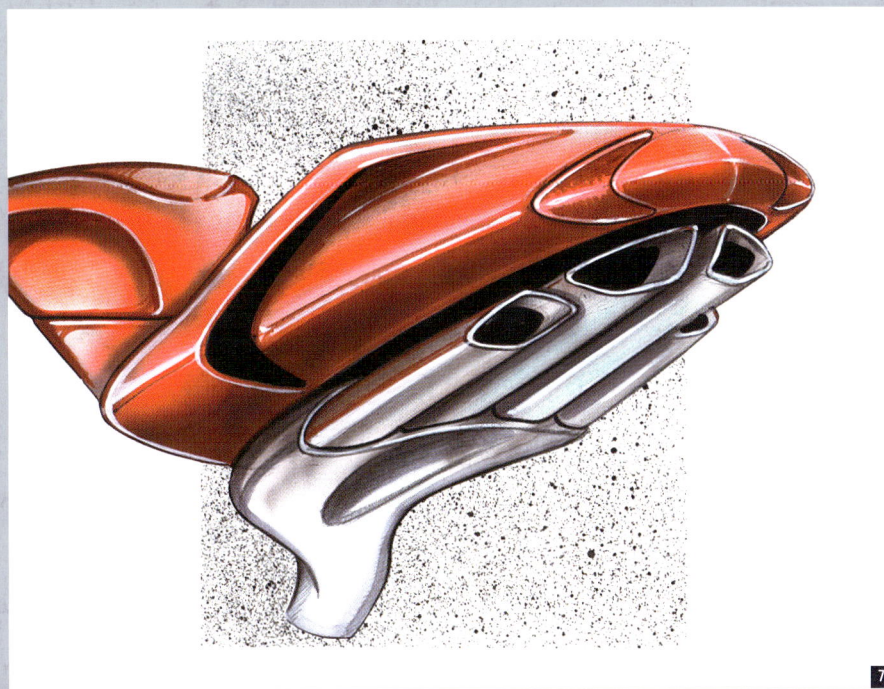

7

MASSIMO TAMBURINI, TOTAL DESIGNER

Massimo Tamburini was born in Rimini on the 28th of November 1943. His father passed on a love of motorcycles and as a boy he had a passion for multicylinder Italian engines but still remembers the Parilla overhead cam singles as the best bikes for the tinkerers and tuners of the era. He graduated from the technical institute, married and had children, Morena, Andrea and Simona, and founded a heating systems company that took the initial letters of the partners' surnames (Valerio Bianchi, Giuseppe Morri, and Massimo Tamburini) to form the name Bimota.

It was after using a second-hand MV Agusta 600 to build his first "special", that our man's Bimota Meccanica began in 1973 and was to continue for the next ten years. He joined Roberto Gallina's team as technical director of the Prototypes department until 1985 when his friend Claudio Castiglioni asked him to direct the Cagiva Operational Centre in Rimini (COR), which was to evolve into the legendary CRC in San Marino, founded on the 1st of April 1993. Working with his "head and heart" (but more than willing to get his hands dirty too), the perfectionist Tamburini modelled masterpieces such as the Ducati Paso 750, the Cagiva Mito 125 and the Ducati 916, but his dream was to design and realise an entire bike, from the mechanicals to the chassis and the superstructure. As he declared in an interview, his ideal bike should have "the displacement of a 750, the power of a 1000 and the weight of a 500."

So it was to be, as one evening in September 1989, Tamburini and Castiglioni decided to create the motorcycle that was to become the MV Agusta F4, a model that first saw the light of day eight years later but was to stun the world with its perfect synthesis of technology and style, functionality and beauty, performance and maniacal attention to detail. Today considered to be one of the world's greatest motorcycle designers, Tamburini is a shy, simple man, passionate but reserved, enthusiastic and rational, competent and modest. He is intolerant of the obvious, the shoddy and the superfluous; a team leader capable of urging his men on towards goals most would consider to be impossible. Massimo praises the CRC environment because, as he says, "it's organized and reserved, qualities that help you work"; in his office, the prints of the F4 models hanging on the walls have precious frames worthy of Renaissance paintings. He's young at heart (he declared in an interview that were he to be reborn he would become a fighter pilot) and now that he is the only designer in the world to have a bike named after him (something of which he is almost ashamed) he is always dreaming about inventing the winning MotoGP of the future.

On the 31st of December 2008, Massimo left the happy band and retired. It is said that he is under an obligation not to design any two-wheeled vehicle for three years. To learn more, we spoke to him in his *buen retiro* in San Marino:

Is it true you've retired and taken up hobbies like any other pensioner?

Yes, that's true, but only until 31st December 2011.

What are you "working" on?

Until the date of the 31st of December 2011, nothing that could be of any interest to bike fans.

What do you think of the latest F4, the 2010 model put into production by your "boys" in your absence? Have they done a decent job? Thumbs up, or thumbs down?

I know the project well at the design level, as around 90% of the work we did together. With regards to its industrialisation, an extremely important phase, while I haven't actually overseen the process, I'm sure, knowing my pupils, they'll have done an excellent job.

Tell us something auspicious for the MV Agusta marque in search of a secure future!

My best wishes go to my friend Claudio Castiglioni in the hope that he finds new investors with an enthusiasm about the motorcycle industry, who will allow him to develop new models capable of fully satisfying the expectations of the MV Agusta clients who have always been extremely demanding.

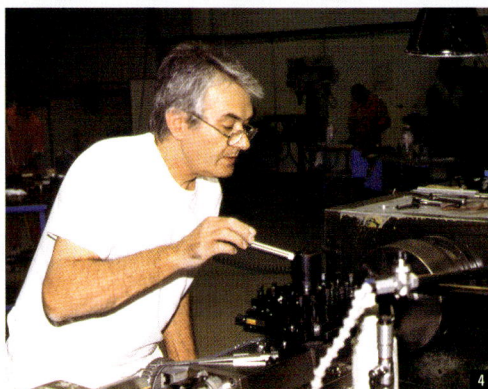

1 Tamburini with typical early Seventies facial hair in the company of the French Bimota rider Michel Rougerie.

2 Tamburini again with his famous first creation: an elegant and aggressive MV 750 (ex-600) with Ceriani Grand Prix dampers and suspension and a massive Fontana quad-shoe front brake.
The gearbox was extractable and, obviously, the final drive was converted to a chain.
This exploit was followed by the Bimota episode (1973-1983) and the MV Agusta adventure (1989-2008) that was to change forever the face of the rarefied super-sports bike segment.

3-5 Three photos of the maestro working on his last creation with the winged cogwheel on the tank: the F4 750 Oro.

The birth of a star:
F4 750 Oro (1997)

A family portrait with the MV Agusta F4 750 Oro. Claudio Castiglioni (left) and Massimo Tamburini pose with their most famous creation. Reliable sources refer to the two shedding tears when the first decal with the MV Agusta script and the gilded cogwheel with blue wings was finally applied to the tank of the show prototype.
This was in early September 1997 and for the new arrival, the world's only production bike with four cylinders and radial valves, a glorious period of worldwide appreciation was beginning.
And to think that it all came about, as is well-known, during a dinner in the summer of 1989 at the Squero restaurant in Rimini, when the designer said to his friend, referring to the Cagiva catalogue: "We've got to get out of the scrum and I'd go for a 750 cc displacement and an in-line four."

TAMBURINI TAKES THE HELM

When in the October of 1994 at Schiranna the staff of the recently closed Cagiva Racing Department were set to work on the F4 project, Rosa divided the technical staff into two working groups: the first, led by the engineer Andrea Goggi, a Cagiva man since 1988 and a veteran of the racing department, dealt with the development of the engine with SBK in mind (eventually featuring conventional heads due to unresolved problems with the "hammerhead" configuration that included overheating of the fuel tank and… the rider) in mind; the second was to revise the power unit in view of serial production, taking into account the new project guidelines. These ranged from wet rather than dry sump lubrication to the extractable gearbox (a feature motivated by prestige but also because it was already available, with the 500 GP unit requiring only slight modification), through to the roller-type rather than Morse cam chain (quieter albeit heavier and requiring lubrication). Furthermore, in view of industrial production, many components (starting with the crankcase) were redesigned to simplify them and lower future casting, machining and assembly costs.

The SBK version soon reached a power output of over 150 hp at 13,400 rpm, obtained with what for the time was very advanced electronic engine management, but the company crisis in the period 1995-1996 inevitably slowed development of this engine in favour of the fine-tuning of the serial production design. To this end, a number of prototypes were built: one of these, produced in 1995, may be defined as the last attempt to create a prototype F4 entirely in-house at Cagiva. The engineer Romano Albesiano, another veteran of the competition department where he had worked since 1991, invested all his experience and passion for technology applied to racing (some years later he was to be the technical director of the magnificent Aprilia RSV4 project). The bike featured an 846.5 cc engine developing around 140 hp and slotted into a frame that as Goggi recalls was a true masterpiece by the former competition department frame builders.

Castiglioni continued to state that it had yet to be decided whether to put this version into produc-

And here she is, the originator of the F4 series: the 750 Oro. Following the presentation in late 1997, we had to wait until 1999 before the first bikes were delivered to clients. During the development period, eight prototypes covered 240,000 kilometres, including many at full throttle on the high speed Nardò ring, without any problems of note emerging. Further evidence of F4's designers painstaking search for quality and originality can be seen in the incredible number of patents (11) that were to be registered along the way and which "covered" mechanical and chassis components and even styling features (in the form of an "ornamental motif"). This contributed to making the model unique among the ultra-elite but also ultra-homologated panorama of international motorcycling in this market segment.

tion or the one on which Tamburini was working at the CRC in San Marino that since 1994 had officially been running the entire F4 project, but everyone at Varese knew that their work would be shelved in favour what the Rimini wizard was preparing in the meantime.

This was because, as we were told by another insider, Gigi De Martini (Cagiva Racing Department from 1988 and then MV Agusta through to 2002), "despite the long years of gestation our F4 was no more than a 'Cagiva 500 GP' while Tamburini's was a bike that was different to all the others." Furthermore, the historic decision to produce a true MV Agusta rather than a new Cagiva had already been taken. The relaunch of the legendary marque had, in fact, been decided early in the spring of 1995, as Tamburini himself recalls:

"I had just recovered in February from a severe illness which had seen me spend long weeks in hospital. During those days I took comfort in outlining and producing a couple of drawings of what was definitively to be the bike that Claudio and I had been thinking about for almost six years, from the under-tail exhausts to all the rest. When I went back to work we immediately decided that our four-cylinder would have to be an MV Agusta. Certainly, the project involving the revival of a marque of this magnitude was enough to give anyone food for thought, but for my part I have to say that everything went smoothly from the word go because Castiglioni gave me the classic blank sheet on which I was substantially free to design what I wanted."

F4

MV AGUSTA

ORLANDI

1-3 The clay model on which Tamburini is working in the centre photo is taking shape, while in the one on the right the famous stacked poly-ellipsoid headlamp is being defined. The multifunctional shell enclosing the lamp also acts as a support for the instrument panel, the front fairing support and the ducts leading to the air-box, as well as the attachment struts for the windscreen and the rear view mirrors: this feature, according to Tamburini, was the fruit of one of Castiglioni's by no means rare design intuitions.

4 and 5 The F4 engine block and exhaust during the preparation of the show prototype.

6 Massimo Tamburini and Claudio Castiglioni with the second, definitive, plaster model.

ONE HOT EVENING IN MILAN

Following Tamburini's return to his desk, work started at CRC on the definitive prototype, two examples of which were to see the light of day based on a brand new perimeter space frame and a power unit with the displacement definitively reduced to 750 cc. This was the last product of the Varese working group charged with its development that since 1996 had been headed by Goggi, the engineer destined to sign off the F4's definitive power unit. The two bikes, rigorously camouflaged as Ducati 916s, were subjected to systematic road and track testing throughout 1996 and 1997 until, in the summer of this last year, the show prototype was ready in technical and stylistic terms for presentation at the classic Milan motorcycle show early in the autumn.

At 8 PM on the 15th of September 1997, a few hours prior to the opening in Milan of the 55th International Cycle and Motorcycle Exposition (16-21 September), the MV Agusta F4 was previewed by the press at the Società del Giardino, the "temple" of Milanese fencing in Via San Paolo 10: alongside Claudio Castiglioni were Giacomo Agostini and Riccardo Agusta, descendent of the family that had founded MV in 1945, as well as riders and mechanics from the former Cascina Costa firm's racing department. When, in a climate (overheated in every sense) of stunned suspension, the bike was "unveiled" and stood in its traditional red and metallic grey racing livery, the comments all revolved around variations on the theme "incredible" for what from the very first glance was hailed by all present as the "Ferrari of motorcycles". While this author was deafened by spontaneous acclamations at the close-up sight of a creation so ethereal (or rather, esoteric) as to seem foreign to any normal production process, and while a Japanese photographer fell off the top of a ladder in front of us, so caught up was he in his work, Castiglioni declared boldly that "we have tried to create something that has never before been seen in the two-wheeled world," in short, "the most beautiful bike in the world, the most technological."

He added that a special Oro series of just 200 numbered examples would be constructed immedi-

ately (in the end there were 300), all of which had already been pre-ordered, and sold at a price of around L.50 million (a figure doubled at the time by the early indiscretions): all the bikes were to be embellished with a gold plaque with the progressive number of that example, while the sale documentation included both a lifetime guarantee and the dual obligation on the part of the purchaser neither to resell the bike nor to race it. What could these last, somewhat unrealistic vetoes bring to mind if not what was the standard practice in the era of Count Domenico Agusta? Clearly, the Vichian theory of historic "occurrences and recurrences" also finds an application in the case of the F4. Then again, it could hardly be otherwise as this bike carries on its tank the same logo, the eight magical letters that for a quarter of a century carried the Italian colours to victory on the tracks of the world. A naturally emotional Agostini admitted that "it had been 20 years that I had hoped to relive a moment like this", while Agusta ensured those present that "my father, my uncles and my grandparents would have been extremely happy to see their marque on this motorcycle."

BEFORE THE EYES OF THE WORLD

Most of the journalists present were to underline in their reports of the evening how in a "stunning, sculptural combination" the two features of the F4 that stood out were the nose and the tail. At the front was a very narrow fairing with two stacked polyellipsoid lamps and indicators incorporated in the rear-view mirrors; at the rear, four incredible exhaust pipes emerge in-line from beneath the saddle, pointing upwards, resembling fighter plane cannons rather than the organ pipes they were officially described as. The two extremes were superbly linked by a wonder-

Cagiva Motor ha il piacere di invitarLa alla presentazione stampa della

Cagiva Motor is pleased to invite you to the press presentation of the

MV AGUSTA

F4

15.09.97 · ore 20:00 · Società del Giardino · Via S.Paolo 10 Milano · Buffet dinner

R.S.V.P segreteria organizzativa (02) 76009711

This wonderful cutaway of the F4 750 Oro from 1999 carries the signature of Guido Campoli of Ferrari Engineering.
The stylist had been present at the meeting in late 1989 between the heads of the Modenese structure directed by Ferdinando Cassese and Massimo Tamburini (accompanied by Massimo Bordi) to establish the maximum dimensions of the F4.

fully original fairing in which predominantly taut lines and sharp angles gave way to curved surfaces that flattened out in a previously unseen synthesis of wheel-to-wheel aesthetic simplicity and stylistic harmony. At the end of the evening, a print media colleague asked out loud, speaking for all of us, whether "it will ever be possible to have the courage to fire up and use on road or track" such an exaggerated concentration of beauty.

A few hours later, on the 16th of September, the Milan Motorcycle Show opened and while through to the following day entrance was reserved for operators in the sector, from the 18th the new bike was revealed to all and immediately acclaimed for what it was: not only the "queen of the show", but an absolutely breath-taking masterpiece. Compact, almost miniaturised and cloaked in the glorious Meccanica Verghera livery, a few hours earlier the F4 had again been honoured with a place on the front page of the *Gazzetta* where a photo was captioned "Rub your eyes. It's an MV." At the show, while the crowds of enthusiasts clambered over and queued up around its stand, everyone instinctively realised that the F4 was not the result of a mere "nostalgia trip," but a truly epochal, avant-garde motorcycle in terms of technology and design and not surprising covered by no less than eleven patents. It was a decidedly uncompromising product with nothing out of place or superfluous and any enthusiast would be ready to swear that it had been worth waiting for: because this truly was "a milestone in the history of world motorcycling" as Goggi was proudly to underline in an interview.

FROM MARANELLO WITH LOVE

Virtually the only relic of the first, legendary prototype power unit built by Ferrari Engineering, the MV Agusta F4 was the first high performance road bike to feature cylinder heads with radially set valves. That is to say, they are set on the same plane but not parallel to one another, converging by 2° towards the centre of the combustion chamber. The radial inclination allows them a movement that, as they rise, carries the external part of the valve away from the cylinder wall, creating less shielding and improving flow and charging characteristics with respect to those obtainable with traditional valves. The result is an optimal combination of power and torque, favouring smooth, peak-free delivery (also helped by particularly highly developed crankshaft rotating masses) while guaranteeing absolute performance.

The valves set into the combustion chamber in a radial configuration are, as mentioned, a recognisable sign of Ferrari's contribution to the initial design of the F4 engine as they are very similar to those fitted to the V12 engines of the Prancing Horse's contemporary Formula 1 cars among others. This was sophistication with distant roots: from the Miller engines (USA) of the late Twenties, through to the Bugattis from the Type 50 onwards and the power units fitted to the contemporary Riley Nine.

Moreover, the twin overhead camshafts of the F4 are directly actuated via bucket tappets and cams machined with a slight truncated cone configuration: while it is known that radial valves necessitate inclined eccentrics, we like to think that in this case their oblique shape is further testimony to the Ferrari influence on the original F4 engine.

In order to obtain extremely compact combustion chambers, the valves have a combined inclination with respect to the axis of the cylinder of just 22° (12.5° for the exhausts and 9.5° for the intakes), the smallest in the category.

As Mario Colombo notes in the fundamental *MV Agusta* (Nada Editore, 2006), written together with Roberto Patrignani: "These are angles that also reveal a close relationship with the most recent F1 technology, signficantly smaller than those used in the past, for example on the famous Rudge engines of the 1930s".

Apart from allowing for an optimal combustion chamber configuration, this valve arrangement also benefits the intake ducts which are steeply inclined to reduce the loss of cool gasses to a minimum: apropos of the ducts, it should be added that the valve guides are machined in such a way as to reduce resistance to gas flow within them.

Although it is clear that the flow dynamics testing conducted at Maranello decreed the superiority of valves with this inclination (albeit with a very limited radiality) compared to a parallel configuration, MV Agusta declared with understandable pride that the system was analysed at Schiranna "with the same equipment and the same technologies successfully used within the ambit of the search for outright performance for the Cagiva 500 GP that in 1994 narrowly missed out on second place overall in the World Championship standings."

1 The most precious heritage of the first stage of the F4 design at Ferrari Engineering: the radial valves. The official press release at the presentation of the F4 750 Oro spoke proudly of this feature and of the crankcase with the extractable cassette gearbox, the other exclusive race-bred component.

2 Gerhard Berger, proud owner of an F4 Tamburini and a Brutale America, at the presentation of the Ferrari 412 T2 (four radial valves per cylinder) for the 1995 season.

3) Jean Alesi in a Ferrari 412 T2 during the Hungarian Grand Prix.

4 The mechanical "heart" of the F4: distinguished not only by the radial valves, but also by general miniaturization efforts. For example, the throttle bodies are particularly compact thanks to painstaking work on the electro-injectors and the butterfly valve.

111

1 The side view of the F4 750 Oro offers the best opportunity to appreciate the model's clean lines and the dimensions worthy of a 500: the styling motifs immediately bring to mind the Cascina Costa GP racing bikes of the golden era.

2 The instrumentation is composed of an analogue electronic rev counter (with a dial running up to 17,000 rpm), a multifunction display and a series of warning lights.
The display acts as a speedometer, milometer, dual trip meter, engine temperature gauge and clock. The units of measure can be set in kilometres per hour and degrees centigrade or miles and Fahrenheit.

3 The specialist press in Italy and abroad dedicated numerous cover stories to the new arrival from Schiranna: in this case, in 2000, it was the Dutch magazine *Moto73* talking about the 750 Oro.

JOURNALISTS… SPEECHLESS

The principal technical data were released: displacement 750 cc, compression ratio 12:1, maximum power 126 hp at 12,200 rpm, maximum torque 7.3 kgm at 9,000 rpm, maximum speed 275 kph, dry weight 180 kg. The four-cylinder, in-line, transverse engine, with twin overhead camshafts, was fabricated entirely in light alloy, with the exception of the crankcase, sand-cast in magnesium alloy, a procedure usually reserved for prototypes and racing bikes. The four valves per cylinder were set radially, lubrication was via a wet sump with an oil cooler and the six-speed gearbox was extractable: this last was another feature of racing bikes rarely used for standard production models. The fuel system was based on a Magneti Marelli integrated electronic ignition and injection system. With regard to the chassis, the enthusiast will already have noted the compound structure with a tubular spaceframe and plates, the enormous inverted Showa fork with 49 mm stems and the stunning single-sided swinging arm in magnesium, like the wheels. The tyres (Pirelli or Michelin) were 120/65-17" at the front (a non-standard, dedicated size placed between the /60 and /70 series with the precise aim of combining the agility in turns of the former and the high speed stability of the latter) and 190/50-17" at the rear (it is known that a 200 was also tested). As the hours passed, more information about the F4 became known: for example, it was announced that following the Oro series, a less expensive F4 S version would be produced (priced at between L.30 and L.35 million). The specialist press naturally accompanied the passionate days of the Milanese show, a true epiphany for the insiders, with articles boldly headlined "Speechless", "The Legend Returns" or "The MV F4 Stuns the World."
What is certain is that the general impression was that of being faced with not so much "a" bike, but "the" bike, the "mother of all bikes" or rather (if you will forgive us these love-struck expressions) the very essence of the motorcycle, in short an epochal icon. Something that would definitively confine to the history books the most exclusive models of the past, from the ineffable

MOTO73
NEDERLANDS GROOTSTE MOTORMAGAZINE

Test Ducati 748R
Racer met
verlichting

Sportreportages
GP wegrace Spanje
ONK wegraces Assen
Superbike/Supersport
Australië + Japan

Bevrijdingsfeest
in GP Zwitserland
Daniel Willemsens
winnende comeback

Bagageberging
Tank- en
zadeltassen

MV Agusta 750S America 1974
versus F4 Serie Oro 1999
TIJDMACHINES

Nederland Motorland
Win een
Aprilia Pegaso

Mammuth built by Friedel Münch, thirty years or so before the all-powerful Wankel-engined Van Veen 1000 OCR from 1978, through to the extremely sophisticated V1000 from 1981, built at the behest of Lord Alexander Hesketh.

In the words of Tamburini, the all-round designer responsible for the F4 "beauty is objective", words that echo many years later those of inimitable masters of the eighth art of aesthetics applied to mechanical engineering, such as Piero Remor or Cesare Bossaglia.

A "ONE-OFF" OUT TO CONQUER THE WORLD

Following the dramatic days of September 1997, the curtain fell on the MV Agusta F4 750 Oro until the repeat presentation at the Bologna Motor Show in December. Nonetheless, while awaiting fresh news (above all the eagerly awaited first road test), the specialist press could hardly restrain itself from publishing a stream of comments, scoops and inferences on the theme some with a few more grains of truth than others. Everyone was feverishly asking the same questions: What'll the F4 be like on the road? And what about on the track? Will it remain an object of desire reserved for a chosen few or, respecting the previously announced programmes, will the manufacturer permit the greatest possible number of enthusiasts to enjoy in the well chosen words of our colleague (and unforgotten maestro) Roberto Patrignani, "the technological finesse of a motorcycle unique in the world"?

The whole of 1998 was rightly devoted to road and track testing by the group of test riders and mechanics led by the engineer Enrico Sanino, Cagiva's head of development and road testing. The aim was to achieve the optimum levels of reliability expected of an exclusive bike such as the

1

2

3

1 This cutaway highlights: the chain driven twin overhead camshafts and the conical cams that actuate the valves via bucket tappets; the radially configured valves and the 6-speed gearbox, extractable like those of racing bikes.

2 The sequence of solids and voids in the carbonfibre fairing, with linear segments alternating with portions of curved and flat areas.

3 The upside down fork with 49 mm diameter stems and a wheel travel of 113 mm: the hub carrier was fixed with a quick release system, while both the spring preloading and the hydraulics (in rebound and compression) were widely adjustable.

4 The concave racing-type radiator cooling the engine.

5 The frame is a separable combination structure, with a tubular front section and plates at the rear.
The photo shows the chrome-molybdenum steel trellis, the same material used on the Varese marque's old GP bikes.

F4 aiming to conquer the market, prior to its "dynamic" presentation. In the meantime, noteworthy events followed one after the other. On the first day of spring in 1998, Cagiva inaugurated in the presence of its chairman Castiglioni its Japanese branch (CagivaJapan) at Shizuoka (Tokyo). This structure, established to market MV Agusta, Cagiva and Husqvarna models in Japan, joined those already up and running in Argentina, the Czech Republic and Thailand.

A further two months passed and Agostini was photographed on the 20th of May during the first official test of the F4 on the runway at Vergiate in the province of Varese, home of an Agusta Group helicopter factory. Mino covered the long straight time after time, mainly for the benefit of the photographers desperate for the first action photos of the new bike.

The sight of the classic MV-Agostini pairing naturally raised a lump in the throats of those present, while widespread incredulity was aroused by the musicality of an exhaust note with more harmonics than decibels.

At the end of the month, the newsstands received the June edition of *Motociclismo* with the "worldwide exclusive" on the test.

Beneath the title "It's a four-cylinder dream..." came the first lines: "And yet it moves. Sceptics and denigrators (and there are always plenty of them) eat your words! The MV F4 exists, she runs and her voice is beautiful and different to any other four-cylinder..." Again in relation to the sound of the four "organ pipes", the author of the article adds that it provides "an emotion that is difficult to translate into words but which has to be experienced almost viscerally."

1

2

3

4

5

OUR CONCERTO

Listen to what Massimo Tamburini had to say to us, his stern face for once split by a beaming smile: the MV Agusta F4 exhaust silencer was designed and realised at the CRC with the help of... an orchestral maestro paid to supervise the work. The aim? To get the best possible sound out of the system (with rigorous measurement of lengths and diameters); that is to say, harmonics rather than decibels. In short, in the era of capitalistic globalization, of markets searching for the most ferocious cuts in production times, that authentic revival of the Bauhaus spirit, the Cagiva Research Centre in San Marino, even went to the trouble of finding an expert in sharps and flats.

Here we have, as ever, aesthetic factors inseparable from technical issues as the foundation of a component developed by the Rimini-born wizard and his disciples, in a search for something that goes beyond the bounds of mere functionality and is the object of yet another patent, in this case actually described as an "ornamental motif." The four exhaust pipes lead, via a sinuous route embracing and perfectly tracing the shape of the engine (clearly, part and parcel of the Tamburinian search for minimum dimensions), to an original expansion-silencing system. This is composed of symmetrical elements in which the two expansion chambers, appropriately diaphragmed and with unmistakeable rounded forms, open to the outside via four silencers of variable lengths and made of diverse materials.

This is the so-called "organ pipe" system that, while permitting optimal reduction of noise levels, lends the bike a highly individual voice, skilfully tuned on the basis of musically derived algorithms.

As Tamburini declared in another interview: "We aimed to obtain an absolutely unique and unmistakeable sound, quiet at low revs and with four distinct tones perfectly tuned at higher engine speeds. The F4 should be not just a bike, but also a sophisticated musical instrument with a sound that is both powerful and melodious and that has nothing in common with that of the Japanese models." The placing of the silencer system in a protected location beneath the saddle (a configuration already seen on the Ducati 916 also designed by Tamburini) and its dual functional and aesthetic value lay behind the above-mentioned patent.

Elsewhere you may read a number of enthusiastic verdicts from the specialist press, foreign titles to the fore, regarding this feature of the F4 that is at least as unusual as the radial valves of Ferrari provenance. All we would say is that the exhaust sound of the Varese four is the most thrilling we have ever heard, with low, musical tones, building continuously to a linear, full-bodied crescendo with no high pitched shrieking if not when past the 10,000 rpm mark when the singing takes on the timbre of a dramatic tenor (or rather the tenor register of a church organ), with a counterpoint provided by a unique intake roar.

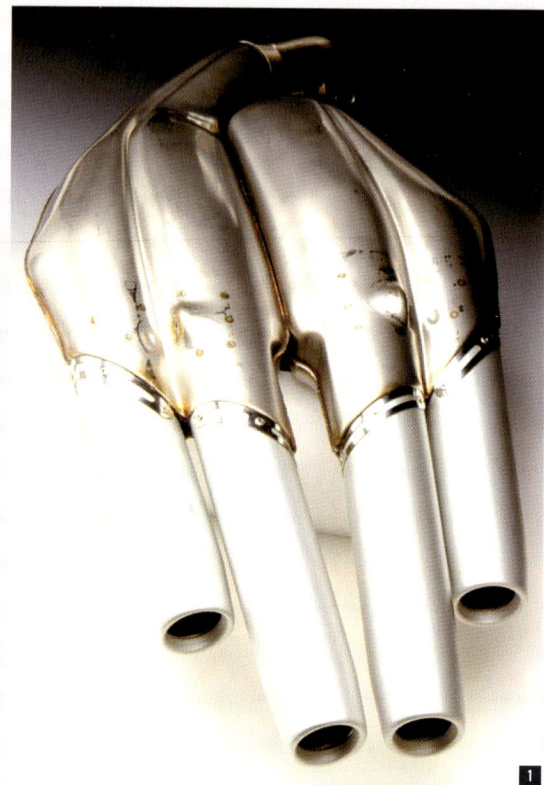

1 The concept of the F4's "organ pipe" exhaust pipes has curious origins that Massimo Tamburini explained to us: "I started thinking about the exhaust pipe and how to give it… a tone, that is, how to lend the rear end of the bike more character, clearly differentiating the sound of the exhaust from that of the Japanese rivals. I was thinking about how to make the sound come from four terminals, perhaps with different timings thanks to differentiated lengths and diameters. It was at this point that I told Claudio Castiglioni that I needed some one who… builds organs. I got what I wanted and we all know the result: harmonics instead of decibels".

2 The exhaust pipes of the 750 Oro, subsequently imitated throughout the world.

3 and 4 "Organ pipes" on the 1000 R 312 Corse and the 1000 R too.

5 Incandescent terminals for the MV Agusta backfire.

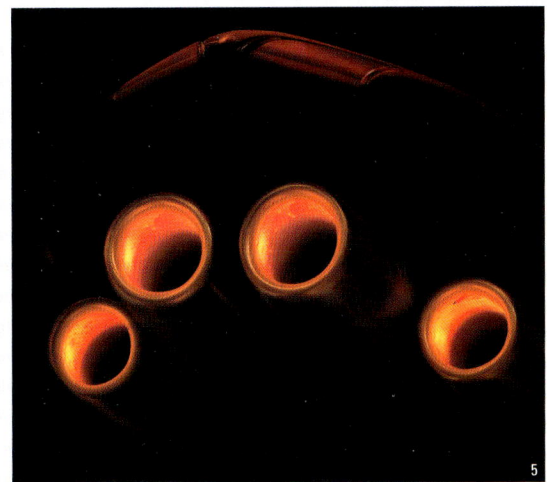

SEARCHING FOR PERFECTION

Exhaustive information regarding the technical characteristics of the first F4 is provided in the appendices, while here we shall look at certain aspects of the Tamburinian guidelines, impressions of the bike on the road and its performance.

It should be said from the outset, that for perhaps the first time in the case of a production bike, the CRC gave absolute precedence in the design process to the integration of the functionality of the power unit, chassis and superstructures. The result? A quintessential and inimitable combination of technical qualities, power and sporting performance exalted by delicious and wholly original styling. Furthermore, in order to avoid last-minute revisions, the entire prototyping process for every component (conducted with almost maniacal perfectionism) was geared to the production of a definitive model characterised by the utmost simplification, in order to facilitate as far as possible both assembly operations and repairs and maintenance.

The engine was labelled by the specialist press in myriad different ways, including that of the "first four-cylinder of the modern era." The unit's reduced transverse dimensions set new records: it was so compact that, thanks in part to the chamfered castings, the cylinder head and block were of the same width, an important factor in terms of both aerodynamics and the centralization of masses and because it permitted the adoption of a particularly narrow and therefore stiffer frame. With regard to the transmission department, a cogwheel is machined from a flywheel on the second crank (as seen looking at the engine from the riding position) and actuates the straight cut primary gear train that engages directly with the clutch basket: a detail which will surely remind those readers who have stayed with us to this point of the system introduced by the engineer Piero Remor no less than 70 years earlier.

The frame was a two-piece composite structure: the main section was composed of a spaceframe in TIG-welded round chrome-molybdenum tubes weighing just 7.2 kg, which lovingly embraced

Giacomo Agostini became the Varese marque's most famous flag bearer thanks to the good offices of Carlo Ubbiali, who in 1965 convinced him to leave the Corse Morini team. Here we are in the April of 1999, on the occasion of the official presentation of the MV Agusta F4 750 Oro at the Monza autodrome. The first "dynamic" appearance for Schiranna's baby had taken place on the runway at Vergiate a few months earlier, but then the popular Ago had restricted himself to a few sprints for the benefit of the photographers.

the engine, linking up at the rear via pins to two fulcrum plates in magnesium alloy in the area of the rear swinging arm mount. The disc braking system was also subjected to special attention from the CRC that, in collaboration with Nissin, the firm which produced it exclusively for the F4 and whose chairman actually travelled from Japan to San Marino to discuss the project, designed it down to the last detail.

RIDING A DREAM

The comments of the first F4 testers were unanimous in recognising the excellence of the bike and their verdicts, frequently involuntarily sensationalist or borderline obsessive, composed an anthology of praise from which it is easy to extract phrases such as "Love at first sight", "Pure Libido". "Pure Gold, "Work of art", "A bike that at a stroke makes its worldwide rivals quake", "The best road bike ever built", "The most fabulous and technical advanced bike of the century", "Riding the F4 you're always aware of what's happening", "It almost lets itself be controlled by thought", "You can lean at 240 kph, with the bike rock solid on the line you have chosen." However, there were also a number of criticisms, starting with the engine's power output, that was nothing out of the ordinary when compared with other sports bike units of similar displacement and architecture that, above all, offered a more rabid throttle response.

Moreover, question marks were placed against the engine's power delivery through to 5-6000 rpm in the higher gears, a certain roughness in rapid on-off throttle manoeuvres, the rather clunky engagement of fifth and sixth gears, the mechanical noise, the handlebar and foot peg vibrations and the generally excessive weight, deriving from the over-engineering of many components.

1-3 Three shots from the first "dynamic" appearance of the MV Agusta 750 Oro, with Agostini in the saddle.
It was no coincidence that the popular Ago had been entrusted from the outset with the role of testimonial for the reborn marque. He is the rider who helped write the most fascinating story in world motorcycling. After his triumphs with MV in the Sixties and Seventies he moved to Yamaha and enjoyed further success before returning to his spiritual home on the 29th of August 1976.
On that day in the German Grand Prix at the Nürburgring, a 500 GP with the winged cogwheel on the tank won for the last time.

The data relating to the F4 750 Oro recorded by *Motociclismo* between the spring and early summer of 1999 on the test bench and at the Nardò track (Lecce) show a power output at the rear wheel of 107.93 hp at 12,600 rpm (118.29 at the crankshaft), maximum torque at the rear wheel of 6.54 kgm at 10,750 rpm (7.17 at the crankshaft), a maximum speed of 278.9 kph at 13,400 rpm and 1000 metres covered from a standing start in 20.37 seconds with an exit speed of 249.7 kph. With regard to acceleration and pick-up, the figures were: 400 metres from a standing start in 10.95", with an exit speed of 214.8 kph, 400 metres in sixth from 50 kph in 14.45" with an exit speed of 154.2 kph. The weight of the bike without fuel was 191.2 kg (102.4 kg on the front wheel, 88.8 kg on the rear).

Leaving aside the verdicts of the experts, what is the F4 like to ride? Once in the saddle you have the immediate impression that for the first time ergonomics and nothing else guided the designer's pencil. You feel that you are sitting inside the bike rather than on top of it, in an embrace capable of generating an immediate sense of reassuring confidence. The 750 Oro has a lightness and ease of handling worthy of a smaller bike: it is relaxed through tight corners and agile and stable through fast curves where you manage to lean in with the bike with one tester declaring "finally it's the rider cornering rather than the bike." The F4 can only be defined as neutral in the way in which it deals with fast curves: the new-found confidence it gives to the rider permits impeccable late braking on the limit with absolute precision, extremely rapid turn-in, irreproachable directional control along the chosen line right the way through the curve. Gear changes are sweet, rapid and precise, facilitated by a hydraulic clutch that is a little heavy but sensitive enough to allow you to slip it when you need to. Braking is extremely powerful but dosable and progressive.

F4 750 ORO

No mere "operation nostalgia", but a truly avant-garde model in terms of technology and aesthetics, in 1997 the F4 750 Oro barnstormed a uniform market, mixing it up and enthralling it.

An extreme design that required eight years of research and development, encouraged the constructor to adopt innovative features for a road bike: from the extractable gearbox to the radial valves, from the composite frame to materials such as carbonfibre and magnesium.

The specification was that of a supersports bike, from the upside down fork to the racing-style tail, from the quick-release fairing to the transverse steering damper, from the pure Ferrari-style star-pattern wheels to the single-side swinging arm that was as beautiful as it was efficient.

Everything caught the eye: the analogue rev-counter reads up to 17,000 rpm, with a yellow ground that screams GP bike, while the aggressive windscreen fairing incorporates the innovative dual stacked headlamps.

And then there was that inimitable logo on the tank to set the enthusiasts' pulses racing after a twenty-year wait!

A thousand thousandths of excellence:
F4 1000 Ago (2002)

1 A memorable new chapter in the story of the reborn MV Agusta was written in 2002 with the appearance of the F4 1000 Ago.

2 and 3 The MV Agusta F4 750 S, that became a classic model like its elder sister, the 750 Oro, as soon as it was launched (September 1999). All the merits of timeless appeal and avant-garde technology are combined in styling motifs capable of resisting ephemeral trends and events, supported by world-beating mechanical and chassis performance. It was thus understandable that the specialist press welcomed the new bikes with titles of sincere if breathless admiration, as in the case of the weekly *Motosprint* whose cover for the 14-20 December 1999 issue shrieked "The world's most beautiful."

MOTORCYCLE ART... FOREVER

Mid-September 1998 saw the first of the sequence of heirs to the original F4: Munich's Intermot was the setting for the launch of the show prototype of the "economical" version, the F4 750 S (126 hp at 12,200 rpm, with a maximum speed of 275 kph). The only differences compared with the Oro concerned the materials employed: for example, the sump and the crankcase covers were in die-cast aluminium, while the rear swinging arm, its attachment plates, the lower front fork yoke and the wheels were also in aluminium rather than magnesium. The F4 Oro's carbonfibre fairing was replaced by a version in a thermoplastic material (Xenoy) also used for the intake box and the front mudguard. These modifications actually resulted in a slight reduction of the overall weight of the bike and a more significant drop in price.

The year closed with a significant honour for the F4 750 Oro: as mentioned previously, it was exhibited at the Guggenheim Museum of Contemporary Art in New York, within the ambit of the exhibition *The Art of the Motorcycle*. Following this event, the tag line "Motorcycle Art" has always accompanied the MV Agusta badge in the company's advertising.

The early months of 1999 were spent awaiting the first complete road test of the F4 750 Oro (the 300 examples of which were about to go into production and to be sold by the end of the year) and at the end of April, *Motociclismo* as usual stole a march on its rivals to offer its latest MV exclusive. June saw the first adverts placed in the specialist periodicals by the exclusive Italian distributors of the F4 (there were around 90 of them). One of the slogans proudly read: "No more sweet dreams for the competition!"

July instead saw the first MV Agusta price list to appear in the motorcycle magazines for almost a quarter of a century, albeit consisting of just a single line relating to the F4 750 Oro (the price of which had in the meantime risen to L.68,750,000). Periodically and with appropriate emphasis, the manufacturer communicated the names of the owners of examples of the first series F4: along

1

2

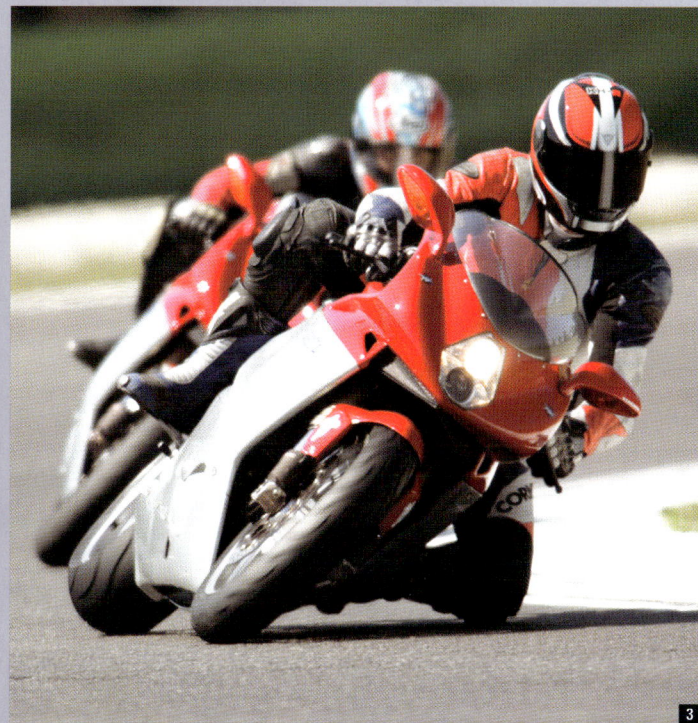

3

with the one that went to enrich the collection of King Juan Carlos of Spain, others ended up with Giacomo Agostini, the collector Ubaldo Elli, Max Biaggi, the Sultan of Brunei, the editorial team of *Motociclismo* and so on.

FROM THE GUGGENHEIM TO THE DEALERS

Alongside the definitive version of the F4 750 S (that went on sale at L.32,000,000), the Milan show in mid-September 1999 saw MV Agusta present the two-seater S 1+1 model (at a list price in January 2000 of L.33,000,000), the fundamental technical characteristics of which (126 hp at 12,200 rpm, maximum speed of 275 kph) were identical to those of the single-seater, while the weight increased by just 1 kg.

In the meantime, enthusiasm, a will to work and an awareness of being part of something unique continued to encourage the Schiranna and CRC staff to give their all. By mid-December around a hundred examples pf the F4 570 S had left the Cassinetta factory in the direction of the dealers. This was a comforting figure that also provided a response to the numerous fans of the marque throughout the world who continued to bombard the specialist magazines with heartfelt requests for information as to when the MV Agusta jewels were to go on sale. The new price list was published late in the year and this time included the F4 750 Oro, the 750 S and the 750 S 1+1. The legend was ready to make in-roads into the market.

In the meantime, the former racers Phil Read, Mario Lega and Eddie Irvine took delivery of their examples of the F4 750 S. For the company it was also also a successful PR operation accompanied by the publication of a two-page advertising spread with a slogan reading: "In the Guggenheim Muse-

1 As had been the case with the Ago, the 1000 cc version of the F4 Senna arrived in 2005 to replace the original 750 (**3**).
While the power output had been increased from 140 to 174 hp, the colours of the elegant livery and the high-spec materials of the earlier bike were retained and part of the profits from the sale of the 300 examples (the same limited edition as the first series, snapped up between June and December 2003) was again donated to the Senna Foundation, the Brazilian humanitarian organization helping the *meninos de rua.*

2 The cover of the important German bi-weekly *Motorrad* exalting the F4 750 S.

4 The star-pattern fire red wheels of the F4 750 Senna.

um. Today also available in the exclusive MV Agusta dealers." A two-page article with colour photos appeared in London's *Financial Times* of 6/7 May 200 under the heading "The Return of the Italian Stallion." As had been the case in the United Kingdom in 1999 with the magazine *Motor Cycle News* and the F4 750 Oro, the German bi-weekly *Motorrad* proclaimed the F4 750 S as the "Sports Bike of the Year" for its technology, style and appeal: these were the first in a long series of national and international honours that continue through to the present day.

REMEMBERING AYRTON SENNA

No less than three prototypes were sent from Varese to the classic German Intermot show in mid-September 2000: the F4 Senna, the F4 SPR and the "naked" Brutale 750 Oro. Such riches surprised most observers as strict business logic suggested that the company should focus on maintaining its position, fine-tuning its existing products. Yet this was not the case: logic went by the board as the fury mid-way between the Dionysian and the Apollonian motivating the Castiglioni and Tamburini duo had yet to abandon them as their all-consuming passion for a challenge held sway.

The F4 Senna (140 hp at 12,600 rpm and a top speed of between 270.9 and 286 kph depending on the final drive ratio) was launched with part of the profits from sales contributing to the foundation named after the Brazilian driver (with whom as is well known Castiglioni was very close friends) created to help the *meninos de rua*, the street kids, an enormous problem for the great South American country. Presented in a stunning black livery with the surname of the departed world champion on the fairing and the frame and wheels finished in a fiery red, the Senna was fitted with a slightly more docile version of the engine from the contemporary and highly aggressive F4 SPR and was produced

1

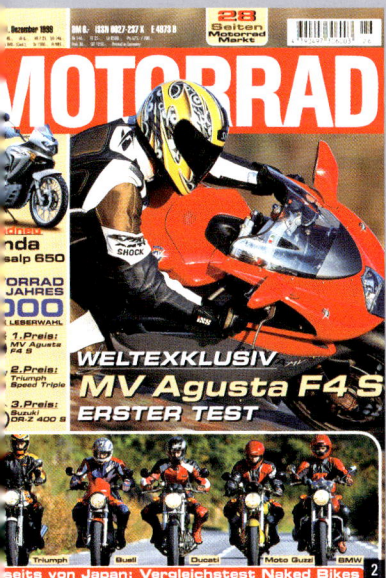

2

3

4

1 The F4 750 S, the "economical" version of the 750 Oro boasted virtually identical mechanical and chassis characteristics to that of its prestigious "sister", while a number of components were changed and the expensive magnesium and carbonfibre were replaced with aluminium alloy (for example in the front fork) and Xenoy thermoplastic (for example in the fairing).

2 The front end was based on the well-known and rock-solid 49 mm upside down fork from the 750 Oro (albeit with the travel extended from 113 to 118 mm).

3 The peculiar "organ pipes" continued to be the signature motif of the rear end.

4 The close-coupled cockpit had a new feature: the gold plate on the upper triple tree with the progressive numbering of each example (300) of the Oro series gave way to an Italian tricolour.

in a series of just 300 examples. A price of L.48,000.000 was announced that became €25,100 when the bike went on sale between the January and February of 2002. One of the fiurst examples went to the Colombian Formula 1 driver Pablo Montoya and by the autumn of the same year all 300 F4 Sennas had all been sold. The F4 SPR (146 hp at 13,000 rpm and a maximum speed of between 270.9 and 293.4 kph depending on the final drive ratio fitted) was the lightweight "race-ready" version of the F4 S, dedicated to MV's more sporting clientele and boasting a revised engine (with new, lighter Mahle pressed pistons with crowns cooled with oil jets) and a fine-tuned chassis. When purchased, the bike was to be supplied with no less than three homologated final drive ratio kits with 15/37, 15/38 and 15/39 crown wheels. An approximate price of L.44,000,000 was indicated and as with the F4 Oro and the F4 Senna, production was to be limited to 300 examples that only went on sale from the June of 2003 (through to December) at €25,370.

"INSANE" DETAILING

The real novelty presented by MV Agusta at the Bavarian show in 200 was, however, the F4 Brutale: finished in a red and metallic grey livery, this two-seater *naked* was initially produced as the customary Oro series in just 300 examples. The manufacturer quoted the following figures: displacement 750 cc, compression ratio 12:1, maximum power 127 hp at 12.500 rpm, maximum torque 7,9 kgm at 9,000 rpm, maximum speed restricted to 250 kph, dry weight 179 kg. An initial price of L.58,350,000 was quoted, which became €29,981 when the bike eventually went on sale in the April of 2003. We should point out straight away that in this account you will find only the most salient facts (along with the complete technical specification in the

1

2

3

4

1 The SPR another of the F4 750s built in just 300 examples, the first of which left the assembly line in June 2003 and remains the property of MV Agusta.

2 and 5 Born as a single-seater, the SPR presented a matte black livery as an alternative to metallic silver or the classic red and silver of the show prototype, with the model name appearing on the flanks or the underside of the fairing.

3 The Brutale 750 Oro, the original model in the naked series presented at Munich in the September of 2000: we know that every example (300, with the progressive number inscribed on the gold plate on the handlebar riser) had been purchased before the model reached the dealers. Example number 12 is personally owned by Claudio Castiglioni.

4 The cover of the Dutch periodical *Motor Magazine* devoted to the F4 SPR.

appendix) about this stunning model and its successive diverse (and successful) variants as so important has it been (not only as a best seller but also as a cult object) in the history of the reborn MV Agusta as to deserve a future monographic study of its own. However, enjoy this little snippet, eloquent testimony to a *naked* of infinite class that has set a benchmark in the sector: the compensation chamber preceding the two characteristic "sawn-off" exhaust pipes is furrowed with narrow stiffening ribs that incorporate the MV logo. This minor aesthetic masterpiece is only visible with the bike jacked up in the workshop or... when leant right over.

In short, "insane" detailing screaming pure Tamburini, the aesthete capable of creating high-tech products with the sole criteria of ars gratia artis.

A propos of Tamburini, when interviewed by *Motociclismo* in the March of 2001, Castiglioni confessed "when Massimo and I placed the first MV decal on the F4 we felt a shiver and had tears in our eyes". On the 24th of July an agreement was signed whereby Piaggio was to take on part of the share capital of MV Agusta Motorcycles Spa, the new firm representing the commercial and production sides of the Varese marque.

For MV, now boasting 560 employees, the last year figures spoke of 23,000 bikes produced for a turnover of L.240 billion, while in the same year Piaggio sold over 480,000 vehicles for a consolidated turnover of L.2,006 billion. Commenting on the agreement, which was designed to allow the development of immediate and brand new synergies of a financial, industrial and commercial nature between the two groups, Castiglioni said that he was convinced that it was "both recognition and a point of departure." We shall see later how the alliance with Piaggio that had seemed to have been concluded was to have a very different destiny.

1

2

3

5

1-3 At last, at the end of 2001, MV Special Parts moved on from the sale of individual special components to offering complete kits for the transformation of an F4 S into something even more exciting and unique.
As a manifesto of this change in direction, the San Marino factory presented a model that was officially named (quite logically) the SP 01 750, but universally known as the Viper: the refined elegance of the blue and metallic grey livery was to contribute to the sale of no less than 50 examples of the kit.
The two photos highlight the typical features of the front and rear ends: the now classic single-sided swing arm with a Sachs monoshock and at the front the "monstrous" 50 mm Marzocchi upside down hydraulic fork, with adjustable extension, compression and spring preloading. Both wheels had a travel of 118 mm.

EXTREME ENGINEERING

At the 59th Milan Cycle and Motorcycle Show in the September of 2001, MV Agusta presented, as had been the case with the F4 Oro, the "economical" version of the Brutale, the S (on sale from April 2003 at €16,500: while the performance figures were similar, the weight rose from 179 to 185 kg. Alongside the S was the F4 750 EV 02, a further evolution of the F4 S, and the new better-finished version of the SPR, the SR (as usual, produced in just 300 examples).

The F4 S EV 02 boasted a more powerful engine (derived from that of the SPR), producing 137 hp at 12,600 rpm, the fruit of the intensive work by the engineers in the R&D department led by Goggi. The increase in power (and torque) was obtained through a series of general mechanical refinements from the combustion chambers to the crankshaft: for example, the crankshaft was lightened by a full kilogram in order to reduce the flywheel effect that had until then prevented the engine from revving more freely and more aggressively and to eliminate the old on-off throttle response hesitations. Priced at €16,334 and €16,475, the new F4 S EV 02 "single" and 1+1 were due to be delivered from the summer of 2002, while the successive EV 03 dual series (on sale from November 2003 to June 2004) was only to offer improvements to the superstructure. In the relative press release the manufacturer spoke with understandable pride of its bikes as "the ultimate in terms of extreme engineering and design choices transferred to serially produced products", underlining once again that "here" there is no separation between technological and aesthetic research.

The 2001 show was also the setting for the launch of MV Agusta Special Parts (the firm founded the previous year within the ambit of the CRC in San Marino and entrusted to the son of Massimo Tamburini, Andrea) with a catalogue of exclusive components such as the parts in magnesium and carbonfibre with which the F4 S could be transformed into the F4 Oro configuration. The show provided an opportunity to exhibit a splendid metallic blue-grey bike celebrating the official launch of the firm: this was the prototype of the stunning F4 SP 01 750, rebaptised by its fans as the Viper

1

2

3

1-4 The world admired the show prototype of the F4 1000 S (single- and two-seater) at the Milan show in the September of 2003 and six months later (May 2004) was able to purchase it from the dealers. Apart from the CRC styling centre's latest matsterly graphics and superstructures (in the four photos, the details, including the widely adjustable right-hand foot peg, bottom left), what struck the industry insiders were the mechanical specs with a power output now reaching 166 hp (for a top speed of 301 kph: food for Japanese thought!) and a torque control system that did away with the classic slipper clutch. With its EBS (Engine Brake System) MV Agusta instead focused on the fuel system: a solenoid valve kept open (when down changing, with the throttle closed) a bypass on the intake tract (downstream of the throttle valve) leading to the second cylinder. The air drawn from the air box and introduced to the cylinder increased the engine speed: torque was therefore generated that worked against and "softened" the engine braking effect from other three cylinders.

thanks to its chromatic resemblance to the well-known Dodge sports car built in the USA. Boasting the same performance figures as the F4 750 S, it was available as just 50 transformation kits. Special Parts also offered components for those F4s that were to be raced, from RG3 exhaust systems and dedicated ignition-injection control units to close-ratio gear sets and racing stands. The San Marino-based firm emphasised the attention it paid to the quality of pre- and post-sales service for MV Agusta bikes: For example maintenance and repairs could be conducted at CRC (by simply knocking on the next door), guaranteeing an extremely professional operation.

It was in mid-July that the Piaggio investors made an about turn. As a bitterly disappointed Castiglioni said: "This is a country in which it is difficult to run a business and this is a situation my workers do not deserve."

A TRIBUTE TO THE CHAMPION OF CHAMPIONS

They held fast at Schiranna and the dynasty of heirs to the original 750 in the MV catalogue continued to expand, maintaining the same high-level finish and specification. The Munich Intermot of September 2002 in fact saw the presentation of the prototype F4 Ago. As the name suggests, the model was dedicated to the marque's greatest champion Giacomo Agostini, with the legendary number 1 inscribed in nostalgic yellow ovals on the sides of the fairing. Initially planned for a limited production run of 500 examples that was subsequently reduced to an edition of 300 (the predicted price of €30,000 for once proving to be correct), the bike was presented in a single red and metallic grey livery. Deriving from the F4 S rather than the Oro, the Ago had no magnesium or sand-cast parts but nonetheless offered a series of exclusive refinements starting with the engine that was based on that of the SPR, the true

1

2

3

4

"The most beautiful in the world". You'll have already seen this title, dedicated by a well-known German specialist weekly to the MV Agusta F4. We've already used it in a caption concerning the F4 1000 S, but we have to roll it out again here because it was used by a monthly (*In Moto*, June 2004) for the 1000 Ago that had just gone on sale to the usual 300 fortunate enthusiasts.
Born as a 750, but subsequently industrialized with a one litre displacement, the model dedicated to the Bergamasco champion of champions led the Schiranna press to say that it was a "figlia d'arte" and that with this model "legend becomes myth."
It was all true; just look at that red and silver livery the fans have seen triumph countless times on circuits around the globe, piloted by the racer with the Hollywood looks. Should further confirmation be required, there's that Number 1 (in the classic yellow oval) on the fairing sides to remind us of the record of the invincible Varese "fighting machines" in a glorious past that could yet return one day.

performance version of the F4. The declared figures were as follows: displacement 750 cc, compression ratio 13:1, maximum power 146 hp at 13,000 rpm, maximum torque 8,2 kgm at 11,000 rpm, maximum speed 270, 278 or 286 kph depending on the final drive ratio, dry weight 188 kg.

The wheels adopted were manufactured by Marchesini to a new design in forged aluminium alloy, while the six-pot Nissin Racing brake calipers were machined from solid billets. The 310 mm front brake discs featured the aluminium flange of the F4 750 Oro, while the Marzocchi fork boasted enormous 50 mm stems treated with titanium nitride to reduce the friction coefficients. Furthermore, the adjustable footpegs were also machined from solid metal, while the air box, the front mudguard and the chainguard were in carbonfibre. Further refinements present on the Ago ranged from titanium shining (a treatment applied to all the aluminium components via immersion in a titanium bath) to an iridescent titanium finish for the rear swinging arm, its pivot plates and the handlebar counterweights. The tubular frame was painted red, the rev-counter had blue figures on a white ground that also carried Agostini's signature and the saddle was upholstered in Alcantara with the F4 logo embroidered on the upper cushion. Lastly, purchasers of the bike were also to receive further exclusive material, from titanium exhaust manifolds to "Ago Racing" silencers, again in titanium, and dedicated Eprom (to adapt the injection-ignition mapping to the changed and improved characteristics of the exhaust system, naturally), through to crown wheels with 15/37 and 15/39 final drive ratios in addition to the 15/38 fitted originally and a paddock-style stand. The Ago was to go on sale from the spring of 2004 at €29,680; however, it was eventually powered by the new 1 litre engine that had been ready from the previous September (and on sale from May 2004 on the 1000 S and 1000 S 1+1) and characterised by the following official figures: displacement 998 cc (bore and stroke 76x55 mm), compression ratio 13:1, maximum power 166 hp at 11,750 rpm, maximum torque 11,1 kgm at 10,200 rpm, maximum speed 301 kph, dry weight 190 kg. On the chassis side there was a new Sachs monoshock adjustable in extension and compression (dual registers for high and low speed damping) and hydraulic spring preloading. In terms of tyres, at the front a 120/70 provided an alternative to the 120/65 that was also homologated and came from the 750 model.

F4 1000 AGO

In spite of styling motifs dating back seven years, the F4 Ago presented that rare form of beauty that some one aptly described as "dynamic rather than aesthetic".

The latest model to come out of Schiranna screamed pure speed, with citations arriving directly from the Grand Prix world, from the superstructures with classic MV Agusta racing colours from the golden age, in which the red (fuel tank, tail, mirrors and front mudguard) immediately captures the eye and heart of the enthusiast.

Then there's the red of the frame, another essential characteristic of the Varese marque's multi-cylinder *bolidi*.

Last but not least, the saddle is also red and a rigorously single-seater, a prerogative in keeping with the nature of a fiery thoroughbred born to be ridden solo. Perhaps with the feet firmly located on stirrups (footpegs) machined from solid metal, as in this case.

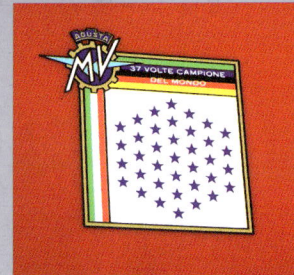

Incomparably exclusive:
F4 CC (2006)

PASSWORD: FULL STEAM AHEAD!

Early in the October of 2002, contacts were re-established with a group of possible new investors headed by Henderson Private Capital (an option previously discarded in favour of the Piaggio offer), while on the horizon appeared a financing plan with Banca Intesa.

Late November then saw a cloud-burst that tried to force the Varese company on its knees: Lake Varese burst its banks and flooded the historic Schiranna factory as a result of the rain that for days had been tormenting northern Italy. Even though the machine tools were not directly affected, significant structural damage led to a halt in production and it was difficult even to estimate a date for when it would restart: the following March was suggested.

Fortunately, late in January 2003, a breath of fresh arrived from the Banca Intesa Group in the form of €25 million: the finance plan announced at the end of the previous summer allowed the company to take the first steps on the road to recovery.

As Castiglioni commented: "This is a result that rewards the strength and prestige of our marques." By the 17th of February a number of production lines were able to restart and at the end of April *La Repubblica* mentioned possible interest in MV Agusta on the part of the financier Roberto Colaninno: the acquisition of the company would fall within a broader plan designed to create an Italian motorcycle pole and would also comprise Piaggio and Ducati.

The news hardly registered with Castiglioni who had already dismissed similar rumours in an interview in the January edition of *Motociclismo*.

In the meantime the specialist magazines continued to show faith in the historic marque by publishing the company's price list comprising no less than five models: the F4 Brutale Oro (on sale at €29,981), the F4 Brutale S (€14,229), the F4 S (€16,542), the F4 S 1+1 (€16,656) and the F4 Ago (€30,000). *Motociclismo* had also introduced a used price list in January 2003, although it was restricted to the F4 S model from 2001 valued at €13,428.

1 The 100 examples of the MV Agusta F CC (the hyper-sporting and hyper-expensive model dedicated to Claudio Castiglioni) were painted by hand one by one. Noblesse oblige for a model that exploded onto the already rarefied MV scene in late 2006 (from the 16th to the 19th of November) and was destined for an elite and passionate few with remarkably deep pockets. Because this F4, the most exclusive of an exclusive range, was priced at a round 100,000 Euros, a world record for a road-going bike. What is all the more incredible is that the figure is hardly exaggerated for a two-wheeler that not only had an "unlimited guarantee" and a platinum plaque on the steering head with its progressive serial number, but is above all characterised by myriad components in high-spec materials.

2 The 1000 S, in single-seater form, conducting the track tests that were to lead to the high performance R version.

3 The 1000 S, in two-seater form, at speed on the straight.

1

2

3

1 and 2 The heir to the 750 models, the 1000 S (here in 1+1 configuration): the original an eye-catching silver and yellow livery characterised the show prototype.

3 The F4 MT4, dedicated to the *maestro*.

4 Massimo Tamburini in what was his office (until 31 December) at CRC in San Marino. On the walls, photos of his "creations", including the F4 750 Oro, of which the guru is proudly indicating a detail.

5 An action shot of the 1000 S, a model born out of long development work that began well before. Realization of the model was facilitated by the fact that the designer had from the outset planned a chassis with dimensions that would comfortably accommodate an engine with a greater displacement than the original three quarters of a litre.

Efforts were focused on producing 24,000 bikes (among the all the group's marques) by the end of the year: although "only" 21,000 were built, they brought with them the first profits. At the same time, in line with the general trends in the sector, it was decided to increase the displacement of the new MV models to 1000 cc.

At the Milan show early in the autumn of 2003, MV Agusta presented the F4 1000 S, the F4 1000 S 1+1 and the ultra-exclusive F4 1000 Tamburini, while MV Agusta Special Parts of San Marino launched the personalised F4 1000 Mamba, Brutale America and Brutale CRC versions. The models that adopted the one litre engine (previously mentioned in relation to the Ago) proved to be the signal that the enthusiasts and the insiders were waiting for: the company was finally on its way to competing on a level playing field (in terms of performance) with the global competitors in the sector and the long chase could be considered to be over. In short, the F4s had achieved maturity because the performance gap with respect to their market rivals, in particular the Japanese, had been definitively closed.

Both the single- and two-seater F4 1000 S were fitted with an engine that had been 70% "revised" by Goggi & Co. with respect to the 750 cc version and boasted the following official statistics: displacement 998 cc (bore and stroke 76x55 mm), compression ratio 13:1, maximum power 166 hp at 11,750 rpm, maximum torque 11.1 kgm at 10,200 rpm, maximum speed 301 kph, dry weight 192 kg (193 kg for the two-seater).

The new engine, work on the design of which began early in 2000, first saw the light of day in 2001 with a displacement of 952 cc, subsequently increased to 998 cc in the interests of increased power and above all more torque: the definitive displacement was obtained by increasing the bore and stroke dimensions of the 750 cc original by just 2.2 mm in the first case and 11.2 mm in the second. This allowed the transverse dimension to remain virtually unchanged, in accordance with the previously mentioned Tamburininan doctrine in this regard.

An important innovation concerned the anti-chatter EBS (Engine Brake System) that restricts the engine braking effect during violent deceleration: it acts directly on the fuel system rather than

1

2

3

4

5

via a dedicated and particularly complicated clutch as in the case of many other models (Aprilia and Kawasaki, for example). The brand new F4s were to go into production in May 2004 with a list price of €18,880 for the single- and €19,080 for the two-seater, in dual red and metallic grey and metallic grey-blue liveries.

MT4: CARRYING THE NAME OF A GENIUS

A true rolling tribute to its designer, the F4 100 Tamburini (or MT4) was also launched in a limited edition of 300 examples. A creation so fabulous as to encourage one journalist to write that this "is the best road bike in the world" and that it will be "untouched by passing time", the MT4 was the most exclusive of the F4s produced to date, in terms of both technology and styling; to save weight wherever possible it was fitted with all the magnesium components of the F4 750 Oro. Regarding the model that carries his name thanks to an autocratic decision by Claudio Castiglioni (the designer would have preferred to dedicate it to the whole of "his" CRC) Tamburini said: "Building the world's most beautiful sports bike is every designer's dream. Making it also the fastest, the most exclusive and the most powerful on the market was my dream. Today that dream came true."

The engine of the F4 Tamburini was derived from that of the F4 1000 S, albeit with various modifications starting with the exclusive, patented TSS (Torque Shift System), previously seen on the Formula 1 Hondas of the early Nineties: the intake trumpets had variable geometry in relation to their length and section, with the result that torque was optimised at all engine speeds.

The manufacturer declared a maximum power output of almost 173 hp at 11,750 rpm (although the engine could spin to 12,850 before the rev limiter kicked in) and a maximum speed of 307 kph

1 The undisputed Queen of the September 2003 Milan Motorcycle Show, the F4 MT4 (or F4 1000 Tamburini), dedicated to the brilliant designer.
The MV Agusta press release accompanying its presentation explicitly spoke of a "magical bike, in which the extreme attention to detailing and the most exclusive componentry are combined with an engine specially configured to obtain thrilling performance."
The roads tests were to highlight these qualities (from the stratospheric maximum speed of 307 kph to acceleration that would stun even the most experienced rider.) that could have made the MT4 an ideal basis for future employment in SBK racing.

2 The instrument panel and the gold plate on the steering head carrying the serial number.

3 An action photo of the MT4 on track, highlighting the front and rear ends of Varese's latest, with the Marzocchi fork displaying titanium nitride treated stems and a rear wheel benefiting from the EBS torque control system.

4 and 6 The front brake is a 321 Nissin dual floating disc unit with calipers with six pistons of differentiated diameters. It was combined with a single 210 mm Nissin disc with a four-pot caliper.
The "gold" you can see in the two photos is titanium: the MT4 in fact boasted all the components cast in an alloy of this lightweight (and expensive material) already seen on the F4 750 Oro.

5 The throttle that actuates the TSS variable geometry intake system, a first for a motorcycle (**7**).

1

2

3

4

5

6

7

1 The F4 1000 Mamba, presented towards the end of 2003, was born as a model destined for 300 (wealthy) enthusiasts who were interested in using their bike on track: the Titanium version featured a titanium exhaust and naturally a dedicated Eprom.

2 The CRC logo well to the fore on the front fairing highlights the fact that this model emerged "personalized" from the legendary "renaissance workshop" in San Marino where Massimo Tamburini worked and taught (to work).

3 The Marchesini wheels are in forged aluminium.

4 The aggressive red and black fairing in carbonfibre (lighter than the aluminium version of the standard 1000 S on which the model is based) is just one of the competition-style components (with many details machined from solid metal) fitted to the Varese snake.

(recorded during the homologation tests with the historic Schiranna test rider Fabrizio Latini in the saddle). In production from the autumn of 2004, the 1000 Tamburini cost €40,005, which rose to around €43,000 with the dedicated kit. As a comment on this jewel of a bike, we would add that as *natura non facit saltus*, not even among designers, it was appropriate that to close the ideal circle opened by MV Agusta with the 500 R19 in 1950 (where the R stood for Remor, its designer) the true heir to that engineering genius, Massimo Tamburini, had a model named after him.

With regard instead to the previously mentioned CRC special versions of the 1000 S and Brutale S models, they marked a sea change in MV Agusta special Parts' business because with them the young San Marino-based company began to market directly on request complete special bikes rather than just dedicated kits or single tuning parts. In particular, the sporting F4 1000 Mamba boasted stunning componentry and an aggressive red and black livery. It was offered in a limited edition of 300 examples and cost, depending on the equipment level, between €21,160 and €29,180. Production began in the May of 2004, immediately after that of the standard 1000 S.

The new one-litre models met with remarkable success at the Munich Show and the press was unanimous in underlining the fact that this was the right moment to attempt the definitive relaunch of the marque. In fact, in the last week of October, Castiglioni (in a constant search for a reliable partner) flew to Malaysia to meet a number of government representatives and managers from Proton, one of the largest Asian automotive groups, quoted on the Kuala Lumpar stock exchange and owner, among others, of the prestigious Lotus marque. On the 28th of October 2003, Castiglioni signed an initial letter of intent with the chairman of Proton regarding an agreement for investment in MV Agusta.

Perhaps the best news came in the April of 2004: the Cassinetta factory was running at full capacity once again with 150 MV, Husqvarna and Cagiva coming off the lines each day (the post-Taylorist, ultra-flexible Kanban method operating on the basis of actual demand from the commercial department). On the 25th of May, a binding offer from Proton to the Schiranna firm of around €70 million suggested that the conclusion of negotiations with the Malaysian group was imminent.

1 and 2 Presented at the NATO base at Cervia on the 29th of August 2005, the F4 1000 Veltro, carries the "signature" of MV Corse, the San Marino structure heir to the Special Parts division.
The occasions for its production in a limited series was the "twinning" with the Italian Air Force's "Veltro" 5th Squadron of the 23rd Fighter Group. There was no coincidence behind the 5-23 numbering and the stylized greyhound symbolizing the Dante-esque Veltro that characterised both series (Strada and Pista) put on sale in 2006.

3 The badge commemorating the event.

4 Colonel Mauro Gabetta and Andrea Tamburini.

5 The Pista differed from the road-going version in that it adopted the titanium exhaust, with dedicate Eprom, closed nose and tail fairings with no headlamp and other lightweight components. Both versions featured carbonfibre fairings with dedicated Veltro graphics, components machined from solid metal and MotoGP-style digital instrumentation.

THOSE MIRACULOUS 10,000 F4S

Early in the summer of 2004 Agusta announced that over 10,000 examples of the F4 had been produced: while clearly not a figure to compare with those of the sector's giants, for the company it represented the most important of achievements, considering the courage displayed over the previous years by everyone at the firm, from the managers to the workers, as they tried to hold it all together and press on despite the looming internal crisis.

On the 7th of July 2004, the company announced that Castiglioni and Proton had signed an agreement regarding the Malaysians' acquisition of a majority shareholding in MV Agusta. The increase in company capital was confirmed as €70 million, subject to debt restructuring and the firm's exit from administration. The insiders were convinced that this partnership would guarantee new industrial and commercial synergies with the objective of achieving further development and enhance the valorization of the group's marques. However, we shall soon see that all that glitters is not necessarily gold.

In mid-September 2004, another sign of the favourable change in the climate came when MV Agusta Special Parts of San Marino became MV Agusta Corse: what better name could have been chosen for the company comprising a dozen people led by Andrea Tamburini?

At the Munich Intermot in September, the Brutale Mamba (produced in 300 examples) was exhibited under the San Marino firm's new name: on sale from March 2005, it was priced at €22,000.

23 GRUPPO CACCIA

1 and 2 The fresh and exciting racing livery of the Corse (with striking white cs in white over the basic "rosso corse" and silver colour scheme) lightens the already slim tail and the crowded area of the left-hand clip-on.
This was the handiwork of the "boys" at CRC of San Marino who personalised a bike destined, as an MV Agusta press release had it, for "assiduous circuit riders."

3 and 4 Two covers from Italian specialist magazines with action shots of the faired (750 S) and naked (Brutale 7590 S) F4s.

5 and 6 The muscular front-end with the incredible 50 mm Marzocchi upside down fork and the rigorously single-seater saddle, clearly reveal the model's sporting soul.

7 and 8 The model was distributed (from late March 2005) by MV Agusta Corse of San Marino, the heir to the Special Parts division.

9 The beautifully crafted heel guard on the right-hand foot peg.

THE ARRIVAL OF THE MALAYSIAN TIGERS

On the 17th of December 2004, it was announced that the court of Varese had declared that MV Agusta had emerged from its period of administration and that the company returned *in bonis*.

At this point, the increase in capital mentioned above was definitively subscribed and paid up by Proton, which provided "suretyship via CityBank for the entire amount." Following the recapitalization, the Malaysian group held a majority shareholding (57.75%), the Castiglioni family 37.25%, Husqvarna AB 3% and Massimo Tamburini 2%. The new structure saw Claudio Castiglioni as chairman of the company with responsibility for both the Marketing and Research and Development sectors, Lorenzo Cocco as managing director, Zaidi Bin Mohd Yusoff as production director and Johnson Liu Wen Jong as head of finance. Castiglioni declared to *Panorama* that the affair had been concluded successfully following "a two-year inferno", thanks to "a forward thinking banker (Corrado Passera, the Banca Intesa CEO ed.), a Malaysian group composed of serious people and a highly competent court."

Early in March 2005, the group's official figures for the first two months of the year indicated a 50.8% increase in registrations compared with the same period the previous year: the best selling model was the Brutale (186 examples out of a total of 1,572 bikes sold). The end of the month saw the introduction of two new models from MV Agusta Corse: the Brutale Gladio and the F4 1000 Corse, both produced in limited editions of 300 examples. The second was to be followed (entering the catalogue in 2007) by the F4 R 312 Corse version, again available only as a single–seater and again in a limited edition of 300 examples.

After the first photos of the new Brutale, the 910 S had appeared in mid-April 2005, the more aggressive R and Starfighter versions went on display at the Milan show late in the year. Alongside them was the stunning (dedicated graphics and a flame red frame!) F4 1000 Senna (174 hp) in 300 examples (at €30,400) and the F4 1000 Veltro (185 hp), produced in just 46 examples (price:

1

CORSE

2

www.superwheels.net

SUPER WHEELS

DUCATI 749S
KAWASAKI Z750
SUZUKI V-Strom
HONDA RC211V

DUCATI DESMOSEDICI
APRILIA PEGASO TUSCANY-TIBET
PATENTE A! Istruzioni per l'uso

PROVA MV Brutale S! la guerra dei sensi

3

TUTTO MOTTO

TUTTO NUOVO!

FANTASTICO 100 LETTORI IN PISTA CON TUTTOMOTO E APRILIA

TEST ANTEPRIMA
MOTO GUZZI
APRILIA
KAWASAKI

MV AGUSTA BRUTALE 750 F4 750
DUELLO ALL'ULTIMA CURVA

ESCLUSIVO! IL MOTOMONDIALE A FUMETTI

4

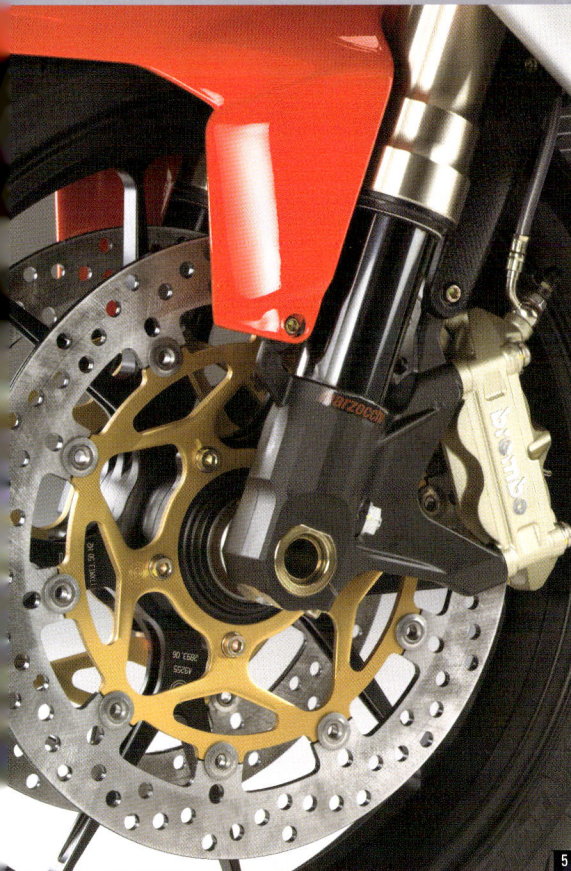

5

AGUSTA MV
CORSE
CRC

6

MV AGUSTA CORSE

7

F4 CORSE

8

9

1 The arrival of the F4 1000 R in May 2006. As an MV Agusta press release proudly noted, 46 publications were present at its launch, with their testers eager to tame the bike's 174 hp on the Misano Adriatico circuit.
The enthusiasm aroused among the insiders was such that shortly afterwards we were to see yet again titles like "The world's most beautiful motorcycle" (*Super Wheels*, June 2006). Another periodical (*In Moto*) went with "Tremble all you Japanese!", recognising what the 1000 R represented in the supersports bike segment: the gap between the rivals was about to be bridged.
The styling motifs (large photo), with the sophisticated new graphics in metallic black and anthracite (or red and silver), renewed the regal aura of the F4 series.

2 and 3 The maniacal attention to detail (some of the finishing was incredible, but the CRC only knows how to work to these levels!) is evident everywhere, from the beautifully enamelled fire red frame to the rev counter that, in the definitive version of the model presented an ineffable new graduated touch of red at the centre.

over €50,000), 23 homologated and 23 for the track: the model came from the MV Agusta Corse stable and took its name from the "strong running" hounds cites by Dante and D'Annunzio as well as from the twinning of MVC and the Italian Airforce's 23rd Squadron. All the new models went into production in 2006. In the meantime, following an announcement in late November, the Malaysian group withdrew from their commitments to MV Agusta: their shareholding (57.75%) passed from Proton to GEVI, a finance company specially created by the CARIGE group of Genoa that paid just €1.00, but agreed to take on frozen debts totalling €106.94 million and the operating debt (the demand for working capital) of 32,5 million.

200 CV, €100,000, 100 EXAMPLES

The first new model of 2006 was the F4 1000 R (single- and two-seater) presented at the Misano Adriatico circuit in late May, a more lavishly equipped, ultra-high performance version of the 1000 S (the cylinder head was new, as was the twin-plate clutch with an aluminium bell housing). Producing 174 hp at 11,900 rpm and good for 301 kph, it went on sale in May 2006 at €19,820 (€19,920 for the two-seater). In late August, we saw the first photos of the very blue Brutale 910 R Italia celebrating the Italy's World Cup triumph.

However, the real star of MV's season was to be seen at the traditional end-of-year Milan show. This was the F4 CC (CC standing for Claudio Castiglioni), a model scheduled to be built in just 100 examples (all hand painted!) and destined to become the world's most expensive bike at €100,000. The power unit was derived from that of the contemporary 1000 R with the displacement increased to 1078 cc (bore and stoke: 79x55 mm), a power output of 315 kph and a top speed of 315 kph (with

1

2

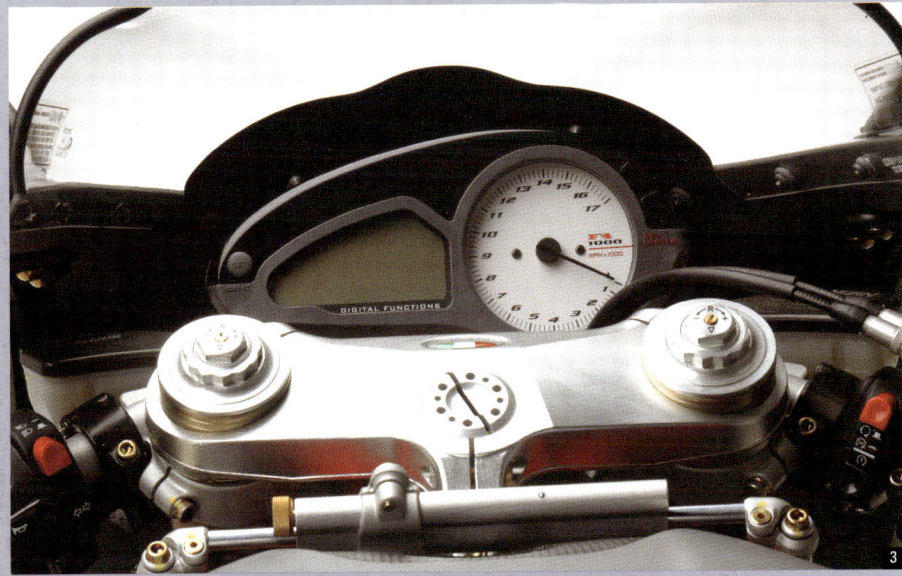

3

a titanium open exhaust) and if it had not been for the delay in the homologation of the Pirelli Dragon Supercorsa Pro tyres... The model was fitted with the renowned TSS variable geometry intake system (optimising torque at all engine speeds) and the similarly patented EBS anti-chatter system, this last combined with a new clutch machined from solid metal and deriving from the company's lengthy racing experience. The suspension was also revised to a racing-style (read: extremely rigid) configuration certainly better suited to the track than the road.

In terms of its mechanical components and chassis, Schiranna's latest jewel (a black pearl with fabulous red highlights) came straight out of the Corse department directed by Goggi and was sculpted by Tamburini in an orgy of precious materials, from the chrome-molybdenum frame to the carbonfibre fairing, from the magnesium swinging arm, frame plates and camshaft, gearbox and clutch casings) to the Del West titanium intake and exhaust valves, with details machined from solid metal (fork ends, footpegs, triple tree, control levers) and meticulously finished. In order to ensure the bike had the best of all possible worlds, the dual valve springs, the valve seats and guides came from Del West of California (well known for its quality standards as a Formula 1 supplier) while the alternator was a Nippondenso oil-cooled neodymion-iron-boron high power unit. A platinum plaque mounted on the steering head carried the serial number of each example, while on delivery the (Euro 3) bike was to be accompanied by a certificate of origin enclosed in a (naturally) bespoke case. As if all this was not enough, the F4 CC was to be accompanied by a number of similarly exclusive accessories including a personalised Girard-Perregaux chronograph.

While publicity generated in the specialist press and elsewhere sang the praises of MV Agusta's latest creation (*Panorama* titled its comment "Every biker's dream"), Castiglioni claimed with renewed pride that he had decided to lend his name to the bike he had "always desired", a "racing bike that can be used not only on the track."

TITANIUM F1

F4 CC

"I decided to lend my name to the bike that I've always wanted, a racing bike that would not be restricted to the track", says Claudio Castiglioni, the proud "sponsor" of the model.

This is probably the ultimate example of a no-holds-barred motorcycle, bringing together the very best components available on the market (for example, the Del West titanium valves) to create a street bike with the specification of racing machine.

Stylistic and technological sophistication of the utmost exclusivity for a model with a displacement of over a litre, a maximum power output of 200 hp and good for 315 kph.

Among the "insane" details: hand-finished titanium exhausts, inscribed mirrors, Alcantara pads hand-stitched with a red thread for the maximum comfort of the rider in the (leather) saddle. race-style fuel filler; hand-punched holes tracing the MV logo on the metal grille covering the intake for the air box; the "cockpit" with the platinum plaque with the serial number; foot pegs and control levers machined from solid billets that look like works of art.

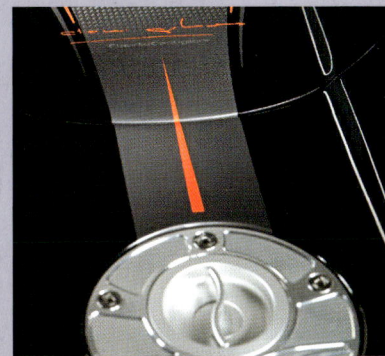

The new dawn at the top:
F4 1000 (2010)

THE CAVALRY'S COMING?

The big news of spring 2007 was the F4 R312 (183 hp at 12,400 rpm) single- and two-seater derived from the F4 1000 R. With regard to maximum speed, the official figures spoke primly of "over 300 kph", but the first magazine tests confirmed the "312 kph" proudly anticipated by Castiglioni and giving rise to the name of the model: a world record for a one-litre production bike given that there was nothing else around to challenge match it, neither the Ducati 1098S nor the four magnificent Japanese members of the "300 club", the Honda CBR 1000RR, the Kawasaki ZX 10R, the Suzuki GSX R1000 and the Yamaha YZF R1.

The former champion Randy Mamola wrote in the magazine *In Moto*: "in the saddle it feels like a 747 ready for take off", going on to praise the usual "fantastic" chassis, from the granitic Marzocchi 50 mm upside down fork to the new Brembo radial brake calipers. A new peak of excellence for a bike that had dominated the dreams of the enthusiasts for 10 years now, the 312 displayed an extremely elegant Bodoni black colour scheme (named after the brilliant typographer from Parma), beneath which could be seen (where they were visible) the perfect competition-style TIG welds to which Tamburini & Co. had accustomed us. The new model cost €20,890 (€20,990 for the two-seater) with a delivery time of one month.

During the course of the following spring, the most powerful version of the 312 was added to the catalogue: the F4 1078 RR 312 (single- and two-seater), with a displacement of 1078 cc, the same as that of the F2 CC from which the new model also stole other details (for example, the Sachs steering damper machined from solid metal). Producing 190 hp at 12,220 rpm, the model cost €21,390 (€21,490 for the two-seater). In the summer, the same engine was fitted to the Brutale 1078 RR (144 hp at 10,600 rpm, 265 kph, according to the manufacturer's figures), the latest stage (along with the contemporary 989 R with 142 hp at 11,000 rpm and 265 kph) in the escalating success of the popular naked. In summer 2008, along with the first rumours about the MV Agusta F3 triple, arrived Harley-

1

2

3

4

5

A year on from the presentation of the F4 R 312 the company was already launching the F4 1078 RR 312 derivation: it boasts the 1078 cc power unit already seen on the ultra-muscular F4 CC, with the power output rising from 183 to 190 hp. The new bike, available in single- and two-seater versions, like its smaller "sister" features an identical Sachs monoshock at the rear end (**1**) with rebound, compression adjustment (high and low speed) and spring preloading, while at the front is the usual oversized Marzocchi 55 mm upside down fork (**4**) equipped with external rebound and compression adjustment and spring preloading. Wheel travel is 130 mm at the front and 120 mm at the rear.

2 Elegantly clothing the mixed frame with its chrome-molybdenum steel tubes and aluminium alloy plates, with anchorage points in conjunction with the cylinder head (**3**), the RR 312's superstructure adopts the same three liveries as the R 312, including the classic red and silver (**5-8**).

Davidson. Castiglioni remained as Chairman with Matthew (Matt) Levatich being appointed as CEO. According to Levatich, the acquisition of such a prestigious marque would reinforce HD's presence in Europe. When he was promoted to president of HD in April 2009, he was replaced by Enrico D'Onofrio.

BYE BYE HD (AND ARRIVEDERCI MASSIMO)

In the meantime, two events characterised the second half of 2008. The first was the transfer, early in the summer, of MV Agusta Corse to Varese. The second was that Massimo Tamburini announced his retirement "effective from the 31st of December 2008". This decision, the origins of which generated myriad rumours, shook the motorcycling world: could you actually imagine some one like the Rimini guru giving up his bikes to cultivate roses and collect stamps in some *buen retiro*?
Returning to 2009, on the 28th of September MV Agusta presented the new versions of the Brutale at the Misano Adriatico circuit: the 990 R and the 1090 RR, producing respectively 139 and 144 hp at 10,600 rpm. The press release accompanying the event stated that "a new era had begun" for the Varese company. This was all too true as just 20 days later Harley-Davidson announced that it was selling the MV Agusta marque (together with Cagiva and the US firm Buell) to focus on the core brand of the famous Wisconsin marque. Once again insiders and enthusiasts alike were thrown into disarray, although a surprised, but ever-optimistic Castiglioni immediately declared that they would continue "to develop new models while awaiting investors"; a few days later he was to speak courageously (talk about optimism of the will!) of 6,500 F4s and Brutale to be sold in 2010.

F4 1000: CHANGE EVERYTHING SO NOTHING CHANGES

Two weeks later, a press release from Schiranna announced the arrival of a new F4, a new generation version that maintained great faith (something that we could never praise too highly) in the original design: defined by the manufacturer as "pure perfection", it was to be the auspicious forebear of MV Agusta's future flagship sports bikes. Named the F4 1000, it was to be the queen of the forthcoming 67th Milan Motorcycle Show (12-15 November) that since 2005 had been held at the Fieramilano site in Rho. In order to prepare the show prototypes, the CRC's peerless team (including Tamburini who through to almost the last was there to lend his designer's eye) worked as ever to the highest standards, albeit with their hearts broken, aware of "the blood and tears" spilt by the phenomenon of capitalistic globalization that had not hesitated to strike hard yet again even here, on the very edges of the empire.

This last two-seater red and silver creation (also sold in matt black, gloss black and titanium liveries) was largely new with respect to models that had preceded it, even though it would take a careful technical examination to notice given that the external appearance had certainly not been revolutionised. The only obvious evidence of change were the quadrangular rather than circular exhaust terminals (equipped with a partial shut-off valve and a new sound that as the throttle was opened passed from a deep throatiness to an ineffable crystalline transparency) and the all-digital instrumentation. Much had changed with the F4 (including a number of components suppliers!) without betraying too much of the past, given that the resulting machine was incredibly aggressive but still exquisitely balanced and a true superbike. Castiglioni likes to see the F4 in the same light as a Porsche that every so often has to evolve while remaining faithful to its innate appeal and timeless styling. In short, in this evolution without revolution (no mean feat, especially as it was the fruit of a new design and not a mere restyling) a masterpiece of the past became the latest icon Made in Italy ready to set about conquering the planet.

From early in 2008, work at MV Agusta was focussed on a single objective: preparing the (exclusively two-seater) model for the Milan Motorcycle Show in the November of 2009.
While Schiranna concentrated on the mechanical assemblies, CRC dealt with all the rest.
The San Marino organization's styling centre began a tour de force demonstration of the "try and try again" method that involved the whole of the new F4, from the tail (**1**)), as usual firstly worked up in clay (**7 and 8**), to the nose (**5**), by way of the instrument panel (**2**) and the rear-view mirrors (**3**).

The evolution of the model that was to lead to the show prototype can be seen in a series of sketches, this one by Adrian Morton (**4**) and one of a hypothetical Oro version (**6**).

9 The 1000 2010 was to prove to be an F4 that had been thoroughly revised without betraying the spirit and substance of the series inaugurated with the 750 Oro.

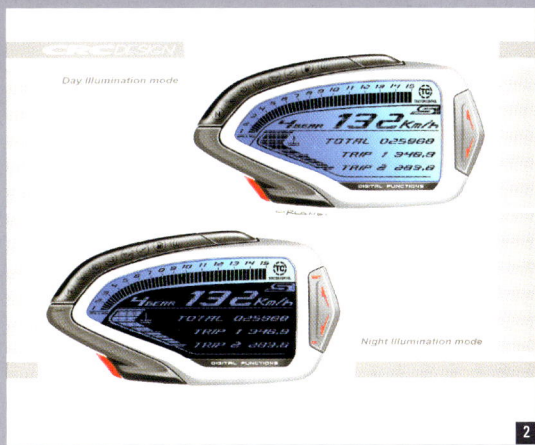

Day Illumination mode

Night Illumination mode

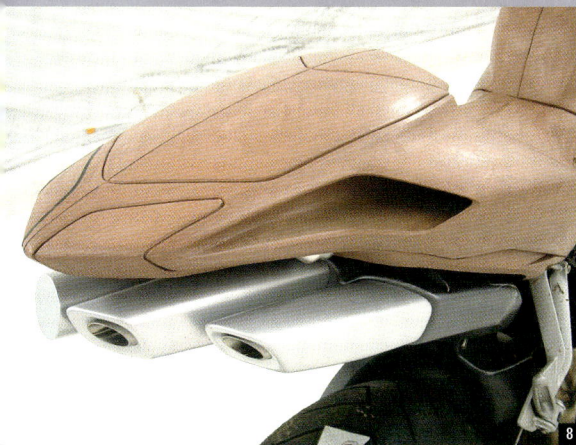

FROM NATIONAL SBK TITLES TO SERIAL PRODUCTION

The twin overhead camshaft engine with radial valves was the 998 cc unit already seen in the Brutale 990 R, but with the block from the 312 RR.

The power output of 186 hp at 12,900 rpm provided a maximum speed of almost 305 kph, remarkably high performance that was controllable (and more importantly always perfectly usable without having to rent the Monza track for half a day) thanks to new electronic systems working on the chassis, starting with the dedicated TC Mk II traction control with dual mapping (Sport/Rain) and adjustable to eight levels of intervention. This was a system developed on the bike that Luca Scassa rode to victory in the Italian SBK championship in 2008 (an F4 312 RR prepared and directly managed by the Research Development department with logistical support from the Unionbike Gimotorsports team).

Maintaining the tradition of sporting marques whereby racing is the best proving ground for production bikes, work began with an analysis of the magnificent performance of the revised (longer and lighter) magnesium swing arm raced by the Arezzo-born rider.

Work on the prototype F4 2010 lasted a couple of years, subdivided between Schiranna (where Goggi's men focused on the development of lighter high performance components) and CRC in San Marino (led by Paolo Bianchi after Tamburini's adieu) that concentrated on the revision of the chassis to improve the riding experience and the updating of the styling. While a declared weight of just 192.5 kg (there was talk of a weight loss of no less than 10 kg) lent a hand to render the chassis more agile, the frame (cro-mo steel tubes with die-cast aluminium plates) was 4 cm narrower (the frontal section of the F4 now resembled that of a twin-cylinder bike), while the single swinging arm was lengthened by 20 mm to favour the bike's already remarkable traction and allow the road-going missile to be controlled more easily at high speed.

Without losing anything in directional control and stability, the granitic front end (the design of

1 At Schiranna, the men led by Goggi worked on lightening and uprating (also focussing on restricting any loss of horsepower) the power unit of the F4 2010. In the crankcase, 600 grams lighter but more capacious than that of the previous models, the rebalanced crankshaft does not require the classic counter-rotating balancer shaft to reduce vibrations.

2 The crowded but extremely ordered area where the front trellis frame and the rear anchorage plates meet, with the beautifully machined foot pegs of rider and passenger displaying the MV logo with understandable pride.

3 The four-cylinder, while retaining the key features of the original model from 13 years previously (first and foremost, the slightly radial configuration of the valves), it was now lighter and higher performing: among the innovations, the oil cooler replacing the previous heat exchanger. (**6**).

4 New 49 mm (rather than 48 mm) Mikuni throttle bodies together with a larger air-box and shorter intake trumpets for the exclusive TSS system inherited from 2005's MT4.

5 and 7 Covering (almost completely) the frame with its perfect TIG welds is an attractive livery of red and silver, gloss and matte black, dark graphite grey and medium graphite grey.

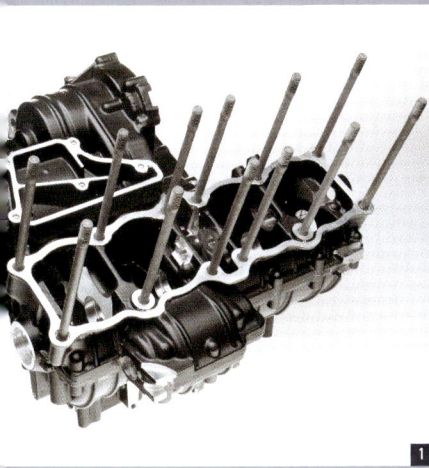

1 A little mechanical engineering: the exhaust system terminating in the new quadrangular "organ pipes" and chassis details from the F4 1000 2010.

2 and 3 Thirteen years on, the rear swinging arm, now 20 mm longer, has lost none of the appeal that led CRC of San Marino to patent it as an "ornamental motif."

4 The twin 320 mm Brembo front discs with monobloc four-pot radial calipers.

5 The Sachs monoshock working as a rocker and equipped with the usual range of adjustments.

6 The chassis (complete with the rear tubular Duraluminium subframe also capable of supporting the exhaust pipes) is now lighter, narrower and shorter than its predecessor, optimized in terms of rigidity and with a narrower steering angle to favour agility.

reference for the segment from the very first F4) now had the front wheel trail reduced from 103.8 to 100.4 mm with the inclination of the steering column reduced from 24°3' to 23°5' (while remaining adjustable within 1 degree).

The suspension was fully adjustable (Marzocchi at the front, Sachs at the rear), while the two Brembo front discs were fitted with monobloc radial calipers (curiously, the master cylinder was still a Nissin axial unit) and the single rear disc was a dedicated Nissin component.

These modifications benefited both manoeuvrability and the riding position, frequently criticised in the past as being unergonomic and rather uncomfortable. In relation to the bike's optimization, the cooling system (which now incorporated an oil radiator in place of the heat exchanger along with the water radiator in order to overcome worrying rise in oil temperature under hard use) and the fuel tank were both redesigned, the latter now being smaller.

BACK TO THE FUTURE

In order to improve efficiency at high revs, the power unit (with redesigned con-rods) adopted a new electronic fuel injection system with the 49 mm Mikuni throttle bodies with dual injectors per cylinder controlled by a new Magneti Marelli ECU that also regulated the above mentioned traction control and, as we shall see, the TSS system. The intake roar had now become so powerful (and enthralling) as to remind the author of the all-Italian aggression of mechanical masterpieces of the Sixties such as the Alfa Romeo Giulia 1600 and the Lancia Fulvia HF 1600.

Everything possible had been done to overcome the well known defect of overly brusque throttle response (that could catch out even the most capable of riders) below 4000 rpm when passing from

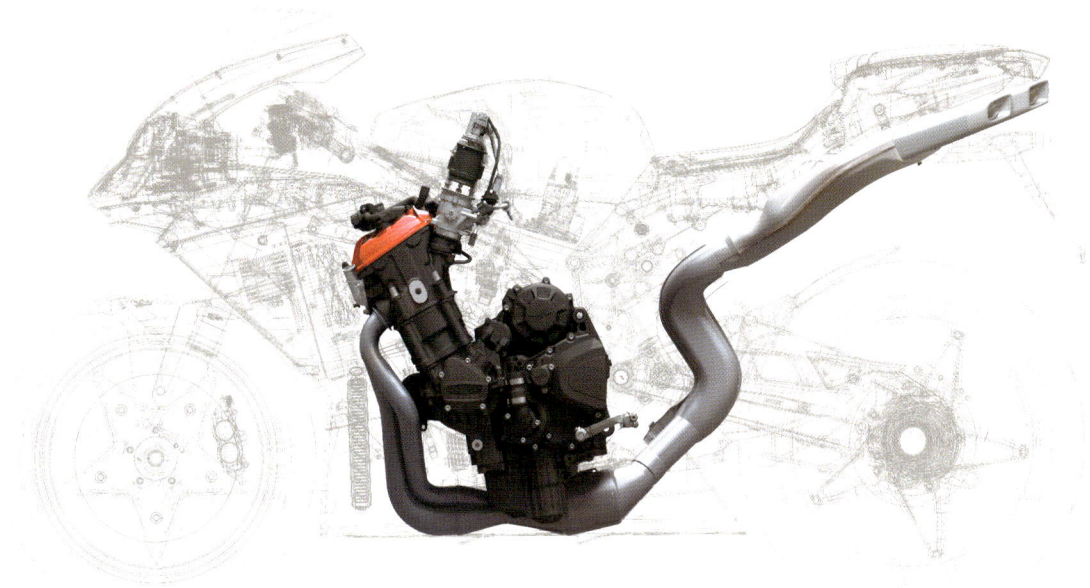

1

2

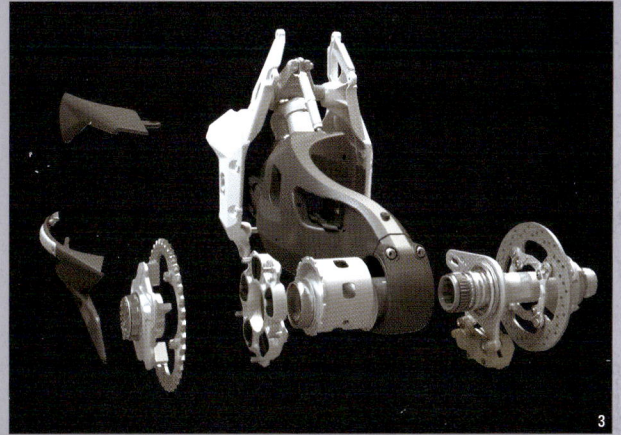

3

4

5

6

ELECTRONICS *IN PROGRESS*

It was above all the extraordinary development of electronics over the last decade (in a progression that, as mentioned previously, passed from arithmetic to geometric and finally exponential) that permitted the engineering of the MV Agusta F4 to attain the current extremely high (albeit still perfectible) levels of performance and electronic management.

We have asked the engineer Mauro Marelli ("in-house" since 1987, formerly at Cagiva Corse and now head of the electrical, electronics and data acquisition fields for MV Agusta) to give us an extremely brief overview of this exciting "work in progress."

Given the experience accumulated with electronic fuel injection with the last Grand Prix Cagiva 500, the staff in the F4 Development department (that derived from the previous Corse or racing department) could hardly fail to develop the new power unit with this kind of fuel system.

The first mass-produced electronic control unit available was the Magneti Marelli P8, already used in the automotive field: it was rather bulky and consequently we only used it for the initial bench testing. Then, for the first laps on the track, we adopted race-derived instrumentation (data acquisition, sensors software), while the need for a much more flexible ECU from the point of view of the calibration parameters oriented us towards an MF3S unit, again produced by Magneti Marelli.

The next stage involved a space-saving process: in place of the P8 ECU we adopted the smaller Magneti Marelli 1.6M, for the first versions of the production engine. It was with this unit that we introduced new software strategies to the F4 such as the EBS torque

control and that of the TSS variable intake system. However, the 1.6M unit restricted the control to a semi-phase condition, while in practise the piloting of the ignition and injection occurred in parallel on the two banks, rather than separately on all four cylinders. This, together with a search for reduced emissions and fuel consumption, led us to adopt a more advanced ECU, again derived from the automotive sector and again produced by Magneti Marelli, the 5SM: it was more compact and offered significantly enhanced performance with respect to the earlier unit.

It was with this unit that we began to talk about phased control of fuel injection and ignition, about Euro 2 and CAN line dialogue with external units (instrument panel). The use of this technology has, furthermore, allowed us to shift from the traditional concave coil and spark plugs to the new plug-top coils inserted directly into the spark plug well.

Lastly, in 2008, a parenthesis that was apparently unrelated to the production side and Claudio Castiglioni's great passion led us back to our old but never completely abandoned vocation for racing: we raced an F4 in the Italian SBK championship, winning the title with Luca Scassa. For these races we decided to use a control unit produced by a Varese firm, Microtec. With it we developed and tested in the competition world new strategies that would also go into production with the latest generation engine management unit, the Magneti Marelli 7BM that thanks to highly evolved hardware provides us electronic management of the two injector banks and traction control. All this together with a new all-digital instrument panel, a smaller, lighter alternator, xenon headlamps and other details such as LED indicators.

1 The Magneti Marelli 7AM control unit is the electronic "heart" of the F4 1000 (**4**); located behind the cylinder block (**2 e 3**) it controls various functions: from the ignition-injection system to ancillary services such as the all-digital instrumentation (**5**), from the new traction control to the lighting system (now with a Xenon lamp, **6**) and the LED indicators (**7-8**).
As the guru of Schiranna's engine development, the engineer Andrea Goggi, says, the development of electronics has, in synergy with the inherent mechanical and chassis qualities of the F4, allowed the latest giant steps to be made with the design of MV Agusta's legendary bike.

3

4

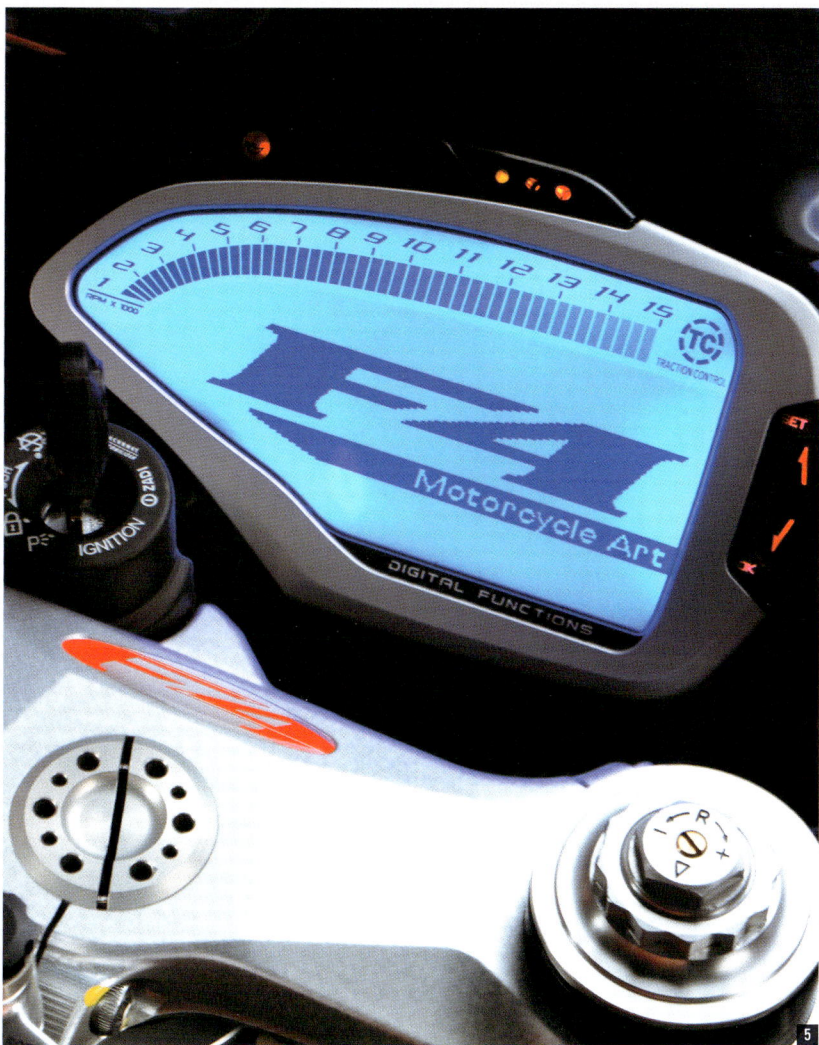

5

6

7

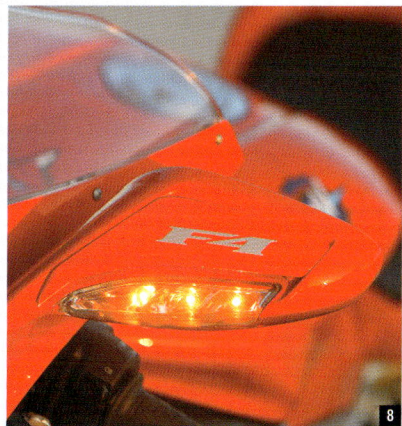

8

a completely closed to a partially open throttle position (the on-off effect), in the knowledge that the problem could not be wholly resolved, as confirmed by the engineer Goggi (head of engine development) in a recent interview, as the electronic injection inevitably had to choose been engine braking and throttle response. In order to optimise power delivery (more low- and mid-range torque as well as high power at the top end, the engine was fitted with the previously mentioned TSS system (variable intake geometry) already seen on the Tamburini and the CC and now further developed (with shorter intake trumpets) and finally industrialised.

Del West 30 mm titanium intake valves, a brand new gear shift (coupled to the customary extractable six-speed-box) with an engaged gear sensor (naturally interacting with the engine mapping) and a slipper clutch are just a few of the myriad measures taken to rationalize the engine, together with new lighter casings, the crankshaft with 50% more inertia and the deeper oil sump equipped with a brand new ecological filter that could be extracted without removing any other component. What design sophistication in this anti-pollution detail!

Apropos of sophistication, just look at the workmanship on the footpegs with their MV logos like those on… the side stand. However, it should also be said that perhaps due to a misunderstanding of the family or rather dynasty brand concept, the F4 1000 continues to transmit considerable vibration (especially through the footpegs due to the elimination of the counter-rotating balancer shaft) and a little too much heat reaches the rider.

When in the February of 2009 an announcement was made that production of the F4 1000 was about to begin (wit a turnkey price dropped to €18,500), an anonymous web surfer declared in a blog that this was a bike that "you don't discuss, you just love." Very true, and emphasised by that decal on the fuel tank commemorating the 37 world titles conquered by MV Agusta in its first lifetime.

On the 6th of August a press release from Schiranna announced that the crisis triggered in mid-October 2009 with MV Agusta being put up for sale by Harley-Davidson had been resolved most satisfac-

1

2

3

4

5

6

torily. The marque was Italian once again, repurchased by Claudio and Giovanni Castiglioni thanks to the family holding company.

A worthy finale to a period that has seen the achievement of a technological pinnacle with the F4 and the rumours of the presentation of new three-cylinder models.

Now we can look ahead with renewed enthusiasm to the future of the "pearl of Italian motorcycling": proudly underlined the much missed Claudio Castiglioni, in his role as chairman, flanked by his son Giovanni (who has now succeeded him at the head of the company) and by the engineer Massimo Bordi. For the motorcycle industry insiders this is exciting news, given that the designer is remembered by all as the artificer since 1987 of the commercial and sporting rebirth of Ducati, thanks to the inspired introduction of the ultra-high performance desmo twin-cam cylinder head with 4 water-cooled valves per cylinder, a glorious emblem of the Borgo Panigale firm for decades.

201 THOROUGHBREDS: AS YOU LIKE IT

Early spring 2011 saw the launch of the Varese marque's latest masterpiece. Tagged with a list price of €22,000, the F4 RR Corsacorta reached the dealers in May: this one-litre model is accredited with over 201 hp at the crank measured at 13,400 rpm, a stratospheric output that would appear to be expressly designed for a tilt at the world 1,000 cc supersport road bike crown. The 200 hp threshold is, after all, currently considered by those in the business to be the true discriminating factor between race and production bikes.

The RR Corsacorta is hardly the fruit of mere updating, no routine makeover: this can be seen in the substantial innovations introduced to the mechanical and chassis specifications, while in terms of

1-3 The three official liveries of the F4 1000 2010.

4 The tester Umberto Rumiano leans hard at Imola aboard MV Agusta's latest product, defined by his colleague Latini as the "apotheosis of accessibility."

5 The "cockpit" (with the handlebars finally close enough to the saddle) and the side view demonstrate that the efforts to "civilize" the mechanical and chassis aspects of the F4 2010 have taken nothing away from the sporting aggression of the model.

6 That "37" on the fuel tank carrying the winged cogwheel logo summarizes the glorious history of the Varese marque: it represents the remarkable number of world championship titles won by the Cascina Costa racing team in the golden age of Ubbiali, Hocking, Hailwood, Agostini and Phil Read.

7 The 11th and 12th of September 2010, saw the presentation of an MV Agusta F4 dedicated to the 50 years of the Frecce Tricolori: the event was celebrated at the Rivolto airfield in the municipality of Codroipo (Udine), where the famous aerobatic team is based. The "Frecce Tricolori" model (196 hp at 12,900 rpm for around 305 kph), boasting numerous components in carbonfibre and titanium, has been produced in just 11 examples, one for each of the team's PAN jets whose distinctive features are taken up in the graphics.

1

2

3

4

5

6

7

1 The F4 RR Corsacorta's racing heritage is evident its name. Its brand new engine, the revised excellence of its chassis and styling that is incredibly even more sophisticated crown the model as the queen of the current crop of 1000 cc supersports bikes. The solid red and white version is flanked by an alternative finished in an elegant pearlescent white.

2 The F4 RR Corsacorta is a bike as happy on road trips as it is on the track where it can express its full potential. Taking it to the limit is not exactly for everyone, but the pilot capable of doing so will experience the utmost expression of biking sensation.

3-5 The chassis specification is close to perfection with the Brembo 320 mm brake discs, the Öhlins NIX upside-down fork with titanium nitrate treated stems, the Öhlins TTX rear swing arm and the fully adjustable rear sets.

6-7 The refinement of the detailing, with the stitching on the saddle, the decal on the tail recalling the race number holder on competition machines, the label that proudly declares that the welding has been done by hand: all elements that make of the Corsacorta an MV Agusta yet again unique and unmistakeable.

8 The rear ¾ view testifies to the elegance of the configuration, starting with the new Marchesini forged aluminium wheel design.

9 Look at that primary drive between the first and second cylinder: a technical detail dating back as far as 1924 and the transverse, in-line four designed by ingegner Piero Remor: evidence of the unbroken design heritage linking the MV Agusta F4 to the masterpiece at the origin of its story.

styling a glance at the fantastic new lines with which the CRC "boys" have cloaked the bike reveals an apparently inexhaustible source of creativity. If the pearlescent white version is exciting, the solid red and white with gold logos is absolutely stunning.

As far as the mechanical side is concerned, the bore has been enlarged from 76 to 79 mm, while the stroke has been shortened from 55 to 50.9 mm, with the average piston speed (RR aerospace alloy components) now dropping from 24.7 to 22.9 m/s (with the rev limiter cutting in at 13,700 rpm). These modifications have also led to a thorough revision of the cylinder head, with the engine breathing through redesigned intake ducts and large (all titanium) valves: the intake and exhaust valves now have respective diameters of 31.8 mm (rather than 29) and 26 mm (rather than 25). The exclusive system of variable length intake trumpets permits improved engine management at low and medium rev speeds. There is also a new primary drive generating less friction (and therefore less power absorption) as both the alternator and the water pump operate a lower speeds, while the traction control has been optimized with new mapping and modes. The system is controlled via new and practical switchgear located on the left-hand handlebar. As always on the MV Agusta F4, the gearbox (with close set ratios) is a removable cassette, one of many race-bred features, while the clutch features a mechanical slipper mechanism. The exhaust adopts the 4-2-1-4 sequence.

With regard to the chassis, the changes might not be as important as those made to the mechanicals, but there is a new Öhlins NIX upside down fork (with 43 mm stems and machined axle carriers) and an Öhlins TTX rear damper: both units are fully adjustable, as is the steering damper, the rear sets, the steering head angle and the height of the rear swing arm pivot point ensuring that the bike is "made-to-measure" in every detail. The forged aluminium wheels provide a weight saving of a full kilo and the Brembo disc brakes (twin 320 mm rotors at the front and a single 210 mm at the rear) feature new monobloc radial callipers. The dry weight remains 192 kg.

In conclusion, if we pull together all the Manzonian threads of this story, we find that not only is MV Agusta alive and well (and is forging ahead together with us, its faithful devotees), but 14 years after we first caught sight of it on a September evening, no one anywhere in the world has yet managed to build a motorcycle as beautiful as the F4.

F4 1000 2010

Why did the F4 need renewing? Essentially, leaving aside all the stratospheric mechanical, chassis and styling prerequisites, because a model was required that was above all easy to ride, something that was never an issue with the earlier F4s.

Starting with a less cramped riding position, between foot pegs, fuel tank and handlebars, that would guarantee a more immediate feeling with the bike, everything was put under the microscope, lightened and optimized.

Much has been done to ensure that an F4 rider pilots a more civilized machine, lighter and more manoeuvrable, with a riding position that caused less stress and… performance anxiety.

More fluidity to the power delivery and a more agile chassis (with suspension finally calibrated to less race-level values) have contributed to this "evolution without revolution."

Styling motifs updated without being altered beyond recognition, this is the masterpiece of the CRC's "golden boys": an F4 that is even more beautiful, lighter and compact to the point of miniaturization.

ANDREA GOGGI, THE DESIGNER SPEAKS: TECHNOLOGY AND ABNEGATION

The engineer Andrea Goggi (born 1963), is the technical director at MV Agusta where he has seen (and contributed to) the birth of every model. There is no one better than him to give us an insight on 15 years of enthralling experience.

I was still a kid when by chance one Sunday, on the occasion of the Grand Prix of Nations at the Monza Autodromo, I met the brothers Gianfranco and Claudio Castiglioni, who had arrived totgether at Lesmo aboard a big Cagiva.
I already had a passion for bikes which gave me the courage to introduce myself and talk to them both, with the result that Claudio asked me to come and see him at the company.
After graduating in mechanical engineering from the Turin Polytechnic (with a thesis based on the Cagiva T engine), I still had to do my military service. I spoke to Claudio again who said: "I'll wait twelve months for you, then come and work for us." So, in 1988, I finally joined Cagiva.
At the end of 1994, with the closure of the Cagiva racing department, I began supervising the development of the F4 engine. This was a period that for me represented a qualitative leap demanding a radical change in mentality.
My first memory of that phase is associated with the arrival of the first F4 750 cc engine.
When I saw it, so large alongside the half-litre Cagiva 500 GP unit, it was a shock that made me realise that we were entering a new world and that I and everyone else working on the new four-cylinder would absolutely have to open our minds to new and exciting horizons that were as yet completely unexplored.

From that initial responsibility I developed an experience that has carried me through to the present day. I can safely say that the F4 engine has proved to be a particularly rich vein of gold that we have been able to exploit to the full and which still has much to give.
This miracle, I have to underline, is so much the fruit of who knows what mechanical prodigies, but rather the uninterrupted application by all those involved in what I would define as an all-Italian perfectionist mentality.
Dulcis in fundo: as a result of my experience with the Cagiva racing department, I have overseen the F4's (as yet rarefied) participation in competition.

In this regard I have to say I fully share Claudio's rigorous conviction that we will only return to top level competition when we are able to do so at the very top level.

The engineer Andrea Goggi is not only the head of engine development at Schiranna, but also a motorcycle racing enthusiast who has followed MV Agusta's (as yet limited) competition activities, culminating in Luca Scassa's conquest of the Italian SBK championship in 2008 in the saddle of an F4 1000 R 312.

FABRIZIO LATINI, THE TESTER SPEAKS: RIDING THE TIGER

We asked Fabrizio Latini (born 1962), the historic head of testing for all the versions of the F4 from the very first top secret prototypes, for a few comments regarding his long experience in the saddle of the Varese masterpiece.

While I'm not a great writer and, like all the testers, I'm a bit of a bear, here are a few thoughts on what it has meant to me to test the F4s.

Like many other things in life, I'd say that you never forget the first time, and it was like that especially with the F4: the birth of the 750 Oro was definitely the most exciting, because that bike in that period was so far ahead in terms of riding sensations that its limits were dictated only by the quality of the components, which back then were not as good as they are now (from the tyres to the brakes and through to the electronic control unit).

Above all, the extraordinary experience of having developed the bike alongside Claudio Castiglioni and Massimo Tamburini has given me an imprinting that is still today an integral part of my way of understanding motorcycles.

The first F4 1000 also represented a significant professional learning experience for me, because the comparison with the best of the rivals in what was the most competitive sector of the period was a fascinating challenge that culminated in 2006 with Luca Scassa's triumph in the Italian Superstock championship, the presence of two bikes on the front row at almost every round of the World Championship and a number of victories.

With the R 312R there was the satisfaction of having developed the fastest 100 sports bike of all, with a maximum speed obtained by me at Nardò of 314 kph.

Coming round to the most recent F4 2010, I should point out that I haven't been the direct protagonist in the testing, but rather I have been coordinating the team responsible for the development of the new product, while I 've been following at first hand the development of the new F3...

In this case too I'm extremely satisfied with the experience, given that our working group has performed an authentic miracle: the complexity of the product and the difficulties of the challenge have demanded commitment, method, experience and above all something that in this wonderful company is never missing: a great HEART!

Fabrizio Latini, MV Agusta's best known tester, is so closely tied to the F 750 Oro, to the development of which he made a decisive contribution, that he keeps an example on show… in his bedroom.

THE PRODUCTION LINE: DREAM FACTORY

Accompanying us on a day-long tour of the entire production process, Fabio Salmoiraghi, head of production at MV Agusta (having joined the firm in 1987 when, on completing his studies he began working on the Cagiva assembly line) explained, "Those who work for us have received rigorous professional training that also plays on a fundamental passion for the product, motorbikes and... for the marque." And he went on to say, "Here we pay particular attention to the human aspect of the work, placing great faith in the professional skills of each employee with respect to what is nonetheless the indispensable support of machinery. In this way every single component and every single bike will be built with maniacal care, while it should be underlined that at any given moment we have full traceability of every detail and every engine and every chassis is associated with a product file (that includes the name of the worker who conducted each operation or test) that follows the production process from the part-finished components through to the completed bike signed off for sale."

Salmoiraghi went on to say, "Here we use the Kanban production method [a Japanese term that means "tag" or "card"] that ensures that the production lines are supplied on the basis of the "just in time" system according to the demands of the market, avoiding expensive stockpiling of part-finished components and fully-assembled bikes. Production takes place on two lines, one in a ring configuration (engine assembly) and one straight (bike assembly), with two or three shifts depending on demand; the end result being that at full capacity around 30 or so units are finished and ready for sale every day. 250 people are currently employed, 150 of them at Schiranna on the production lines and in the stores and around 40 at CRC (the Cagiva Research Centre) in San Marino."

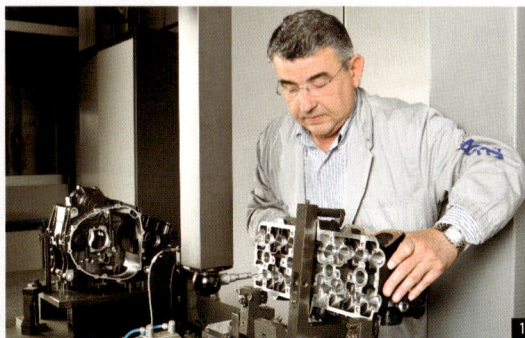

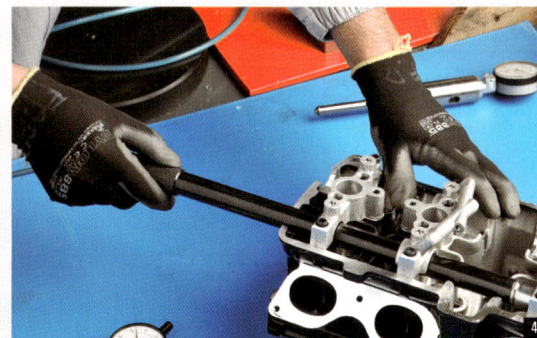

1-3 The part-finished crankcase half-shells and cylinder heads are prepared for machining on the Heller MC 16: the castings arrive at Schiranna from a foundry in Reggio Emilia (the crankcases) and from Brescia (the heads).
The last operation on the cylinder heads is performed on a SERDI 330 machine tool and concerns the grinding of the valve guides and seats.
All these are initial phases in a process (engine pre-assembly) that is completed in the measurements department after ultrasound cleaning of the parts: here the Brown&Sharpe CNC Dea machine makes a three-dimensional scan (checking one cylinder head and one crankcase every four) to check that the tolerances are within acceptable limits, in relation to the high quality demanded of the end product.

4-6 After machining, it is the specialist worker who intervenes to finish the components by hand, eliminating every metal residue. Then again, combining this highly skilled craft aspect with the most advanced automated procedures is an integral part of the MV Agusta corporate philosophy.

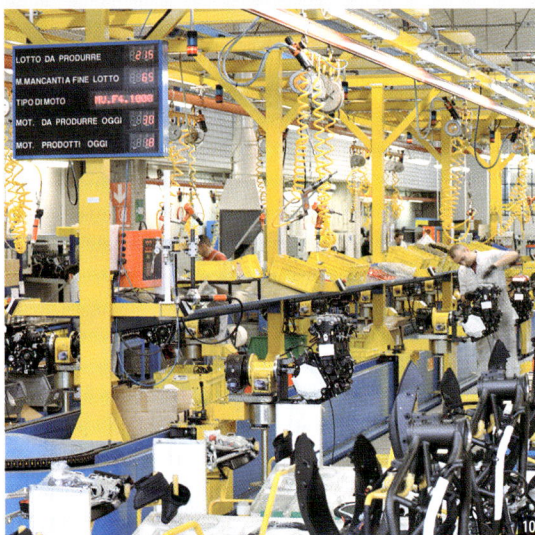

7 The insertion of the valve guide is effected with the aid of a press, while that of the seats is still effected manually. It is preceded by the heating of the heads in an oven to 200° for 40 minutes, while the seats are immersed in liquid nitrogen to cool them.

8 and 9 The human touch is indispensable in the assembly of the camshaft bearings and checking the assembly of the crankshaft.

10 and 11 The engine assembly line is characterised by a ring configuration and is semi-automatic, with external workstations for the assembly of the sub-groups (cylinder head, crankcase, crankshaft). At the top can be seen the illuminated panel monitoring the daily production.

12-14 Both the engine assembly and that of the bike itself is based on the Kanban method described in the text. The procedure in this phase is absolutely craft-based: proceeding in the classic itinerary from crankcase up to the cylinder head, the F4's four-cylinder power unit takes shape under the careful eye of the specialist. Every solution that raises the qualitative level of the final product is adopted.

15-17 With the assembly complete, each unit moves on to the engine testing room (dominated by the Api Com test bench) where it will be tested, at operating temperature, for 20 minutes, at different engine speeds (from 2,500 to 13,000 rpm, the point where the rev-limiter kicks in).
At the control station, all the operating parameters are verified and checks are made to ensure that all the values are within the established and homologation norms, before entrusting the engine to the bike assembly line.

18 and 19 The bike assembly procedure is configured in a straight line, with the automated aspect serving only to facilitate and objectify the quality of the product. In accordance with the most modern philosophies, the line exploits a Lean Production system and every bike is accompanied by a kit of components making up a single unit.

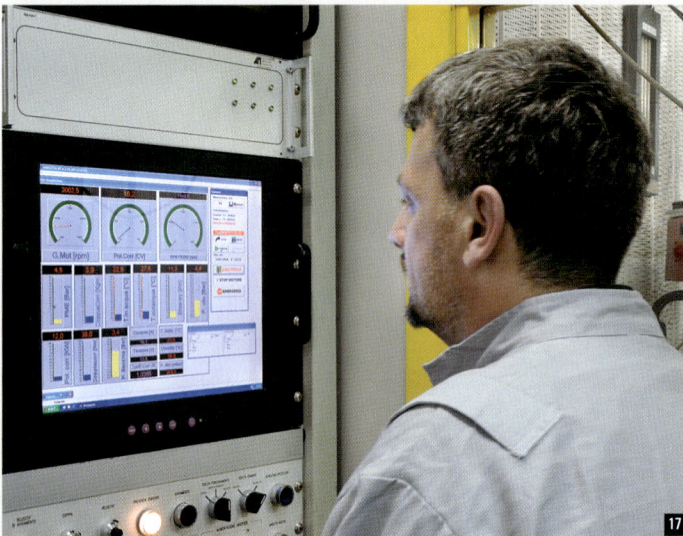

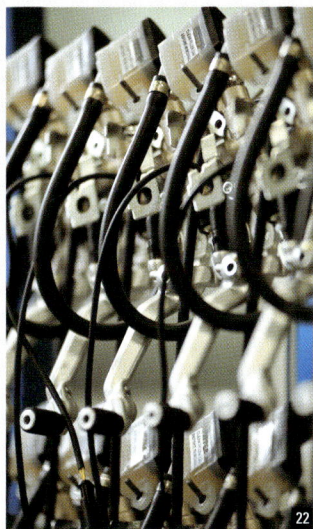

20-24 Extreme care is dedicated to the brakes: prior to introducing the brake fluid, the circuit is subjected to extremely severe preliminary checks with automated machinery (but always under the watchful eye of a specialist worker. Only after this check are the brakes ready to be mounted and the system is charged with fluid.

25 Fork assembly: the stem covers are united by the triple trees. The manual intervention of the specialist worker is essential, as in similar operations such as the assembly of the handlebars with the levers, switchgear and throttle control.

26 and 27 Then comes the fitting to the frame of the monoshock and the single-sided swinging arm: this last is one of the many (11) F4 components patented by the CRC of San Marino from 1997, the of the presentation of the original model in the series, the 750 Oro.

28 This is the last stage in the assembly of the bike: the kit trolley is empty. Now follow the last three passages in the production process: the final test, the clothing and the official signing off for sale.

29 The "waiting room" for the F4 following its assembly and prior to moving on to the final testing.

30 The final testing: after an initial check (with the engine running and all gears engaged) on the rollers to simulate a five-kilometre road trip, the conformity of the components (from the brakes to the headlamp) to the qualitative standards are verified via around 30 tests. Should any problems be found, the bike moves on to a check and diagnosis station for the appropriate remedial work before being declared available for sale.

31 With extreme care, the F4 is finally "dressed" with the last superstructure components (fairing, saddle, side panels, tail): the bike is now ready for the last stage in its production process, the signing off for sale.

32 The signing-off area: the last phase in the MV Agusta quality control in which a final check up is conducted and every bodywork element is carefully examined. This done a quality stamp on the product file will allow an employee to sign off the bike, ready for it to be transferred to the packing and shipping store.
Note that some bikes travel to their fortunate owners in dedicated wooden chests that are so elegant they appear to be works of art themselves.

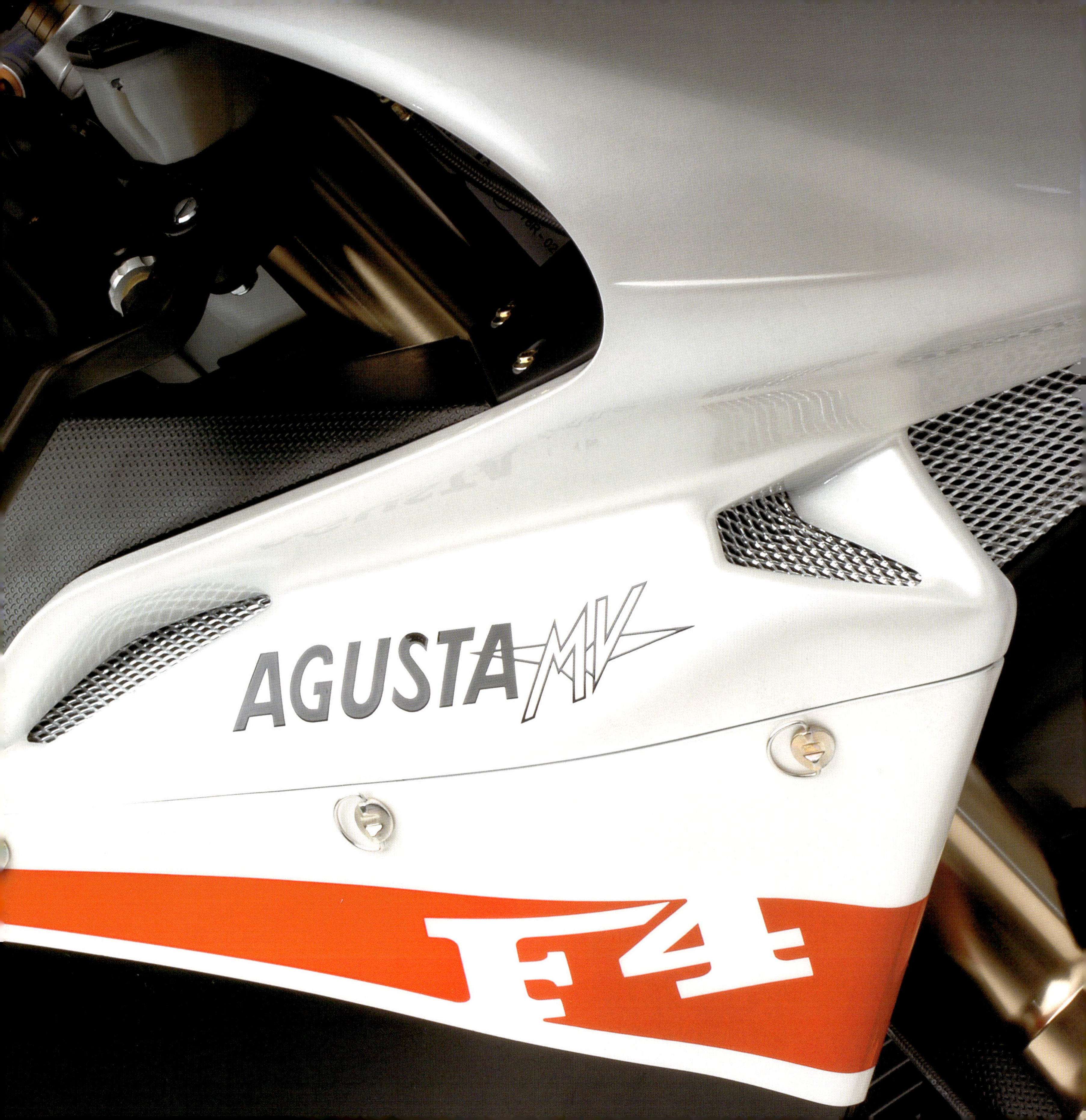
AGUSTA MV
F4

A DIALOGUE WITH THE PROTAGONISTS

Massimo Tamburini

"FROM WHEN I WAS VERY LITTLE I HAD A PASSION

FOR BIKES: I HAD A REAL PREDILECTION

FOR THE FOUR-CYLINDER MODELS".

(From an interview given to the author

in the summer of 2007)

CRC in San Marino: technology and imagination
THE RENAISSANCE TITANIUM WORKSHOP

CRC (the Cagiva Research Centre) located at No. 35 Via Ovella in the Republic of San Marino, was born on the 1st of April 1993 from the ashes of Cagiva's COR (Rimini Operations Centre), founded at Cerasolo Ausa di Coriano (RN) in 1985 and directed by Massimo Tamburini. The designer was called to direct (and was to do so until the 31st of December 2008) what was no longer merely an operational offshoot, but an autonomous structure.

Here, the Varese-based group's new models were researched, designed, tested and built in prototype form (giving birth to epochal models from the Cagiva Mito to the Ducati 916 and through to the MV Agusta F4), with the utmost professionalism and a unique combination of high aesthetics, fine craftsmanship and technological perfectionism.

The atmosphere at CRC was that of a modern-day renaissance workshop, or rather a reborn Bauhaus, given that the design and executive quality of the work systematically led to products whose efficient beauty is only equalled by the painstaking, not to say maniacal, care devoted to them.

There is a genetic imprinting, a constant search for perfection that the San Marino engineers have adopted as their fundamental strategy that is quite clearly the most precious heritage left by the Rimini-born designer. Hence the list of CRC patents applied to the MV Agusta F4 and announced with understandable pride from the presentation of the very first version, the 750 Oro, ten of then relating to "chassis applications" and one to "an engine application": the headlamp composed of stacked tandem polyellipsoid lights; a conical locking device for the steering bearing assembly; a steering damper with an axis constantly perpendicular to the vehicle's longitudinal plane of symmetry; a front brake-clutch lever assembly with a multiple safety system; front brake-clutch pump assembly mounted low to reduce overall dimensions; a front brake-clutch pump-reservoir assembly with a quick-release security mount; a multiple tank assembly with "sequential" configuration of components; a footpeg support assembly with an adjustment facility; a single-sided rear swinging arm; the exhaust silencer; and lastly, the manifold with multiple specific geometry sections for internal combustion engine intake and exhaust systems.

For the record and for future honour and memory, the list (through to 1997, when the employees numbered 30, while subsequently the number rose to the current 40 or so) of the heads of those offices and departments that, under the leadership of Massimo Tamburini, were responsible for the F4 miracle: Dervis Macrelli (metalwork-frames), Marcello Marchetti (composite materials-painting), Fabio Orlandi (Styling Centre), Massimo Parenti (technical direction), Gioacchino Rossini (machine tooling), Nicola Tagliaventi (modelling) and Andrea Tamburini (quality control).

EVOLUTION WITHOUT REVOLUTION

During a recent visit to CRC, we recorded a conversation about the evolution of the F4 theme with a number of the protagonists: Present, along with the author of this book, Otto Grizzi, were Paolo Bianchi, head of CRC from the November of 1992, Fabio Olandi, alongside Massimo Tamburini from 1988 as a designer and now head of the CRC Styling Centre, and Adrian Morton, forty-year-old British designer (with experience working at Benelli), seconded to CRC from the MV Agusta headquarters.

O.G. *Let's begin with the F4 2010, regarding which there is talk of around a hundred modifications for an evolution without revolution of the original design.*

P.B. The objective of the F4 2010 project was certainly a drastic revision of the old F4, born, as a concept ready for industrialization, no less than 12 or 13 years ago. Since then, many things have changed, many technologies have

improved, computer-aided design included, and we have been able to push on. Among our objectives was an improvement in the riding position, the shedding of around 10 kilos in weight from the bike and so on; in short, the minor defects recognised in a masterpiece. Transforming the old F4 into the new was a demanding task that took up the whole of the last two years, with the project being initiated before 2009, that is, early in 2008: back then, in fact, we were already running prototypes with chassis configurations different to those of the old F4.

O.G. *So, while they were working on the mechanical assemblies at Schiranna, here at CRC you started with the chassis.*

P.B. Yes. We had to because the old F4 had always retained, albeit evolving over time, the original chassis born with the 750 cc engine: the new one had a displacement of a litre and we configured it so as to be better able to handle the increased power we had to play with. We started at the back, with the swinging arm lengthened by 20 mm, while at the same time closing by half a degree the steering's angle of incidence (with a consequent reduction in the front wheel trail) and, in relation to a more comfortable riding position closer to the handlebar controls, we also loaded the front by around an extra 1% (we're now at 52%) and modified the old fuel tank (that for one thing interfered with the rider's belly too much...), creating one that is smaller and shorter and in a thermoplastic material rather than steel.

O.G. *From sheet steel to a synthetic material for the fuel tank?*

P.B. Yes. It's a nylon injected in a liquid state into a mould that spins, with the centrifugal effect causing the material to stick to the walls: it's a modification that has resulted in a significant saving of weight with the tank that, being the central element of the bike, influences its centre of gravity. Moving on, we widened the saddle: the rider's now got more room to move around more naturally and find the best riding position (previously it was more or less imposed upon you) in relation to their size and stature. The angle of the handlebars was corrected, advancing them by 10 mm and raising them by a further 10 mm.
It was a huge job, even though it might be hard to believe, just to eliminate much of the vibration felt through the handlebars: we worked both on the weight and the position of the end sections, redesigning them and locating them a few millimetres further out.

...G. In short, the front end remains the strong suit of the F4's chassis...

P.B. Yes, but with the result that the bike is more harmoniously balanced, with the aim of providing greater possibilities for varying your trajectory with gentle movements.

O.G. *In detail, where have you managed to save weight?*

P.B. In terms of the chassis again, we worked hard on the unsprung weight, the front wheel and rear wheels above all: now that compared with ten years ago we can be more confident about the casting processes and the calculation phase while guaranteeing great systemic integrity, between the two of them, we were able to eliminate 1.2 kilos of aluminium through thinner sections.

We worked hard on the front fork, losing another 1.2 kilos here too. It's still in aluminium alloy and we haven't touched its flexional and torsional rigidity values, while we have worked on achieving the values of the 20 mm longer fork in magnesium used by Luca Scassa in his victorious Italian SBK campaign in 2008. Then we moved on to the silencer, shaving off a further few hundred grammes, with the same going for the frame and frame plates too. Weight was saved with a fuel pump that was practically redesigned ex novo, an object that is never seen but which nonetheless contributes to the weight of the bike around the centre of gravity. Then there's the headlamp, from which a kilo and a half was trimmed, as among other things, the die-cast support attached to the frame was eliminated: now the unit has an external shell in plastic and there are no longer the two stacked polyellipsoids that the old F4

had, as a new single polyellipsoid unit has been introduced with a xenon bulb (a world first for a bike). Lastly, we saved a good three kilos from the plastics.

O.G. *Could we now talk about something out of the ordinary?*

P.B. Sure. Let's talk, with a few examples, about our significant efforts to miniaturize the bike. The F4 2010 has a narrower frame than the old bike by 4 cm in its frontal section, but the engine section has not been reduced by a single millimetre so, in order to make something smaller we had to look at all the rest. Just think, for example, that we allowed the water piping to run along the left-hand side of the fairing by creating a small niche in the air intake: in order to be able to this, the pipe is no longer round in section but elliptical! Another very delicate operation was performed on the temperature "aspect", in one of the most critical points of the bike, where the exhaust manifold exits and 450° are reached. With the plastic of the air intake just 7-9 millimetres away there was a real risk it would melt: we resolved the problem by adopting an upgraded plastic and introducing within the intake itself a pad in ceramic fibre with an elevated capacity for reducing the heat.

Moreover, in order to favour heat extraction, where on the fairing there is an extraction vent, during the course of the work we adopted a small appendix in the lower part, an extractor profile with no other function than that of accelerating a little the extraction of air...

Sure, they're all minor aids, but put them all together... To give another example, everyone here has contributed to the invention of something to further insulate the rider's legs from

the heat arriving from the engine (after all we're talking of values of around 250-300°!) so, we came up with a shield in aluminium, inside which we placed a pad in ceramic fibre while on the other side there's another shield... The problem, in all these cases, has been that we're working in extremely restricted areas that we wanted to reduce even further so as to obtain an even smaller, more compact and narrower bike, truly extreme!

O.G. *In short, the F4 2010's extreme in terms of this refinement, extreme in its optimization, but at the same time, in some ways, it's more flexible than earlier versions, more user-friendly if you like, or as user-friendly as a bike of this kind can be...*

P.B. In effect, we've recovered every little space the bike made available and I like to say in this respect, that it's a bike that won't get dirty because there's no room for dust; and all this helps make it more "civil", more usable on a daily basis... But to finish this discussion of the extreme miniaturization and the optimization of the F4, here are a few more facts.

For example, we've used the prow of the forward part of the fairing to house the coolant expansion tank, and we were struggling for two months because we couldn't work out where to run the brake pipes!

And then, you see those slots on the mudguard? They're not just stylish, they actually allow the fairing to dip when, under heavy braking, the fork reaches the end of its travel. Lastly, another interesting trick was redesigning the routing of the wiring to the rear light and the brake light: now they actually run through the silencer, they actually run through the exhaust!

Details of the F4 750 Oro: the vertical tandem polyellipsoid headlamp was retained without variations through to the 1000 2010; the riding position with which Massimo Tamburini intended to make every biker a GP racer; the magnesium swinging arm, the fruit of intensive computer studies via a special FEM (Finite Element Modelling) software package, with over 80 analyses reproducing every possible condition of use; the adjustable rider's foot pegs, with the cams clearly visible in the photo.

Let's just say we were inspired by the cabling of domestic ovens, but the wiring of the F4 is in nickel covered with a dual layer of PTFE fabric sinterized on silicone...

O.G. *It would be interesting to hear about the relationship between CRC and Schiranna at a design decision level.*

P.B. We work in complete synergy, in the sense that for some time we have been conducting a hour's video conference every morning, during which we discuss everything: for example, the whole chassis of the bike was developed in collaboration with the Varese testers.

O.G. *Shall we move on to the question of styling?*

F.O. The point of departure was the definition of a new aesthetic that took into account the fact that the F4 was to become easier to ride. This entailed no extreme clip-on bars too far from the foot pegs or the rider overheating and suffering too much turbulence on his back and so on. And again, an end to the fuel tank interfering with the rider's belly and no more rear view mirrors in which you can hardly see anything! I repeat that everything was to be done, along with the reduction in weight and a better balanced chassis, with a single objective: making the new F4 easier to ride.

A.M. Yes, the old F4 was a heavy bike that was hard to ride and we took steps to correct this. But while we were at it, we also worked on further levels of "lightening", lending the appearance of the bike a little of that "tension" it previously lacked, shaving off a little "weight" from the image, from the surfaces as well as from the mass... I'm talking about a succession of tauter surfaces, without sharp edges, however, simply with more pronounced styling lines with respect to the old style. Hence our search for revised volumes, for a tauter line throughout the bike, through to the tail, through to the new exhaust terminals that were redesigned, not by chance and not without in-house debates, with a quadrangular form.

O.G. *Was it harder to create the first, legendary F4 or keep the Tamburinian guide lines alive for 13 years in the successive versions?*

F.O. I'll talk about the origins, and at the outset it truly was the stuff of legends. One day Massimo said to us, "Boys, it's going to be an MV Agusta." We had nothing to start out from, not even an MV decal from which to derive a logo as at the time we only had the Cagiva and Ducati marques. So he sent me to scour the second-hand markets (as far afield as Switzerland) in search of all the MV logos possible...

O.G. *And then?*

F.O. And then we put all the badges we'd found on the drawing board and we corrected them, retouching the proportions, optimizing them, completing a restyling. All by hand, before a single computer was even switched on: then we codified everything with a pantone scale.
Claudio Castiglioni arrived one day and pulled a bunch of valves out of his pockets saying, "You see these? These are the valves of the Ferrari Formula 1 car and they'll be the radial valves of the new MV Agusta F4 engine." And so we set off on the F4 adventure that has led us to the 2010 version.

A.M. The old bike had dated in terms of its configuration: just because the F4's a sports bike shouldn't mean that you have to suffer to ride it. We were asked to make the new bike easier to ride (while remaining extremely powerful and fast), more docile and more comfortable as the better you feel on the bike the better it is to ride and. the easier it is to sell.
To this end we started by shifting the chassis slightly further forwards to "free-up" the bike's tail and position the rider closer to the front end, ever at the "heart" of the F4 ride.

O.G. *Weren't you worried about "laying hands" on a bike that had already achieved legendary status such as the original F4?*

A.M. The old F4 had already earned its place in motorcycling history as one of the most beautiful bikes ever. We treated it as you would treat a beautiful woman, intervening only where necessary, and in this respect I'll mention just one example, the new front headlamp. This rhomboid unit is something that only we had, even though many have tried to copy it, becoming a dominant characteristic in the genome of sports bikes. But look at the evolution of the species, with the surface of the lamp all prismatic and surfaced, polished on one side, opaque on the other! It's definitely a characteristic that in my opinion should be retained on the future models.

F.O. Yes, I agree. I fact, I'd like the details that we've created to be recognized as carrying the CRC "signature" on the F4 2010, from the new rear-view mirror with its aerodynamic flap to the slots on the front mudguard accommodating the fairing at the end of the fork travel. Details we've made beautiful because our maestro [Massimo Tamburini] taught us that styling and function can and must coexist.

O.G. *With regard to the CRC "signature", I'd like to finish with a question that I'm particularly interested in and that concerns the past but above all the future of the Cagiva Research Centre. What was the atmosphere like when Massimo Tamburini was here and how did your approach to the work change when he left?*

F.O. We're tailors, we clothe what others design. Tamburini instead designed the bike in the sense that he provided the overall dimensions and references, from the degree of inclination of the steering head to the engine mounting points. His great strength was that he had a strategic vision that we always knew we could count on.

P.B. Sure, he had that overall "grasp" and with Tamburini you could be sure that he always knew what he was doing and where we would arrive by doing something in a certain way. This is what we tried to learn from him.
In the early months of 2009, without him, there were a few concerns, then the group drew together, it reacted well and efficient teamwork pulled us through. Because we had to finish, and quickly, the bikes for the end of year show... Which is exactly what we did.
After 20 years working together, losing him was like losing a family member. But we want to move on; we've got plenty more bikes to design.

F4

CRC

1 Family portrait with the F4: standing on the extreme right, the head of CRC, Paolo Bianchi.

2 Paolo Bianchi again, visibly satisfied with the work done.

3 The work is conducted in clean and tidy surroundings that approach… sterility: undoubtedly a "logistical" decision by Tamburini.

4 Fabio Orlandi (left) and Adrian Morton from the Styling Centre.

5-7 Front end, rear end and fairing of the FA 1000 2010, the final result of the rigorous experimentation successfully completed despite dark clouds on the horizon.

A round table at Schiranna
ENGINES RUMBLE ON THE ENCHANTED LAKE

In late spring 2010, we gathered a number of the protagonists in the F4 story round a table (in the main building at the MV Agusta factory on Lake Varese).

The aim of the encounter was to reflect on themes from product identity to the path followed by technical evolution, from market analysis to the prospects for the marque. The author of this book, Otto Grizzi, was joined by Roberto Godone (technical direction), Andrea Goggi (head of engine development) and Fabrizio Latini (head of testing).

O.G. *Can we define in a few key points, the essence, the concept of the first F4, the 750 Oro, and then compare that design with the latest version, the F4 2010?*

R.G. It's only right to remember where in effect we started out from; that is, from the approval of the industrial plan relating to the MV Agusta F4: it was May-June 1997 and just 100 days later we presented that model as a show prototype!

A.G. What struck me most about that period was the change in mentality, a true revolution that was demanded of the factory, of the entire company in fact, involving the conversion of production from the Cagiva marque to MV Agusta.

F.L. That's right, an entire generation had to

"change job!" However, talking about beginnings, one of my first memories concerns the fact that when we started developing the model, the 90 hp of the F4 was never going to cause rivals such as the Kawa 900 and the Honda 900 CBR any sleeplesss nights! Then, in the August of 1995, on the occasion of a test at Mugello, we were already producing 156 hp: this, I believe, was the exact moment of the passing of the baton between two stories, that of the Cagiva GP 500 and that of the MV Agusta 750.

R.G. It was the precise wish of Claudio Castiglioni and Massimo Tamburini that the F4 should be a unique point of reference in the sector. Inside and out, our bike was to represent something completely different (both in terms of function and styling) to anything else on the market.

F.L. In effect, for example, when in 1997 we adopted a /65 front tyre we were introducing something absolutely new, something cutting edge in the sector in dynamic terms. We had to wait until the arrival of the SBK models in 2006 to see any others around...

O.G. *How did you proceed, once the rigid guidelines regarding the originality of the model had been established?*

A.G. In the early years, we focussed on the search for power. It was hard work, because

the bore and stroke dimensions of the 750 cc engine, determined by the design brief calling for minimum transverse dimensions, were very restrictive. In short, only when we decided to move to the one litre displacement, could we also begin to search for performance. With Claudio Castiglioni's constant and systematic support, we began years of painstaking research and development work to bridge the performance gap between us and the best of our competitors of the time: in this regard, the experience that was being accumulated in the field by the Belgian rider Steven Casaer in endurance racing from 2000 was essential.

F.L. They were heroic times, I remember that to support Steven during the races, I'd leave on the Friday morning with the bike, cover maybe 1,000 kilometres to reach the circuit and then be ready to lend a hand during the Saturday practice sessions.

A.G. Yes, they were heroic times, your heart was in your work and you never let up thanks to the constant encouragement of Claudio Castiglioni.

O.G. *In those arduous but exciting years, were there times when you had give up on certain technical features?*

A.G. It happened occasionally, for example with the dry plate clutch, tested at length and then abandoned in favour of the oil bath unit.

In the front row, Enrico D'Onofrio and Claudio Castiglioni embraced by Matt Levatich. Behind them, the numerous group of employees and collaborators from the MV Agusta factory at Schiranna.

O.G. *It would be interesting at this point to hear from each of you which were the best and worst of moments of the F4 saga.*

F.L. For me, the worst memory coincides with the most exciting. I'm referring to certain times when the lack of financial resources looked like preventing us from moving forward with the work. And yet, that apparently insuperable obstacle gave us the impetus to start over and recover each time in grand style.

R.G. What a great and exciting battle it was with the competition, but truly hard work!

E.D'O. I've only been here for 14 months, I don't have all your memories, and maybe I see things in a slightly different light, with a gaze fundamentally directed towards our future, an industrial future; that relaunching of the company of which the premises can found in the history you all mention. I'm speaking on the basis that the MV Agusta F4 is something different to anything else available on the market; for example in the attention to detail on which the F4 legend is founded. Our workers are not just workers, but craftsmen capable of producing objects with an artistic content. Our clients are not just clients, but great enthusiasts and collectors who have recognised that the F4 is more than a beautiful bike, it's a bike that generates emotion...
That said, I'd put to one side the romantic notion of the beautiful and damned F4, because I really

believe that the time has come to focus on the industrialization of the models, in part as a solution to our recurrent moments of crisis. In fact, my worst moment came with the sense of abandonment when Harley-Davidson announced it was putting the MV Agusta marque up for sale.

A.G. For me, the best thing was seeing the development of a bike born in the previous century. The works, every time something broke: it was always a blow to the heart.

O.G. *After this look at the past, a few words about the future?*

A.G. We've been working hard over the last few years to create a more usable product, I'd say more... civilized, and to expand the available model range. It has to be said that the first objective has been achieved thanks to electronics, which has made giant steps since the introduction of the first F4.

F.L. We've analyzed the Japanese competition in depth, because a fundamental requisite for winning over clients faithful to Japanese marques (all people who take a load of technical features for granted) was to overtake them not only in terms of performance but also in the detailing. So, when we were able to say that our componentry was better than theirs it came as no surprise to us to hear a Honda CBR owner say "I tried the MV Agusta F4: it goes as well as my Honda, but looks better".

ON TRACK!

"FOR ME IT'S A DEEPLY EMOTIONAL MATTER OF GREAT PRIDE

TO SEE ON TRACKS AND ROADS AROUND THE WORLD

THIS ITALIAN BIKE WITH THE CHARACTERISTIC LOGO

OF THE UNIQUE AND INIMITABLE MV AGUSTA!"

Giacomo Agostini

750 ORO, 1000 AGO AND "MODEL YEAR 2010" ON THE ASPHALT

Mid-July 2010. The heat at the Pirelli track No. 2 at Vizzola Ticino is truly torrid on the occasion of our extraordinary photo session. It isn't just the climate but also the "hot-blooded" nature of the three F4s (in the words of one of the testers present) that, thanks to the collaboration of the MV Agusta management we've managed to bring together on the tiny circuit next to Malpensa airport.

These are three irreplaceable benchmarks of the series born in 1997 and two are privately owned: the 750 Oro of Luigi Genoni, six years in the MV engine-testing room and now President of the Moto Club Internazionale MV Agusta, and the Ago of Roberto Orlandini, a super-enthusiast from Pisa and a Piaggio employee. The third is the 2010 that arrives directly from Schiranna, accompanied by Fabrizio Latini, head of F4 testing, and two technicians from the company's R&D department (Massimo Furnari and Fabio Re) acting as his assistants and testers.

Off we go.
First the static photos, then the camera-car, the downhill shots, the laps and so on...

We gather some impressions from the day's protagonists.

Fabrizio Latini is a happy man: "14 years of work to achieve great joy. That's what I feel today when trying these three bikes. Then again, these three F4s for me are something of a metaphor for life, with bikes in place of... women. The 750 Oro is the first, the one you'll never forget; the 1000 Ago is the one for "good sex"; the 1000 2010 is the latest and always the most stimulating".

Luigi Genoni steps in: "They're all models with one thing in common: they're all beasts to be tamed." Roberto Orlandini confirms: "When you get off a bike like that after a hard ride you feel like you've been out running."
As one of his companions observes, "They're track-ready bikes, just take off the number plate..." Fabio Re is more or less of the same opinion: "I'd say that fundamentally they're bikes for... men capable of dominating."

We hand the question over to Fabrizio Latini.

The latest F4, is it really still so demanding?

"No, the 1000 2010 is the apotheosis of friendliness, a tame SBK, a model motivated by evident compromises. In short, it's the end of the Tamburini philosophy, that is, the F4 as a vehicle allowing an ordinary biker, at least for a few hours, to become a racer through the exasperation of the riding experience and through the realization that everything happens at faster than normal speeds, almost a school of life. And then, that 13,900 rpm scream of the SPR engine...

Right, first and foremost what hits home is the sound: today the most exciting is that of the 1000 Ago, at least according to Sansai "Karzai" Zappini, the graphic designer-photographer-biker who was part of today's expedition to the Varese heath.

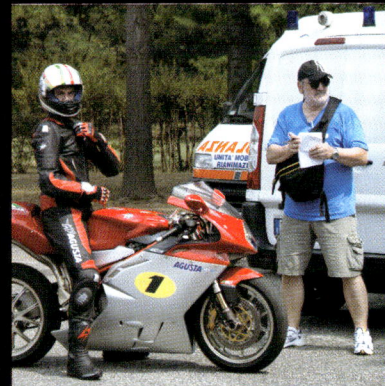

In the large photo, from the left: the F4 750 Oro, the 1000 Ago and the F4 1000 2010, protagonists of the track day.
Right, from the top: Gigi Soldano, the photographer who took the photos for these (and many of the other) pages of this book; the F4 1000 2010 returns to the Schiranna R&D department for the research and testing that will lead to the 2011 heir; Otto Grizzi (standing), the former *Motociclismo d'epoca* journalist and the author of this book.

by Giacomo Agostini

It was time a book reached the shops that would bear witness to the MV Agusta F4 adventure. That book has now arrived and its readers can explore all the details of a remarkable story.

They will hear about the birth of a grandiose idea, that of reviving a marque dear to millions of enthusiasts. They will learn about the iron will of two men, Claudio Castliglioni and Massimo Tamburini, determined to produce a motorcycle unlike any other. They will immerse themselves in the heroic atmosphere of those months of gruelling labour preparing the show prototype. They will relive the feverish hours of the model's presentation, one September evening 14 years ago. They will witness once again the stunned admiration of the industry insiders when the MV masterpiece was unveiled. They will read once again the enthusiastic titles the specialist press were to devote to the event.

They will experience the tens of thousands of road testing kilometres covered to perfect a product born virtually without defects. They will be moved by the early attempts to revive the racing career a marque that was already the stuff of legends thanks to its barnstorming past victories on tracks around the globe, ahead of the "great return" to competition.

They will see the Varese marque's struggles for survival in the face of the ruthless laws of the global market, witnessing it rise time after time like a phoenix from the ashes.

They will once again be filled with pride by this symbol of Italian craftsmanship when the chronometer demonstrates that the performance gap with respect to its rivals had been definitively closed.

The whole of this adventure is condensed in the pages written by Otto Grizzi with love (the same love that I shall always carry in my heart) for the blue wings and gilded cogwheel. .

I know that these pages will remain for ever as documentation of the birth of the world's most beautiful motorcycle, the MV Agusta F4.

APPENDICES

THE F4 AND RACING

There was a passion for racing in Claudio Castiglioni's DNA, but when asked about a competition future for the MV Agusta F4 his answer was always: "We'll only race when we're sure that the results will live up to our glorious heritage."

Nonetheless, the Varese "four" has for some time been lapping the tracks, albeit for experimental purposes and without ever having raced in the marque's official colours. What follows is a summary of the wait for the "great return".

2000

The Belgian rider Steven Casaer rides the F4 on its debut in the Shell Cup.

2001

On the 8th of April 2001 Andrea Mazzali (a former Italian 750 cc Super Production champion in 1996) started the first round of the new founded CIV's SBK championship at Misano Adriatico, racing a standard F4 Oro and finishing 13th in a field of 36. He completed the championship season 12th overall. In 2002, Mazzali actually raced using the old engine, while in 2003, taking advantage of changes to the SBK regulations, competed with an F4 fitted with the new 1000 cc engine that he considered "better performing than the Japanese units." In 2004, the rider again participated in the CIV's SBK championship, this time with an F4 1000 S and a team now wholly independent of the Varese manufacturer: unfortunately,

Mazzali fell in the opening race at Mugello, fracturing a rib. On the 17th of April 2005, at Vallelunga (first round of the CIV SBK championship) he crashed out in the early stages, while on the 8th of May he courageously took part in an SBK World Championship round: he started 30th on the grid and, after retiring in Race 1 on the 4th lap, finished Race 2 in 20th place. Despite all kinds of difficulties, Mazzali was to remain faithful to the MV Agusta F4 because, as he says, "I just can't leave this bike." In the meantime, at 3 PM on the 14th of April 2001, the 120,000 spectators at the Bugatti circuit at Le Mans witnessed an extraordinary event: the return of an MV Agusta to a World Championship event, a quarter of a century after Giacomo Agostini's victory with the 500 GP at the Nürburgring in 1976. At the famous 24 Hours, the first round in the World Endurance Championship, an F4 1000 entered and run by the Belgian Maxim Experience team (riders: S. Casaer, J. Elisson and D. Scheers) raced with number 104 in the Open class (a non-competitive entry as the bike was still a prototype) and succeeded in completing the race.

2002

In the same colours, the bike finished in 7th place (riders S. Casaer and B. Pister and D. Schildermans) in the Liege 24 Hours at Spa-Francorchamps. This performance had been preceded by a fantastic first place in the warm-up held in wet conditions.

2003

A coloured American rider, Dwight Mitchell, raced in the TT (F1 and Senior) with an F4 750 painted yellow and red, the colours of the M&A Racing team.

2004

Again at the TT, Umberto Rumiano of Brescia raced an F4 750 SPR: he finished 38th out of 54 riders to finish in the F1 class. That same year, the German team MV Agusta-Burger King-Lust participated in the World Endurance Championship with an F4 1000 S: on its debut in the Albacete 12 Hours 5th – 6th June) the bike retired with electrical problems. Again in 2004, an F4 1000 S was run in the German SBK championship by the MV Agusta Deutschland team, with the 2000 World Supersport champion Jörg Teuchert in the saddle. Debuting on the 9th of May at the Sachsenring, Teuchert qualified 4th in a field of 41. Victory was finally achieved by the German rider and the Italian bike on Sunday the 30th of August on the Schleizer-Dreieck track, that success being repeated 15 days later at Oschrsleben.

2005

Following the Malaysian Tigers' landing on the shores of Lake Varese, MV Agusta established a semi-works racing programme in which Teuchert was the obvious candidate for a shot at the German SBK championship. However, Castiglioni's principal objective was victory in

Above, Steven Casaer competing in a round of the World Endurance Championship at the Le Mans circuit in 2001 aboard an F4 entered by the Maxim team. The Belgian rider shared with Andrea Mazzali from the Reggiano district (right) the great merit of having contributed to the development of the F4 masterpiece with irreplaceable feedback from the track.
With regard to Mazzali, mention should be made of both his courage and loyalty to the marque, despite myriad difficulties, and his ability to "treat the bike well", a rare quality among racers.

the FIM Superstock 1000 World Cup for under-24 riders, a series with global visibility in which MV Agusta was to be represented by the Gimotorsports team coordinated by Gigi D'Esposito.

At the end of April (that is to say, from the race at Valencia in Spain, the first European GP of the series), the team, which could count for the entire season on the proven support of Bruno Sacchi's Unionbike, as well as that of the Schiranna technicians for the management and development of the engine, was to enter two examples of the F4 1000 S for the young riders, Vittorio Iannuzzo and Fabrizio De Marco. For the second part of the season a joint Italian-German project had instead been set up to develop the F4 1000 World SBK with which MV Agusta was to make its eagerly awaited return to world championship racing.

It was in this context that *Motociclismo*, interpreting the illicit desire of massed enthusiasts from all four corners of the globe, shot off an article by the chief editor Adalberto Falletta explicitly entitled "An MV for Valentino."

At the end of March 2005, the Gallina team (directed by the former racer Roberto) announced Michele Gallina's participation in the Italian SBK championship aboard an MV Agusta F4 1000 Tamburini prepared with the chassis kit produced by CRC and marketed by MV Agusta Corse: was this the first step in the company's direct involvement in the historic marque's return to racing? The bike delivered 185 hp at the rear wheel and weighed 165 kg, including the electric starter. In its debut race on the 17th of April at Vallelunga, the La Spezia-born rider conquered a remarkable 2nd place overall in the rain.

At exactly 10:43 on the 24th of April 2005 (witnessed by this author), the hearts of enthusiasts leapt when they saw at the start of a World Championship race, the aforementioned round of the FIM 1000 Superstock World Cup at Valencia, not one but four MV Agustas. Along with the F4 1000 Ss of Iannuzzo and De Marco, in fact, there were also those of Ayrton Baldovini and Daniele Vaghi of the Biassono EVR Corse team.

Early in May 2005, on the crest of the wave of enthusiasm, those in the know began to suggest names and surnames of a future works racing team, with Giacomo Agostini as the point of reference, Loris Capirossi or Troy Bayliss as rider and Carlo Pernat as race manager. Speaking to us from Monte Carlo, the former World Champion Virginio Ferrari offered his private structure for the "great return."

Again in May 2005, confirmation of an increasingly important competition component in the marque image came in the form of the 14th place obtained by the Meyer-Meyer-Heiler MV Agusta F4 (team Burger King) in the Albacete 8 Hours (Spain) in the SBK category of the World Endurance Championship and the success achieved in the Russian Open SBK Championship by an F4 1000 Tamburini ridden to a victorious debut by Bruno Rozkalns, a rider and the MV Agusta importer for the Baltic countries.

In late June 2005, history actually repeated itself and what had seemed to be an unachievable Utopia instead took shape. At 10:50 on the morning of the 26th, almost 30 years after the aforementioned race won by Agostini at the Nürburgring, an MV Agusta was once again leading a World Championship event. The event occurred at Misano during the San Marino GP, a round in the FIM Superstock 1000 World Cup. On the eighth lap, Vittorio Iannuzzo (who had started from the front row with the second fastest time in qualifying and broke the track record on the second lap) took his F4 1000 S No. 31 into the lead ahead of 32 other competitors.

2006

2006 saw Luca Scassa's triumph in the Italian Superstock Championship aboard his MV Agusta F4 1000. The same rider and Ayrton Baldovini narrowly missed out on victory in the STK World Championship.

2007

In the first half of 2007, there were rumours regarding Carl Fogarty's possible appointment as MV Agusta's team manager in the SBK World Championship. Nothing came of it and the champion rider restricted himself to piloting an F4 R 312 in the celebration of the centenary of the Tourist Trophy on the Isle of Man.

At the end of a season's racing in the USA in the AMA SBK series, Luca Scassa was crowned Rookie of the Year.

2008

Luca Scassa triumphant again: after a season spent out in front, he recorded the final victory in the CIV SBK aboard the F4 1000 R 312. The bike was prepared by the Schiranna R&D department, with the support of the Unionbike-Gimotorsports team.

2009

For 2009, MV Agusta announced that its colours would be defended by the FIM STK Cup by Davide Giuliano and Alan Lowes riding for the Unionbike-Gimotorsports team.

Results were disappointing, but nonetheless (while awaiting the day of the "great return"), well dug, old Mole!

Three shots of Luca Scassa, the Aretino rider who, after his STK triumph in 2006, rode his MV Agusta F4 R 312 to victory in the Italian SBK Championship in 2008, with the support of the Gimotorsports Unionbike team founded in 1990 and specialised in racing four-stroke bikes.
The racing model provided numerous design cues that led to the F4 1000 2010.

THE F4 "SPECIALS": TUNING THE BEST

Given that even Ferraris and Lamborghinis can be tuned, the F4 was hardly likely to have escaped the attentions of those bike tuners capable of improving on what might have seemed to be perfection. Here are just a few examples.

Poggipolini

At Munich's Intermot in 2000, Poggipolini of Bologna (a well known firm specialising in machining titanium) presented its F4 "special" that was 20 kg lighter than the original. Titanium was used for the upper yoke, the front brake and clutch reservoir brackets, the rear swinging arm, the spring of the monoshock, the rear hub, the crown wheel, the exhaust, the fairing and saddle subframes, the footpegs and various nuts and bolts. The bike also featured twin Brembo 320 mm carbon brakes discs at the front with forged aluminium radial calipers and four pistons in titanium as well as woven mesh pipework, and a carbonfibre fairing (preimpregnated with an epoxy resin) and tail. Total price for the makeover: 140 million of the old Italian lire!

Febur

In 2002, Febur of Mantua, specialising in exclusive accessories for motorcycles, proposed a "weight-loss" programme for the F4 based on special components in titanium, magnesium, carbon and Ergal: the end result was a bike weighing 163 kg in running order, around 40 less than the original.

Cemes

The thorough revision of the MV Agusta F4 S proposed by Cemes of Treviso appeared in 2003 and offered 30 extra horsepower while weighing 30 kg less. Apart from the chassis side, virtually all of the internal engine components had been revised, with the displacement being increased to 847.5 cc. The price for a complete kit (of which around 15 examples were put on sale)? Over 35,000.

R.D.M.

In 2004, the R.D.M. team of Rome presented the most "explosive" of the special versions of the Varese "four": an MV Agusta F4 750 fuelled by nitrous oxide! The chemical supercharging was achieved via a Nitrous Works kit distributed in Italy by Protoxide and composed of a canister of liquid N2O (located on the passenger seat, while the red button used to "arm" the system was a conspicuous addition to the handlebars), a high pressure electric fan, woven metal pipework, a filter and four Y injectors located on the intake ducts. A number of modifications were naturally made to the engine, from valve springs in titanium (manufactured, like the nuts and bolts by Cemes) to the induction system, from the exhaust to the copper rings adopted in place of the cylinder head gaskets, through to the NGK CR8 EK spark plugs, "colder" than the originals. Furthermore, the exhaust system with the manifolds deriving from the F4 Ago featured Galassetti carbonfibre terminals. An additional Dynojet Power Commnder III CPU was entrusted with management of the engine in its non-supercharged configuration only. On straights, once the button was pressed (the operation being effected with the throttle fully open otherwise a safety device prevented firing) one could enjoy the remarkable increase in power provided by the homogeneous mixture of petrol and N2O (which the Y injectors supplied directly to the intake ducts with a strict combustive agent/fuel ratio of 14.7:1): 153.1 hp at 12,470 at the rear wheel! The thrust is incredibly powerful, the gear ratios seem to have shortened but the thrill (that is to say the nitrous oxide) is over all too quickly. The conversion costs 4,737 and also comprises Febur carbonfibre bodywork and modifications to the chassis allowing the road rocket to be controlled: a WP fork kit and Discacciati radial front brake pump.

HRT

Following the summer of 2005, the most enthusiastic tuners were rewarded with a kit for the F4 1000 produced by HRT, a true "shadow" racing department for MV Agusta. Displacement bored out to 1078 cc (an extra 3mm per cylinder), rechromed sleeves, new pistons, a higher compression ratio (13:2 instead of 13:1) and a new Eprom: this was the "recipe" for the SPR version (price: 4,200) offering over 180 hp at the crankshaft. The more aggressive SBK version instead boasted new gear ratios (a taller first, the other five being closer set) and lost the exhaust catalyser (cost: 1,440).

Ioannoni

I the autumn of 2005, the enthusiasts received word of another F4 1000 tuning project, the work of Giuseppe Ionnani and his son Mario, MV Agusta importers at Ingolstadt (Germany) since 2004. The objective was that of creating a bike (the F4 1000 R) ready to race in SBK: while numerous carbonfibre bodywork elements were fitted, the greatest attention was paid to the mechanical and chassis components. The engine (completely revised, from the induction system with a carbonfibre air-box to the dedicated Arrow exhaust, by way of the titanium valves and other racing delicacies) churned out 207 hp at the crankshaft. The front fork was a WP Superbike unit (like the rear monoshock), the magnesium rear swinging arm and yokes came from the F4 Tamburini, while the brakes had a Brembo radial pump and Zanzani ventilated discs.

Motocorse

2006 saw the presentation of the F4 1080 Platino. It was built by Motocorse (a well-known Japanese-

Sammarinese manufacturer of racing components) using a 1078 cc engine with pistons and complete exhaust system in titanium (and remapped electronics), thanks to which a compression ratio of no less than 13.3:1 and a power output of "over 190 hp" were rumoured. Almost as if to justify the stratospheric price approaching 65,000, there were countless premium components such as parts in carbonfibre, an Öhlins rear monoshock, Brembo radial calipers and Marchesini forged wheels.

Renovatio Garage

At Modena, under the name Renovatio Garage, Alessandro Binni has for some time been creating special parts for the MV Agusta F4 and Brutale to be used on the track.

In 2009 he presented examples of complete craft-built bikes: the Brutale Corse T1 Titanium and the F4 Viper Titanium.

In 2010, the Ghirlandina "factory" presented the F4 Viper Revolution that, based on the F4 R 312, "redefines the concept of across the board personalisation." The styling catches the eye through the use of a pearlescent paint finish allowing the underlying carbonfibre to show through.

The mechanical specification features cooling via two radiators (water and oil) and a new water pump rotor, while TSS (variable geometry intake tracts) was adopted for the first time on this engine and the gearbox was fitted with

close ratios and a slipper clutch. The chassis features a front-end with a reduced steering head inclination and a new pressurised 50 mm fork, while the rear benefits from a perfectly rated Öhlins monoshock and different suspension kinematics.

Dulcis in fundo, the weight of the motorcycles has dropped by over 20 kg thanks to widespread use of parts in ergal, carbonfibre, magnesium and titanium.

Alka Design

In 2010, Alka Design of Normandy (Déville lès Rouen) presented the F4 Libeccio, the latest graphic restyling of the F4.

The design studio run by the architect and collector Alexander Dauly and the painter Sébastian Noré has shown great respect for the original aesthetic parameters; that is, the "Italianness" of the motorcycle designed by Tamburini. The creations, made to order, are almost always one-offs.

TECHNICAL DATA TABLES

500 R19

(NB: the technical specifications of this model, while presented in an abbreviated and non-orthodox form, represent the only official data communicated at the time by the manufacturer).

ENGINE: four-stroke, transverse four cylinders, inclined forwards by 10°; bore and stroke: 54x54 mm x 4 = 494.4 cc; twin overhead camshafts actuated by a central gear train; compression ratio 9:1; magneto ignition; fuel system: two x Dell'Orto SSI-2&DS-DD carburettors; lubrication via a gear pump; gear primary drive on the left-hand side; in-unit gearbox with transverse selector; multiple plate clutch; cardan shaft final drive with constant velocity joints on the left; pedal starting; dynamo and contact breaker ignition.

CHASSIS: continuous tubular duplex cradle frame with box-section central uprights; telescopic fork; deformable parallelogram rear suspension with torsion bars and friction dampers; wheelbase 1,520 mm; central drum brakes, 230 mm front and 220 mm rear; light alloy wheels with 3.00x19" and 3.50x19" front and rear tyres.

LIQUIDS: 18-litre pressed steel fuel tank, 2.5-litre oil sump.

DECLARED PERFORMANCE AND WEIGHT: power: 40 hp at 8,500 rpm, maximum speed: 170 kph, dry weight: 155 kg.

600 4C6

ENGINE: four-stroke, transverse four cylinders inclined through 20°; single cylinder head, separate cylinders in light alloy with cast iron sleeves. Light alloy crankcase. Composite crankshaft on six main bearings. Forged steel con-rods. Bore and stroke 58x56 mm; displacement: 592 cc; compression ratio: 9.3:1; maximum power: 52 hp at 8,000 rpm. Two overhead valves per cylinder, with an 80° angle between them and actuated by twin camshafts and bucket tappets driven by the crankshaft via a gear chain. Intake valve diameter: 30 mm; exhaust valve diameter: 28.6 mm. Valve lift: 7.5 mm Play between cam and tappet with the engine cold: intake +/- 0.25; exhaust +/- 0.30. Valvegear diagram: intake aperture: 48° before TDC; intake closure: 68° after BDC; exhaust aperture: 70° before BDC; exhaust closure: 36° after TDC.

IGNITION: distributor. Fixed advance: 18/20°; automatic advance: 29/30°; total advance 46/50°. Distance between contacts: 0.4 mm. Spark plugs: Bosch W275 or Marelli CW275L. Distance between contacts: 0.6 mm.

LUBRICATION: for engine and gearbox, pressurised via gear pump and oil in crankcase sump. Sump capacity: 4 kg. Oil: SAE 20 (winter) and SAE 40 (summer). Replaced every 6,000 km. Mesh filter, cleaned every oil change. Filter cartridge, replaced every 12,000 km. For rear crown wheel and pinion: 0.4 kg of Agip F.1 Rotra SAE 90 oil. Replaced every 12,000 km.

FUEL SYSTEM: high octane petrol. Fuel tank capacity: 20 l. of which 2 l. reserve. Carburettors: four x Dell'Orto MB 24 and MB/S 24. 24 mm diameter. Jet max. 120. Jet min. 45. Fuel valve 70. E 10 needle valve on second notch. 260 B vaporiser. 44 L60 inclined trumpets. Choke screw open by two turns.

PRIMARY TRANSMISSION: helicoid gears, 1.75:1 (56/98 teeth).

CLUTCH: multiple plates, oil bath, with seven unlined driving plates and seven lined driven plates, along with the lined thrust plate.

GEARBOX: in-unit, five speed and direct drive, with straight cut constant mesh gears and dog clutches. Pedal actuation, with lever and rocker on the right. Internal ratios: First = 3.57; second = 2.43; third = 1.68; fourth = 1.24; fifth = 1.

SECONDARY TRANSMISSION: crown wheel and pinion from the gearbox, ratio 1.066:1 (15/16 teeth); shaft with cardan joint; final drive ratio 3:1 (12/36 teeth). Total ratios: First = 20; second = 13.6; third = 9.43; fourth = 6.96; fifth = 5.60.

ELECTRICAL SYSTEM: 12 V, Marelli 130W dynamotor. 12 V/18 Ah battery. Front headlamp with asymmetric 40/45 W dual filament bulb and 2.5 W position light. Rear lamp with 5/21 W spherical dual filament bulb for position and brake lights. 2.5 W instrument panel light. Horn: electric.

FRAME: duplex tubular closed cradle.

SUSPENSION: Hydraulic front fork; Shell Tellus 33 oil, 180 cc per stem, replaced every 24,000 km. Rear swinging arms and hydraulic telescopic dampers, hub bearing play checked every 12,000 km.

WHEELS AND TYRES: Front and rear wire wheels in light alloy, 3.00x18". Front tyre: 3.50x18", ribbed; pressure: 1.5 bar. Rear tyre: 4.00x18", treaded; pressure: 1.8 bar (2 bar with a passenger).

BRAKES: front dual Campagnolo 216 mm mechanically actuated discs; rear Ceriani drum with single cam and two shoes; effective dimensions: 200x45 mm.

DIMENSIONS AND WEIGHT: wheelbase: 1390 mm; length 2110 mm; handlebar width: 810 mm; max. height: 1110 mm; handlebar height: 850 mm; saddle height: 800 mm; minimum ground clearance: 170 mm; declared dry weight: 221 kg.

DECLARED PERFORMANCE AND FUEL CONSUMPTION: maximum speed 177 kph. Fuel consumption: 5 l/100 km according to the Cuna norms. Engine-gearbox oil consumption: 0.500 kg/100 km.

750 SPORT 4C75

ENGINE: four-stroke, transverse four cylinders inclined through 20°; single cylinder head, separate cylinders in light alloy with cast iron sleeves. Light alloy crankcase. Composite crankshaft on six main bearings. Forged steel con-rods. Bore and stroke: 65x56 mm; displacement: 743 cc; compression ratio: 9.5:1; maximum power: 69 hp at 7,900 rpm. Two overhead valves per cylinder, with an 80° angle between them and actuated by twin camshafts and bucket tappets driven by the crankshaft via a gear chain. Intake valve diameter: 31.80 mm; exhaust valve diameter: 29 mm. Valve lift: 8 mm Play between cam and tappet with the engine cold: intake +/- 0.25; exhaust +/- 0.30. Valvegear diagram: Intake aperture: 48° before TDC; intake closure: 68° after BDC; exhaust aperture: 70° before BDC; exhaust closure: 36° after TDC.

IGNITION: distributor. Fixed advance: 18/20°; automatic advance: 29/30°; total advance 46/50°. Distance between contacts 0.4 mm. Spark plugs: Bosch W260 or Marelli CW260L. Distance between electrodes: 0.6 mm. Replaced every 12,000 km.

LUBRICATION: for engine and gearbox, pressurised via gear pump and oil in crankcase sump. Sump capacity: 4 kg. Oil to be used in all seasons: Agip Sint 2000 (SAE 20-50). Replaced every 6,000 km. Mesh filter, cleaned every oil change. Filter cartridge, replaced every 12,000 km. For rear crown wheel and pinion: 0.4 kg of Agip F.1 Rotra SAE 90 oil. Replaced every 12,000 km.

FUEL SYSTEM: high octane petrol. Fuel tank capacity: 24 l. of which 4 l. reserve. Carburettors: four x Dell'Orto UB 24 B2 and UB 24 BS2. 24 mm diameter. Jet max. 105. Jet min. 45. Fuel valve 70. E 8 needle valve on second notch. 260 A vaporiser. 44 L60 inclined trumpets. Choke screw open by one turn.

PRIMARY TRANSMISSION: helicoid gears, 1.75:1 (56/98 teeth).

CLUTCH: multiple plates, oil bath, with seven unlined driving plates and seven lined driven plates, along with the lined thrust plate.

GEARBOX: in-unit, five speed and direct drive, with straight cut constant mesh gears and dog clutches. Pedal actuation, with single lever on the right. Internal ratios: First = 2.38; second = 1.69; third = 1.29; fourth = 1.09; fifth = 1.

SECONDARY TRANSMISSION: Crown wheel and pinion from the gearbox, ratio 1.066:1 (15/16 teeth); shaft with cardan joint; final drive ratio 2,668:1 (32/12 teeth). Total ratios: first = 11.68; second = 8.45; third = 6.47; fourth = 5.44; fifth = 4.98.

ELECTRICAL SYSTEM: 12 V, Marelli 130W dynamotor. 12 V/18 Ah battery. Front headlamp with 40/45 W asymmetric dual filament bulb and 2.5 W position light. Rear lamp with 5/21 W spherical dual filament bulb for position and brake lights. 2.5 W instrument panel light. Horn: electric.

FRAME: duplex tubular closed cradle.

SUSPENSION: hydraulic front fork; Shell Tellus 33 oil, 180 cc per stem, replaced every 24,000 km. Rear swinging arms and hydraulic telescopic dampers, hub bearing play checked every 12,000 km.

WHEELS AND TYRES: Front and rear wire wheels in light alloy, 3.00x18". Front tyre 3.50x18", ribbed; pressure: 2 bar. Rear tyre: 4.00x18", treaded; pressure: 2.2 bar (2,5 bar with a passenger).

BRAKES: central drums; front: Grimeca with dual cams and four shoes; effective dimensions: 230x30 mm; rear: Grimeca with single cam and two shoes, effective dimensions: 200x45 mm.

DIMENSIONS AND WEIGHT: wheelbase: 1390 mm; length: 2110 mm; handlebar width: 660 mm; max. height: 1020 mm; handlebar height: 850 mm; saddle height: 800 mm; minimum ground clearance: 150 mm; declared dry weight: 230 kg.

DECLARED PERFORMANCE AND FUEL CONSUMPTION: maximum speed 200 kph. Fuel consumption: 7.8 l/100 km according to the Cuna norms. Engine-gearbox oil consumption: 0.500 kg/100 km.

800 AMERICA

ENGINE: four-stroke, transverse four cylinders inclined through 20°; single cylinder head, separate cylinders in light alloy with cast iron sleeves. Light alloy crankcase. Composite crankshaft on six main bearings. Forged steel con-rods. Bore and stroke: 67x56 mm; displacement: 789,7 cc; compression ratio: 10:1; maximum power: 75 hp at 8500 rpm. Two overhead valves per cylinder, with an 80° angle between them and actuated by twin camshafts and bucket tappets driven by the crankshaft via a gear chain. Intake valve diameter: 31.8 mm; exhaust valve diameter: 29 mm. Valve lift: 8.5 mm. Play between cam and tappet with the engine cold: intake: +/- 0.25; exhaust: +/- 0.30. Valvegear diagram: intake aperture: 48° before TDC; intake closure: 68° after BDC; exhaust aperture: 70° before BDC; exhaust closure: 36° after TDC.
IGNITION: distributor. Fixed advance: 16°; automatic advance: 29/30°; total advance: 46. Distance between contacts: 0.4 mm. Spark plugs: Bosch W260 or Marelli CW260L. Distance between electrodes: 0.6 mm. Replaced every 12,000 km.
LUBRICATION: for engine and gearbox, pressurised via gear pump and oil in crankcase sump. Sump capacity: 5 kg. Oil to be used in all seasons: Agip Sint 2000 (SAE 20-50). Replaced every 6,000 km. Mesh filter, cleaned every oil change. Filter cartridge, replaced every 12,000 km. For rear crown wheel and pinion: 0.4 kg of Agip F.1 Rotra SAE 90 oil. Replaced every 12,000 km.
FUEL SYSTEM: high octane petrol. Fuel tank capacity: 19 l. of which 2 l. reserve. Carburettors: four x Dell'Orto VHB 26 D with central dashpot and single cartridge-type air filter. Diameter: 26 mm. Jet max. 118. Jet min. 45. Fuel valve 40. E 4 needle valve on second notch. 262 AE vaporiser. 44 L60 inclined trumpets. Choke screw open by one turn.
PRIMARY TRANSMISSION: helicoid gears, 1.75:1 (56/98 teeth).
CLUTCH: multiple plates, oil bath, with seven unlined driving plates and seven lined driven plates, along with the lined thrust plate.
GEARBOX: in-unit, five speed and direct drive, with straight cut constant mesh gears and dog clutches. Pedal actuation, with single lever on the right. Internal ratios: First = 2.38; second = 1.69; third = 1.29; fourth = 1.09; fifth = 1.
SECONDARY TRANSMISSION: Crown wheel and pinion from the gearbox, ratio 1.066:1 (15/16 teeth); shaft with cardan joint; final drive ratio: 2.668:1 (32/12 teeth). Total ratios: First = 11.84; second = 8.40; third = 6.36; fourth = 5.52; fifth = 4.97.
ELECTRICAL SYSTEM: 12 V, Marelli 130W dynamotor. 12 V/32 Ah battery. Front headlamp with 40/45 W asymmetric dual filament bulb and 2.5 W position light. Rear lamp with 5/21 W spherical dual filament bulb for position and brake lights. 2.5 W instrument panel light. Horn: electric.
FRAME: duplex tubular closed cradle.
SUSPENSION: Ceriani hydraulic front fork; Shell Tellus 33 oil, 180 cc per stem, replaced every 24,000 km. Rear swinging arms and hydraulic dampers: hub bearing play checked every 12,000 km.
WHEELS AND TYRES: front and rear wire (cast spokes on request) wheels in light alloy, 3.00x18". Front tyre 3.50x18", ribbed; pressure: 2 bar. Rear tyre: 4.00x18", treaded; pressure: 2.2 bar (2.5 bar with a passenger).
BRAKES: Front: dual 280 mm hydraulically actuated Scarab discs; rear: Grimeca drum with single cam and two shoes; effective dimensions: 200x45 mm (on request: with light alloy spoked wheels, single Scarab disc brake).
DIMENSIONS AND WEIGHT: wheelbase: 1390 mm; length: 2150 mm; handlebar width: 720 mm; max. height: 1080 mm; handlebar height: 880 mm; saddle height: 770 mm; minimum ground clearance: 150 mm; declared dry weight: 230 kg.
DECLARED PERFORMANCE AND FUEL CONSUMPTION: maximum speed: 208 kph. Fuel consumption: 8 l/100 km according to the Cuna norms. Engine-gearbox oil consumption: 0.500 kg/100 km.

F4 750 Oro

ENGINE: four-stroke; four in-line transverse cylinders inclined forwards through 20°; cylinder head in aluminium alloy; block in aluminium alloy with closed deck architecture and cast-in liners with ceramic composite bore plating; aluminium alloy pistons; forged steel con-rods; sand-cast magnesium crankcase; forged steel one-piece crankshaft on six main bearings. Displacement: 749.4 cc; bore and stroke: 73,8x43.8 mm; compression ratio: 12:1; maximum power: 126 hp at 12,200 rpm; maximum torque: 7.3 kgm at 9,000 rpm. Four radially configured valves per cylinder inclined at 22° and directly actuated via bucket tappets by two overhead camshafts driven off the crankshaft by a central chain. Valve diameters: intake: 29 mm; exhaust: 25 mm. Tolerances: intake: +/- 0.15-0.24; exhaust: +/- 0.20-0.29. Valvegear diagram: intake aperture: 12° before TDC; intake closure: 42° after BDC; exhaust aperture: 30° before BDC; exhaust closure: 10° after TDC. Valve lift: intake: 8.5 mm; exhaust: 7.6 mm.
FUEL SYSTEM: Weber-Marelli 1.6M multipoint integrated electronic fuel injection and ignition. 46 mm throttle bodies.
IGNITION: electronic inductive discharge. Spark plugs: Champion G59C or NGK CR9EB.
COOLING: liquid with water-oil heat exchanger.
LUBRICATION: wet sump with lobed oil pump. Oil capacity and type: SAE 10w-60 with filter, 3,5 kg.
PRIMARY TRANSMISSION: straight cut gears, ratio: 50/79.
CLUTCH: hydraulically actuated, multiple plates in oil bath.
GEARBOX: extractable cassette-type with six speeds with constant mesh gears. Pedal actuation, on the left. Ratios: First = 13/38; second = 14/31; third = 18/32; fourth = 20/30; fifth = 22/29; sixth = 21/25.
SECONDARY TRANSMISSION: chain; ratio: 14:41.
ELECTRICAL SYSTEM: 12 V, 12 V/9Ah battery, 650W alternator at 5,000 rpm.
FRAME: combination of chrome-molybdenum steel tubes and cast magnesium swinging arm pivot sections.
SUSPENSION: front Showa upside down 49 mm fork equipped with adjustable compression and rebound damping and spring preload; wheel travel: 118 mm. rear single-sided swinging arm in magnesium alloy with progressive leverage and an Öhlins (later Sachs) monoshock equipped with compression and rebound damping (high and low speed damping) and spring preload; wheel travel 120 mm.
WHEELS AND TYRES: magnesium alloy rims; front: 3.50x17"; rear: 6.00x17". Tyres: Pirelli Dragon Evo or Michelin Pilot Sport or Metzeler MEZ3 Racing; front: 120/65-17"; rear: 190/50-17" (or 180/55-17").
BRAKES: front: Nissin 310 mm dual floating discs, caliper with six differentiated diameter pistons; rear: Nissin 210 mm single disc, caliper with four pistons.
DIMENSIONS AND WEIGHT: wheelbase: 1,398 mm; length: 2,007 mm; width: 685 mm; saddle height: 790 mm; minimum ground clearance: 130 mm; trail: 98.5 mm; declared dry weight: 184 kg.
DECLARED PERFORMANCE: maximum speed: 275 kph.

F4 750 S

(in brackets the data relating to the 750 S 1+1)
ENGINE: four-stroke; four in-line transverse cylinders inclined forwards through 20°; cylinder head in aluminium alloy; block in aluminium alloy with closed deck architecture and cast-in liners with ceramic composite bore plating; aluminium alloy pistons; forged steel con-rods; aluminium alloy crankcase; forged steel one-piece crankshaft on six main bearings. Displacement: 749.4 cc; bore and stroke: 73,8x43.8 mm; compression ratio: 12:1; maximum power: 137 hp at 12,600 rpm; maximum torque: 8.3 kgm at 10,500 rpm. Four radial valves per cylinder inclined at 22° and directly actuated via bucket tappets by two overhead camshafts driven off the crankshaft by a central chain. Valve diameters: intake: 29 mm; exhaust: 25 mm. Tolerances: intake: +/- 0.15-0.24; exhaust: +/- 0.20-0.29. Valvegear diagram: intake aperture: 12° before TDC; intake closure: 42° after BDC; exhaust aperture: 30° before BDC; exhaust closure: 10° after TDC. Valve lift: intake: 8.5 mm; exhaust: 7.6 mm.
FUEL SYSTEM: Weber-Marelli 1.6M multipoint integrated electronic fuel injection and ignition. 46 mm throttle bodies.
IGNITION: electronic inductive discharge. Spark plugs: Champion G59C or NGK CR9EB.
COOLING: liquid with water-oil heat exchanger.
LUBRICATION: wet sump with lobed oil pump. Oil capacity and type: SAE 10w-60 with filter, 3.5 kg.
PRIMARY TRANSMISSION: straight cut gears, ratio: 47/81.
CLUTCH: hydraulically actuated, multiple plates in oil bath.
GEARBOX: extractable cassette-type with six speeds with constant mesh gears. Pedal actuation, on the left. Ratios: First = 13/38; second = 14/31; third = 18/32; fourth = 20/30; fifth = 22/29; sixth = 21/25.
SECONDARY TRANSMISSION: chain; ratio: 15:40.
ELECTRICAL SYSTEM: 12 V, 12 V/9Ah battery, 650W alternator at 5,000 rpm.
FRAME: combination of chrome-molybdenum steel tubes and aluminium alloy swinging arm pivot sections.
SUSPENSION: front Showa upside down 49 mm fork equipped with adjustable compression and rebound damping and spring preload; wheel travel: 118 mm. rear single-sided swinging arm in aluminium alloy with progressive leverage and a Sachs monoshock equipped with compression and rebound damping (high and low speed damping) and spring preload; wheel travel 120 mm.
WHEELS AND TYRES: aluminium alloy rims; front: 3.50x17"; rear: 6.00x17". Tyres: Pirelli Dragon Evo or Michelin Pilot Sport or Metzeler MEZ3 Racing; front: 120/65-17"; rear: 190/50-17" or 180/55-17".
BRAKES: front: Nissin 310 mm dual floating discs, caliper with six differentiated diameter pistons; rear: Nissin 210 mm single disc, caliper with four pistons.
DIMENSIONS AND WEIGHT: wheelbase: 1,398 mm; length: 2,007 mm; width: 685 mm; saddle height: 790 mm; minimum ground clearance: 130 mm; trail: 98.5 mm; declared dry weight: 191 (192) kg.
DECLARED PERFORMANCE: maximum speed: 283 kph.

F4 Senna

(in brackets the data relating to the Senna 1000)

ENGINE: four-stroke; four in-line transverse cylinders inclined forwards through 20°; cylinder head in aluminium alloy; block in aluminium alloy with closed deck architecture and cast-in liners with ceramic composite bore plating; aluminium alloy pistons; forged steel con-rods; aluminium alloy crankcase; forged steel one-piece crankshaft on six main bearings. Displacement: 794.4 (998) cc; bore and stroke: 73.8 (76) x 43.8 (55) mm; compression ratio: 12:1; maximum power: 140 (174) hp at 11,900 rpm; maximum torque: 8.3 (11.3) kgm at 10,500 (10,000) rpm. Four radial (2°) valves per cylinder inclined at 22° and directly actuated via bucket tappets by two overhead camshafts driven off the crankshaft by a central chain. Valve diameters: intake: 29 mm; exhaust: 25 mm. Tolerances: intake: +/- 0.15-0.24; exhaust: +/- 0.20-0.29. Valvegear diagram: intake aperture: 18° before TDC; intake closure: 56° after BDC; exhaust aperture: 50° before BDC; exhaust closure: 14° after TDC. Valve lift: intake: 9.7 mm; exhaust: 8.5 mm.

FUEL SYSTEM: Weber-Marelli 1.6M (5S) multipoint integrated electronic fuel injection and ignition. 46 mm throttle bodies.

IGNITION: electronic inductive discharge. Spark plugs: Champion G54V or NGK CR9EKB or NGK R 0045-J10.

COOLING: liquid with water-oil heat exchanger.

LUBRICATION: wet sump with lobed oil pump. Oil capacity and type: SAE 10w-60 with filter, 3.5 kg.

PRIMARY TRANSMISSION: straight cut gears, ratio: 47/81 (50/79).

CLUTCH: hydraulically actuated, multiple plates in oil bath.

GEARBOX: extractable cassette-type with six speeds and constant mesh gears. Pedal actuation, on the left. Ratios: First = 14/37 (13/38); second = 16/33 (16/34); third = 15/27 (18/32); fourth = 19/30 (20/30); fifth = 23/33 (22/29); sixth = 18/24 (21/25).

SECONDARY TRANSMISSION: chain, ratios available: 15x39, 15x38, 15x37.

ELECTRICAL SYSTEM: 12 V, 12 V/9Ah battery, 650W alternator at 5,000 rpm.

FRAME: combination of chrome-molybdenum steel tubes and aluminium alloy swinging arm pivot sections.

SUSPENSION: front Marzocchi upside down hydraulic fork with 50 mm titanium nitride treated stems and equipped with adjustable compression and rebound damping and spring preload; wheel travel: 118 mm. rear single-sided swinging arm in magnesium alloy with progressive leverage and a Sachs monoshock equipped with compression and rebound damping (high and low speed damping) and spring preload; wheel travel 120 (129) mm.

WHEELS AND TYRES: aluminium alloy rims; front: 3.50x17"; rear: 6.00x17". Tyres: Pirelli Dragon Evo (Pirelli Dragon Supercorsa Pro), front: 120/65 (120/70)-ZR 17"; rear: 190/50 (190/55)-ZR 17" or 180/55-17".

BRAKES: front: Nissin 310 (320) mm dual floating discs, caliper with six differentiated diameter pistons (radial with four pistons); rear: Nissin 210 mm single disc, caliper with four pistons.

DIMENSIONS AND WEIGHT: wheelbase: 1,398 (1,408) mm; length: 2,007 mm; width: 685 mm; saddle height: 790 (810) mm; minimum ground clearance: 130 mm; trail: 98:5 (103.8) mm; declared dry weight: 188 (190) kg.

DECLARED PERFORMANCE: maximum speed: 270, 278 or 286 (301) kph depending on the final drive ratio.

F4 SPR

ENGINE: four-stroke; four in-line transverse cylinders inclined forwards through 20°; cylinder head in aluminium alloy; block in aluminium alloy with closed deck architecture and cast-in liners with ceramic composite bore plating; aluminium alloy pistons; forged steel con-rods; aluminium alloy crankcase; forged steel one-piece crankshaft on six main bearings. Displacement: 749.4 cc; bore and stroke: 73,8x43.8 mm; compression ratio: 13:1; maximum power: 146 hp at13,000 rpm; maximum torque: 8.2 kgm at 11,000 rpm. Four radial (2°) valves per cylinder inclined at 22° and directly actuated via bucket tappets by two overhead camshafts driven off the crankshaft by a central chain. Valve diameters: intake: 29 mm; exhaust: 25 mm. Tolerances: intake: +/- 0.15-0.20; exhaust: +/- 0.20-0.25. Valvegear diagram: intake aperture: 18° before TDC; intake closure: 56° after BDC; exhaust aperture: 50° before BDC; exhaust closure: 14° after TDC. Valve lift: intake: 9.7 mm; exhaust: 8.5 mm.

FUEL SYSTEM: Weber-Marelli 1.6M multipoint integrated electronic fuel injection and ignition. 46 mm throttle bodies.

IGNITION: electronic inductive discharge. Spark plugs: Champion G54V.

COOLING: liquid with water-oil heat exchanger.

LUBRICATION: wet sump with lobed oil pump. Oil capacity and type: SAE 10w-60 with filter, 3.5 kg.

PRIMARY TRANSMISSION: straight cut gears, ratio: 47/81.

CLUTCH: hydraulically actuated, multiple plates in oil bath.

GEARBOX: extractable cassette-type with six speeds and constant mesh gears. Pedal actuation, on the left. Ratios: First = 15/37; second = 16/33; third = 15/27; fourth = 19/30; fifth = 23/33; sixth = 18/24.

SECONDARY TRANSMISSION: chain, ratios available: 15x39, 15x38, 15x37.

ELECTRICAL SYSTEM: 12 V, 12 V/9Ah battery, 650W alternator at 5,000 rpm.

FRAME: combination of chrome-molybdenum steel tubes and aluminium alloy swinging arm pivot sections.

SUSPENSION: front Marzocchi upside down hydraulic fork with 50 mm titanium nitride treated stems and equipped with adjustable compression and rebound damping and spring preload; wheel travel: 118 mm. rear single-sided swinging arm in aluminium alloy with progressive leverage and a Sachs monoshock equipped with compression and rebound damping (high and low speed damping) and spring preload; wheel travel 120 mm.

WHEELS AND TYRES: aluminium alloy rims; front: 3.50x17"; rear: 6.00x17". Tyres: Pirelli Dragon Evo, front: 120/65-17"; rear: 190/50-17" or 180/55-17".

BRAKES: front: Nissin 310 mm dual floating discs, caliper with six differentiated diameter pistons; rear: Nissin 210 mm single disc, caliper with four pistons.

DIMENSIONS AND WEIGHT: wheelbase: 1,398 mm; length: 2,007 mm; width: 685 mm; saddle height: 790 mm; minimum ground clearance: 130 mm; trail: 98.5 mm; declared dry weight: 188 kg.

DECLARED PERFORMANCE: maximum speed: 270, 278 or 286 kph depending on the final drive ratio.

F4 Brutale Oro

ENGINE: four-stroke; four in-line transverse cylinders inclined forwards through 20°; cylinder head in aluminium alloy; block in aluminium alloy with closed deck architecture and cast-in liners with ceramic composite bore plating; aluminium alloy pistons; forged steel con-rods; aluminium alloy crankcase; forged steel one-piece crankshaft on six main bearings. Displacement: 749.4 cc; bore and stroke: 73,8x43.8 mm; compression ratio: 12:1; maximum power: 127 hp a12,500 rpm; maximum torque: 7.9 kgm at 10,500 rpm. Four radial (2°) valves per cylinder inclined at 22° and directly actuated via bucket tappets by two overhead camshafts driven off the crankshaft by a central chain. Valve diameters: intake: 29 mm; exhaust: 25 mm. Tolerances: intake: +/- 0.15-0.24; exhaust: +/- 0.20-0.29. Valvegear diagram: intake aperture: 12° before TDC; intake closure: 42° after BDC; exhaust aperture: 30° before BDC; exhaust closure: 10° after TDC. Valve lift: intake: 8.5 mm; exhaust: 7.5 mm.

FUEL SYSTEM: Weber-Marelli 1.6M multipoint integrated electronic fuel injection and ignition.

IGNITION: electronic inductive discharge. Spark plugs: Champion G59C or NGK CR9EB.

COOLING: liquid with oil cooler.

LUBRICATION: wet sump with lobed oil pump. Oil capacity and type: SAE 10w-60 with filter, 3.5 kg.

PRIMARY TRANSMISSION: straight cut gears, ratio: 47/81.

CLUTCH: hydraulically actuated, multiple plates in oil bath.

GEARBOX: extractable cassette-type with six speeds and constant mesh gears. Pedal actuation, on the left. Ratios: First = 13/38; second = 14/31; third = 18/32; fourth = 20/30; fifth = 22/29; sixth = 19/23.

SECONDARY TRANSMISSION: chain; ratio: 14:41.

ELECTRICAL SYSTEM: 12 V, 12 V/9Ah battery, 650W alternator at 5,000 rpm.

FRAME: combination of chrome-molybdenum steel tubes and cast magnesium swinging arm pivot sections.

SUSPENSION: front Marzocchi upside down hydraulic fork with 50 mm titanium nitride treated stems and equipped with adjustable compression and rebound damping and spring preload; wheel travel: 135 mm. rear single-sided swinging arm in magnesium alloy with progressive leverage and a Sachs monoshock equipped with compression and rebound damping (high and low speed damping) and spring preload; wheel travel 120 mm.

WHEELS AND TYRES: magnesium alloy rims; front: 3.50x17"; rear: 6.00x17". Tyres: Dunlop Sport Max D207, front: 120/65-17"; rear: 190/50-17" or 180/55-17".

BRAKES: front: Nissin 310 mm dual floating discs, caliper with six differentiated diameter pistons; rear: Nissin 210 mm single disc, caliper with four pistons.

DIMENSIONS AND WEIGHT: wheelbase: 1,410 mm; length: 2,020 mm; width: 760 mm; saddle height: 805 mm; minimum ground clearance: 135 mm; trail: 101.5 mm; declared dry weight: 179 kg.

DECLARED PERFORMANCE: maximum speed restricted to 250 kph.

F4 1000 Ago

ENGINE: four-stroke; four in-line transverse cylinders inclined forwards through 20°; cylinder head in aluminium alloy; block in aluminium alloy with closed deck architecture and cast-in liners with ceramic composite bore plating; aluminium alloy pistons; forged steel con-rods; aluminium alloy crankcase; forged steel one-piece crankshaft on six main bearings. Displacement: 998 cc; bore and stroke: 76.55 mm; compression ratio: 12:1; maximum power: 166 hp at 11,750 rpm; maximum torque:11.1 kgm at 10,200 rpm. Four radial (2°) valves per cylinder inclined at 22° and directly actuated via bucket tappets by two overhead camshafts driven off the crankshaft by a central chain. Valve diameters: intake: 29 mm; exhaust: 25 mm. Tolerances: intake: +/- 0.15-0.20; exhaust: +/- 0.20-0.25. Valvegear diagram: intake aperture: 18° before TDC; intake closure: 54° after BDC; exhaust aperture: 18° before BDC; exhaust closure: 46° after TDC. Valve lift: intake: 9 mm; exhaust: 8 mm.
FUEL SYSTEM: Weber-Marelli 1.6M multipoint integrated electronic fuel injection and ignition. 46 mm throttle bodies.
IGNITION: electronic inductive discharge.
COOLING: liquid with water-oil heat exchanger.
LUBRICATION: wet sump with lobed oil pump. Oil capacity and type: SAE 15w-50 with filter, 3.5 kg.
PRIMARY TRANSMISSION: straight cut gears, ratio: 50:79.
CLUTCH: hydraulically actuated, multiple plates in oil bath.
GEARBOX: extractable cassette-type with six speeds and constant mesh gears. Pedal actuation, on the left. Ratios: First = 13/38; second = 16/34; third = 18/32; fourth = 20/30; fifth = 22/29; sixth = 21/25.
SECONDARY TRANSMISSION: chain, ratios available: 15x39, 15x38, 15x37.
ELECTRICAL SYSTEM: 12 V, 12 V/9Ah battery, 650W alternator at 5,000 rpm.
FRAME: combination of chrome-molybdenum steel tubes and aluminium alloy swinging arm pivot sections.
SUSPENSION: front Marzocchi upside down hydraulic fork with 50 mm titanium nitride treated stems and equipped with adjustable compression and rebound damping and spring preload; wheel travel: 118 mm. Rear single-sided swinging arm in aluminium alloy with progressive leverage and a Sachs monoshock equipped with compression and rebound damping (high and low speed damping) and spring preload (hydraulic actuation); wheel travel 120 mm.
WHEELS AND TYRES: aluminium alloy rims; front: 3.50x17"; rear: 5.50x17". Tyres: Michelin Pilot Power, front 120/65-17, rear 190/50-17 or 180/55-17".
BRAKES: front: Nissin 310 mm dual floating discs, caliper with six differentiated diameter pistons; rear: Nissin 210 mm single disc, caliper with four pistons.
DIMENSIONS AND WEIGHT: wheelbase: 1,408 mm; length: 2,007 mm; width: 685 mm; saddle height: 810 mm; minimum ground clearance: 130 mm; trail: 98.5 mm; declared dry weight: 190 kg.
DECLARED PERFORMANCE: maximum speed: 301 kph.

F4 1000 S

(in brackets the data relating to the 1000 S 1+1)

ENGINE: four-stroke; four in-line transverse cylinders inclined forwards through 20°; cylinder head in aluminium alloy; block in aluminium alloy with closed deck architecture and cast-in liners with ceramic composite bore plating; aluminium alloy pistons; forged steel con-rods; aluminium alloy crankcase; forged steel one-piece crankshaft on six main bearings. Displacement: 998 cc; bore and stroke: 76x55 mm; compression ratio: 12:1; maximum power: 166 hp at 11,750 rpm; maximum torque 11.1 kgm at 10,200 rpm. Four radial (2°) valves per cylinder inclined at 22° and directly actuated via bucket tappets by two overhead camshafts driven off the crankshaft by a central chain. Valve diameters: intake: 29 mm; exhaust: 25 mm. Tolerances: intake: +/- 0.15-0.20; exhaust: +/- 0.20-0.25. Valvegear diagram: intake aperture: 18° before TDC; intake closure: 54° after BDC; exhaust aperture: 18° before BDC; exhaust closure: 46° after TDC. Valve lift: Intake: 9 mm; exhaust: 8 mm.
FUEL SYSTEM: Weber-Marelli 1.6M multipoint integrated electronic fuel injection and ignition. 46 mm throttle bodies.
IGNITION: electronic inductive discharge.
COOLING: liquid with water-oil heat exchanger.
LUBRICATION: wet sump with lobed oil pump. Oil capacity and type: SAE 15w-50 with filter, 3.5 kg.
PRIMARY TRANSMISSION: straight cut gears, ratio: 50:79.
CLUTCH: hydraulically actuated, multiple plates in oil bath.
GEARBOX: extractable cassette-type with six speeds and constant mesh gears. Pedal actuation, on the left. Ratios: First = 13/38; second = 16/34; third = 18/32; fourth = 20/30; fifth = 22/29; sixth = 21/25.
SECONDARY TRANSMISSION: chain; ratio: 16:41.
ELECTRICAL SYSTEM: 12 V, 12 V/9Ah battery, 650W alternator at 5,000 rpm.
FRAME: combination of chrome-molybdenum steel tubes and aluminium alloy swinging arm pivot sections.
SUSPENSION: front Marzocchi upside down 50 mm fork equipped with adjustable compression and rebound damping and spring preload; wheel travel: 118 mm. rear single-sided swinging arm in aluminium alloy with progressive leverage and a Sachs monoshock equipped with compression and rebound damping (high and low speed damping) and spring preload; wheel travel 120 mm. Engine Brake System for torque control.
WHEELS AND TYRES: aluminium alloy rims; front: 3.50x17"; rear: 6.00x17". Tyres: Michelin Pilot Power, front 120/65-17, rear 190/50-17 or 180/55-17".
BRAKES: front: Nissin 310 mm dual floating discs, caliper with six differentiated diameter pistons; rear: Nissin 210 mm single disc, caliper with four pistons.
DIMENSIONS AND WEIGHT: wheelbase: 1,408 mm; length: 2,007 mm; width: 685 mm; saddle height: 810 mm; minimum ground clearance: 130 mm; trail: 98.5 mm; declared dry weight: 192 (193) kg.
DECLARED PERFORMANCE: maximum speed: 301 kph.

F4 1000 Tamburini

ENGINE: four-stroke; four in-line transverse cylinders inclined forwards through 20°; cylinder head in aluminium alloy; block in aluminium alloy with closed deck architecture and cast-in liners with ceramic composite bore plating; aluminium alloy pistons; forged steel con-rods; aluminium alloy crankcase; forged steel one-piece crankshaft on six main bearings. Displacement: 998 cc; bore and stroke: 76x55 mm; compression ratio: 13:1; maximum power: 172.8 hp at 11,750 rpm; maximum torque 11.5 kgm at 9,200 rpm. Four radial (2°) valves per cylinder inclined at 22° and directly actuated via bucket tappets by two overhead camshafts driven off the crankshaft by a central chain. Valve diameters: intake: 29 mm; exhaust: 25 mm. Tolerances: intake: +/- 0.15-0.20; exhaust: +/- 0.20-0.25. Valvegear diagram: intake aperture: 18° before TDC; intake closure: 54° after BDC; exhaust aperture: 18° before BDC; exhaust closure: 46° after TDC. Valve lift: intake: 9 mm; exhaust: 8 mm.
FUEL SYSTEM: Weber-Marelli 1.6M multipoint integrated electronic fuel injection and ignition. 46 mm throttle bodies. Torque Shift System with variable geometry intake tracts.
IGNITION: electronic inductive discharge.
COOLING: liquid with water-oil heat exchanger.
LUBRICATION: wet sump with lobed oil pump. Oil capacity and type: SAE 15w-50 with filter, 3.5 kg.
PRIMARY TRANSMISSION: straight cut gears, ratio: 50:79.
CLUTCH: hydraulically actuated, multiple plates in oil bath.
GEARBOX: extractable cassette-type with six speeds and constant mesh gears. Pedal actuation, on the left. Internal ratios: First = 13/38; second = 16/34; third = 18/32; fourth = 20/30; fifth = 22/29; sixth = 21/25.
SECONDARY TRANSMISSION: chain; ratio: 16:41.
ELECTRICAL SYSTEM: 12 V, 12 V/9Ah battery, 650W alternator at 5,000 rpm.
FRAME: combination of chrome-molybdenum steel tubes and aluminium alloy swinging arm pivot sections.
SUSPENSION: front Marzocchi upside down hydraulic fork with 50 mm titanium nitride treated stems and equipped with adjustable compression and rebound damping and spring preload; wheel travel: 118 mm. Rear single-sided swinging arm in aluminium alloy with progressive leverage and a Sachs monoshock equipped with compression and rebound damping (high and low speed damping) and spring preload (hydraulic actuation); wheel travel 120 mm. Engine Brake System for torque control.
WHEELS AND TYRES: aluminium alloy rims; front: 3.50x17"; rear: 5.75x17". Tyres: front 120/65-ZR 17, rear 180/55-ZR 17" or 190/50 ZR 17".
BRAKES: front: Nissin 310 mm dual floating discs, caliper with six differentiated diameter pistons; rear: Nissin 210 mm single disc, caliper with four pistons.
DIMENSIONS AND WEIGHT: wheelbase: 1,408 mm; length: 2,007 mm; width: 685 mm; saddle height: 810 mm; minimum ground clearance: 130 mm; trail: 98.5 mm; declared dry weight: 184 kg.
DECLARED PERFORMANCE: maximum speed: 307 kph.

F4 1000 MAMBA
(in brackets the data relating to the 1000 Mamba 1+1)
ENGINE: four-stroke; four in-line transverse cylinders inclined forwards through 20°; cylinder head in aluminium alloy; block in aluminium alloy with closed deck architecture and cast-in liners with ceramic composite bore plating; aluminium alloy pistons; forged steel con-rods; aluminium alloy crankcase; forged steel one-piece crankshaft on six main bearings. Displacement: 998 cc; bore and stroke: 76x55 mm; compression ratio: 12:1; maximum power: 174 hp at 11,900 rpm; maximum torque 11.3 kgm at 10,000 rpm. Four radial (2°) valves per cylinder inclined at 22° and directly actuated via bucket tappets by two overhead camshafts driven off the crankshaft by a central chain. Valve diameters: intake: 29 mm; exhaust: 25 mm. Tolerances: intake: +/- 0.15-0.20; exhaust: +/- 0.20-0.25. Valvegear diagram: intake aperture: 18° before TDC; intake closure: 54° after BDC; exhaust aperture: 18° before BDC; exhaust closure: 46° after TDC. Valve lift: intake: 9 mm; exhaust: 8 mm.
FUEL SYSTEM: Weber-Marelli 5SM multipoint integrated electronic fuel injection and ignition. 46 mm throttle bodies.
IGNITION: electronic inductive discharge.
COOLING: liquid with water-oil heat exchanger.
LUBRICATION: wet sump with lobed oil pump. Oil capacity and type: SAE 15w-50 with filter, 3.5 kg.
PRIMARY TRANSMISSION: straight cut gears, ratio: 50:79.
CLUTCH: hydraulically actuated, multiple plates in oil bath.
GEARBOX: extractable cassette-type with six speeds and constant mesh gears. Pedal actuation, on the left. Ratios: First = 13/38; second = 16/34; third = 18/32; fourth = 20/30; fifth = 22/29; sixth = 21/25.
SECONDARY TRANSMISSION: chain; ratio: 15:40.
ELECTRICAL SYSTEM: 12 V, 12 V/9Ah battery, 650W alternator at 5,000 rpm.
FRAME: combination of chrome-molybdenum steel tubes and aluminium alloy swinging arm pivot sections.
SUSPENSION: front Marzocchi upside down 50 mm fork equipped with adjustable compression and rebound damping and spring preload; wheel travel: 120 mm. rear single-sided swinging arm in aluminium alloy with progressive leverage and a Sachs monoshock equipped with compression and rebound damping (high and low speed damping) and spring preload; wheel travel 120 mm. Engine Brake System for torque control.
WHEELS AND TYRES: aluminium alloy rims; front: 3.50x17"; rear: 6.00x17". Tyres: front 120/70-ZR ", rear 190/55-ZR 17".
BRAKES: front: 320 mm dual floating discs, caliper with six differentiated diameter pistons; rear: 210 mm single disc, caliper with four pistons.
DIMENSIONS AND WEIGHT: wheelbase: 1,408 mm; length: 2,007 mm; width: 685 mm; saddle height: 810 mm; minimum ground clearance: 130 mm; trail: 98:5 mm; declared dry weight: 184 (185) kg.
DECLARED PERFORMANCE: maximum speed: 301 kph.

F4 1000 CORSE
(in brackets the data relating to the 1000 Corse with updated R 312 engine)
ENGINE: four-stroke; four in-line transverse cylinders inclined forwards through 20°; cylinder head in aluminium alloy; block in aluminium alloy with closed deck architecture and cast-in liners with ceramic composite bore plating; aluminium alloy pistons; forged steel con-rods; aluminium alloy crankcase; forged steel one-piece crankshaft on six main bearings. Displacement: 998 cc; bore and stroke: 76x55 mm; compression ratio: 13:1; maximum power: 174 (183) hp at 11,900 (12,400) rpm; maximum torque 11.3 (11.5) kgm at 10,000 rpm. Four radial (2°) valves per cylinder inclined at 22° and directly actuated via bucket tappets by two overhead camshafts driven off the crankshaft by a central chain. Valve diameters: intake: 29 mm; exhaust: 25 mm. Tolerances: intake: +/- 0.15-0.20; exhaust: +/- 0.20-0.25. Valvegear diagram: intake aperture: 12° before TDC; intake closure: 42° after BDC; exhaust aperture: 30° before BDC; exhaust closure: 10° after TDC. Valve lift: intake: 8.5 mm; exhaust: 7.5 mm.
FUEL SYSTEM: Weber-Marelli 5SM multipoint integrated electronic fuel injection and ignition.
IGNITION: electronic inductive discharge.
COOLING: liquid with oil cooler.
LUBRICATION: wet sump with lobed oil pump. Oil capacity and type: SAE 15w-50 with filter, 3.5 kg.
PRIMARY TRANSMISSION: straight cut gears, ratio: 50:79.
CLUTCH: hydraulically actuated, multiple plates in oil bath.
GEARBOX: extractable cassette-type with six speeds and constant mesh gears. Pedal actuation, with single lever on the left. Ratios: First = 13/38; second = 14/31; third = 18/32; fourth = 20/30; fifth = 22/29; sixth = 19/23.
SECONDARY TRANSMISSION: chain; ratio: 15:40.
ELECTRICAL SYSTEM: 12 V, 12 V/9Ah battery, 650W alternator at 5,000 rpm.
FRAME: combination of chrome-molybdenum steel tubes and aluminium alloy swinging arm pivot sections.
SUSPENSION: front Marzocchi upside down 50 mm fork equipped with adjustable compression and rebound damping and spring preload; wheel travel: 120 mm. rear single-sided swinging arm in aluminium alloy with progressive leverage and a Sachs monoshock equipped with compression and rebound damping (high and low speed damping) and spring preload; wheel travel 120 mm.
WHEELS AND TYRES: aluminium alloy rims; front: 3.50x17"; rear: 6.00x17". Tyres: front 120/70-ZR ", rear 190/55-ZR 17".
BRAKES: front: 320 mm dual floating discs, caliper with six differentiated diameter pistons; rear: 210 mm single disc, caliper with four pistons.
DIMENSIONS AND WEIGHT: wheelbase: 1,414 mm; length: 2,026 mm; width: 820 mm; saddle height: 805 mm; minimum ground clearance: 135 mm; trail: 101.5 mm; declared dry weight: 192 kg.
DECLARED PERFORMANCE: maximum speed: 301 kph (Over 300 kph).

F4 1000 VELTRO STRADA
(in brackets the data relating to the 1000 Veltro Pista)
ENGINE: four-stroke; four in-line transverse cylinders inclined forwards through 20°; cylinder head in aluminium alloy; block in aluminium alloy with closed deck architecture and cast-in liners with ceramic composite bore plating; aluminium alloy pistons; forged steel con-rods; aluminium alloy crankcase; forged steel one-piece crankshaft on six main bearings. Displacement: 998 cc; bore and stroke: 76x55 mm; compression ratio: 13:1; maximum power: 177 (185) hp at 12,000 (12,100) rpm; maximum torque: 11.9 (12.3) at 9,000 rpm. Four radial (2°) valves per cylinder inclined at 22° and directly actuated via bucket tappets by two overhead camshafts driven off the crankshaft by a central chain. Valve diameters: intake: 29 mm; exhaust: 25 mm. Tolerances: intake: +/- 0.15-0.20; exhaust: +/- 0.20-0.25. Valvegear diagram: intake aperture: 12° before TDC; intake closure: 42° after BDC; exhaust aperture: 30° before BDC; exhaust closure: 10° after TDC. Valve lift: intake: 8.5 mm; exhaust: 7.5 mm.
FUEL SYSTEM: Weber-Marelli 5SM multipoint integrated electronic fuel injection and ignition. 46 mm throttle bodies. Torque Shift System with variable geometry intake tracts.
IGNITION: electronic inductive discharge.
COOLING: liquid with oil cooler.
LUBRICATION: wet sump with lobed oil pump. Oil capacity and type: SAE 15w-50 with filter, 3.5 kg.
PRIMARY TRANSMISSION: straight cut gears, ratio: 50:79.
CLUTCH: hydraulically actuated, multiple plates in oil bath.
GEARBOX: extractable cassette-type with six speeds and constant mesh gears. Pedal actuation, with single lever on the left. Ratios: First = 13/38; second = 16/34; third = 18/32; fourth = 20/30; fifth = 22/29; sixth = 21/25.
SECONDARY TRANSMISSION: chain; ratio: 15:40.
ELECTRICAL SYSTEM: 12 V, 12 V/9Ah battery, 650W alternator at 5,000 rpm.
FRAME: combination of chrome-molybdenum steel tubes and aluminium alloy swinging arm pivot sections.
SUSPENSION: front Marzocchi upside down 50 mm fork equipped with adjustable compression and rebound damping and spring preload; wheel travel: 120 mm. rear single-sided swinging arm in aluminium alloy with progressive leverage and a Sachs monoshock equipped with compression and rebound damping (high and low speed damping) and spring preload; wheel travel 120 mm.
WHEELS AND TYRES: aluminium alloy rims; front: 3.50x17"; rear: 6.00x17". Tyres: front: 120/70 ZR 17" (R 17 NHS Tubeless), rear 190/55-ZR 17" (R 17 NHS Tubeless).
BRAKES: front: Brembo Racing 320 mm dual floating discs with Brembo Racing monobloc radial caliper; rear: Brembo Racing 210 (218) mm single disc, caliper with four pistons (Brembo Racing caliper with four pistons).
DIMENSIONS AND WEIGHT: wheelbase: 1,414 mm; length: 2,026 mm; width: 820 mm; saddle height: 805 mm; minimum ground clearance: 135 mm; trail: 101:5 mm; declared dry weight: 170 (159) kg.
DECLARED PERFORMANCE: maximum speed: 307 kph.

F4 1000 R
(in brackets the data relating to the 1000 R 1+1)

ENGINE: four-stroke; four in-line transverse cylinders inclined forwards through 20°; cylinder head in aluminium alloy; block in aluminium alloy with closed deck architecture and cast-in liners with ceramic composite bore plating; aluminium alloy pistons; forged steel con-rods; aluminium alloy crankcase; forged steel one-piece crankshaft on six main bearings. Displacement: 998 cc; bore and stroke: 76x55 mm; compression ratio: 13:1; maximum power: 174 hp at 11,900 rpm; maximum torque 11.3 kgm at 10,000 rpm. Four radial (2°) valves per cylinder inclined at 22° and directly actuated via bucket tappets by two overhead camshafts driven off the crankshaft by a central chain. Valve diameters: intake: 29 mm; exhaust: 25 mm. Tolerances: intake: +/- 0.15-0.20; exhaust: +/- 0.20-0.25. Valvegear diagram: intake aperture: 12° before TDC; intake closure: 42° after BDC; exhaust aperture: 30° before BDC; exhaust closure: 10° after TDC. Valve lift: intake: 8.5 mm; exhaust: 7.5 mm.
FUEL SYSTEM: Weber-Marelli 5SM multipoint integrated electronic fuel injection and ignition. 46 mm throttle bodies. Torque Shift System with variable geometry intake tracts.
IGNITION: electronic inductive discharge.
COOLING: liquid with oil cooler.
LUBRICATION: wet sump with lobed oil pump. Oil capacity and type: SAE 15w-50 with filter, 3.5 kg.
PRIMARY TRANSMISSION: straight cut gears, ratio: 50:79.
CLUTCH: hydraulically actuated, multiple plates in oil bath.
GEARBOX: extractable cassette-type with six speeds and constant mesh gears. Pedal actuation, with single lever on the left. Ratios: First = 13/38; second = 16/34; third = 18/32; fourth = 20/30; fifth = 22/29; sixth = 19/23.
SECONDARY TRANSMISSION: chain; ratio: 15:40.
ELECTRICAL SYSTEM: 12 V, batteria 12 V/8,6 A, alternatore 350W a 5000 giri.
FRAME: combination of chrome-molybdenum steel tubes and aluminium alloy swinging arm pivot sections.
SUSPENSION: front: Marzocchi upside down 50 mm fork equipped with adjustable compression and rebound damping and spring preload; wheel travel: 120 mm. Rear: single-sided swinging arm in aluminium alloy with progressive leverage and a Sachs monoshock equipped with compression and rebound damping (high and low speed damping) and spring preload; wheel travel 120 mm.
WHEELS AND TYRES: aluminium alloy rims; front: 3.50x17"; rear: 6.00x17". Tyres: Pirelli Dragon Supercorsa Pro or Pirelli GP Racer: front 120/70-ZR ", rear 190/55-ZR 17".
BRAKES: front: 320 mm dual floating discs, caliper with six differentiated diameter pistons; rear: 210 mm single disc, caliper with four pistons.
DIMENSIONS AND WEIGHT: wheelbase: 1,408 mm; length: 2,007 mm; width: 685 mm; saddle height: 810 mm; minimum ground clearance: 130 mm; trail: 103:8 mm; declared dry weight: 192 (193) kg.
DECLARED PERFORMANCE: maximum speed: 301 kph.

F4 CC
ENGINE: four-stroke; four in-line transverse cylinders inclined forwards through 20°; cylinder head in aluminium alloy; block in aluminium alloy with closed deck architecture and cast-in liners with ceramic composite bore plating; aluminium alloy pistons; forged steel con-rods; aluminium alloy crankcase; forged steel one-piece crankshaft on six main bearings. Displacement: 1078.37 cc; bore and stroke: 79x55 mm; compression ratio: 13:1; maximum power: 200 hp at 12,200 rpm; maximum torque 12.75 kgm at 9,000 rpm. Four radial (2°) valves per cylinder inclined at 22° and directly actuated via bucket tappets by two overhead camshafts driven off the crankshaft by a central chain. Valve diameters: intake: 29 mm; exhaust: 25 mm. Tolerances: intake: 0.15-0.20; exhaust: 0.20-0.25. Valvegear diagram: intake aperture: 12° before TDC; intake closure: 42° after BDC; exhaust aperture: 30° before BDC; exhaust closure: 10° after TDC.
FUEL SYSTEM: Weber-Marelli 5SM multipoint integrated electronic fuel injection and ignition. Torque Shift System with variable geometry intake tracts. 46 mm throttle bodies.
IGNITION: electronic inductive discharge.
COOLING: liquid with oil cooler.
LUBRICATION: wet sump with lobed oil pump. Oil capacity and type: SAE 15w-50 with filter, 3.5 kg.
PRIMARY TRANSMISSION: straight cut gears, ratio: 50/79.
CLUTCH: hydraulically actuated, multiple plates in oil bath.
GEARBOX: extractable cassette-type with six speeds and constant mesh gears. Pedal actuation, with single lever on the left. Ratios: First = 13/38; second = 16/34; third = 18/32; fourth = 20/30; fifth = 22/29; sixth = 21/25.
SECONDARY TRANSMISSION: chain; ratio: 15:39.
ELECTRICAL SYSTEM: 12 V, 12 V/9Ah battery, 365W alternator at 6,000 rpm.
FRAME: combination of chrome-molybdenum steel tubes and cast magnesium swinging arm pivot sections.
SUSPENSION: front Marzocchi upside down 50 mm fork equipped with adjustable compression and rebound damping and spring preload; wheel travel: 129 mm. rear single-sided swinging arm in magnesium alloy with progressive leverage and a Sachs monoshock equipped with compression and rebound damping (high and low speed damping) and spring preload; wheel travel 120 mm.
WHEELS AND TYRES: forged aluminium alloy rims; front: 3.50x17"; rear: 6.00x17". Tyres: front 120/70-ZR ", rear 190/55-ZR 17".
BRAKES: front: Brembo Racing 320 mm dual floating discs, with Brembo Racing monobloc radial caliper with four pistons; rear: 210 mm single disc, caliper with four pistons.
DIMENSIONS AND WEIGHT: wheelbase: 1,408 mm; length: 2,007 mm; width: 685 mm; saddle height: 810 mm; minimum ground clearance: 130 mm; trail: 103:8 mm; declared dry weight: 187 kg.
DECLARED PERFORMANCE: maximum speed: 315 kph.

F4 R 312
(in brackets the data relating to the R 312 1+1)

ENGINE: four-stroke; four in-line transverse cylinders inclined forwards through 20°; cylinder head in aluminium alloy; block in aluminium alloy with closed deck architecture and cast-in liners with ceramic composite bore plating; aluminium alloy pistons; forged steel con-rods; aluminium alloy crankcase; forged steel one-piece crankshaft on six main bearings. Displacement: 998 cc; bore and stroke: 76x55 mm; compression ratio: 13:1; maximum power: 183 hp at 12,400 rpm; maximum torque 11.5 kgm at 10,000 rpm. Four radial (2°) valves per cylinder inclined at 22° and directly actuated via bucket tappets by two overhead camshafts driven off the crankshaft by a central chain. Valve diameters: intake: 29 mm; exhaust: 25 mm. Tolerances: intake: 0.15-0.20; exhaust: 0.20-0.25. Valvegear diagram: intake aperture: 12° before TDC; intake closure: 42° after BDC; exhaust aperture: 30° before BDC; exhaust closure: 10° after TDC.
FUEL SYSTEM: Weber-Marelli 5SM sequentially phased multipoint integrated electronic fuel injection and ignition. 46 mm throttle bodies.
IGNITION: electronic inductive discharge.
COOLING: liquid with oil cooler.
LUBRICATION: wet sump with lobed oil pump. Oil capacity and type: SAE 15w-50 with filter, 3.5 kg.
PRIMARY TRANSMISSION: straight cut gears, ratio: 50/79.
CLUTCH: hydraulically actuated, multiple plates in oil bath.
GEARBOX: extractable cassette-type with six speeds and constant mesh gears. Pedal actuation, with single lever on the left. Ratios: First = 13/38; second = 16/34; third = 18/32; fourth = 20/30; fifth = 22/29; sixth = 21/25.
SECONDARY TRANSMISSION: chain; ratio: 15:40.
ELECTRICAL SYSTEM: 12 V, 12 V/9Ah battery, 650W alternator at 5,000 rpm.
FRAME: combination of chrome-molybdenum steel tubes and aluminium alloy swinging arm pivot sections.
SUSPENSION: front Marzocchi upside down 50 mm fork equipped with adjustable compression and rebound damping and spring preload; wheel travel: 129 mm. rear single-sided swinging arm in magnesium alloy with progressive leverage and a Sachs monoshock equipped with compression and rebound damping (high and low speed damping) and spring preload; wheel travel 120 mm.
WHEELS AND TYRES: forged aluminium alloy rims; front: 3.50x17"; rear: 6.00x17". Tyres: front 120/70-ZR ", rear 190/55-ZR 17".
BRAKES: front: 320 mm dual floating discs, caliper with four pistons; rear: 210 mm single disc, caliper with four pistons.
DIMENSIONS AND WEIGHT: wheelbase: 1,408 mm; length: 2,007 mm; width: 685 mm; saddle height: 810 mm; minimum ground clearance: 130 mm; trail: 103:8 mm; declared dry weight: 192 (193) kg.
DECLARED PERFORMANCE: maximum speed: 312 kph.

F4 1078 RR 312

(in brackets the data relating to the 1078 RR 1+1)

ENGINE: four-stroke; four in-line transverse cylinders inclined forwards through 20°; cylinder head in aluminium alloy; block in aluminium alloy with closed deck architecture and cast-in liners with ceramic composite bore plating; aluminium alloy pistons; forged steel con-rods; aluminium alloy crankcase; forged steel one-piece crankshaft on six main bearings. Displacement: 1078.37 cc; bore and stroke: 79x55 mm; compression ratio: 13.1:1; maximum power: 190 hp at 12,200 rpm; maximum torque:12.4 kgm at 8,200 rpm. Four radial valves per cylinder inclined at 22° and directly actuated via bucket tappets by two overhead camshafts driven off the crankshaft by a central chain. Valve diameters: intake: 29 mm; exhaust: 25 mm. Tolerances: intake: 0.15-0.20; exhaust: 0.20-0.25. Valvegear diagram: intake aperture: 12° before TDC; intake closure: 42° after BDC; exhaust aperture: 30° before BDC; exhaust closure: 10° after TDC.
FUEL SYSTEM: Weber-Marelli 5SM sequentially phased multipoint integrated electronic fuel injection and ignition. 46 mm throttle bodies.
IGNITION: electronic inductive discharge.
COOLING: liquid with oil cooler.
LUBRICATION: wet sump with lobed oil pump. Oil capacity and type: SAE 15w-50 with filter, 3.5 kg.
PRIMARY TRANSMISSION: straight cut gears, ratio: 50:79.
CLUTCH: hydraulically actuated, multiple plates in oil bath.
GEARBOX: extractable cassette-type with six speeds and constant mesh gears. Pedal actuation, with single lever on the left. Ratios: First = 14/37; second = 16/33; third = 18/31; fourth = 20/30; fifth = 22/29; sixth = 21/25.
SECONDARY TRANSMISSION: chain; ratio: 15:40.
ELECTRICAL SYSTEM: 12 V, 12 V/9Ah battery, 650W alternator at 5,000 rpm.
FRAME: combination of chrome-molybdenum steel tubes and aluminium alloy swinging arm pivot sections.
SUSPENSION: front: upside down 50 mm fork equipped with adjustable compression and rebound damping and spring preload; wheel travel: 130 mm. Rear: single-sided swinging arm in aluminium alloy with progressive leverage and a Sachs monoshock equipped with compression and rebound damping (high and low speed damping) and spring preload; wheel travel 120 mm.
WHEELS AND TYRES: aluminium alloy rims; front: 3.50x17"; rear: 6.00x17". Tyres: front 120/70-ZR ", rear forged 190/50-ZR 17".
BRAKES: front: 320 mm dual floating discs, monobloc radial caliper with four pistons; rear: 210 mm single disc, caliper with four pistons.
DIMENSIONS AND WEIGHT: wheelbase: 1,408 mm; length: 2,007 mm; width: 685 mm; saddle height: 810 mm; minimum ground clearance: 130 mm; trail: 103:8 mm; declared dry weight: 192 (193) kg.
DECLARED PERFORMANCE: maximum speed: over 300 kph.

F4 1000 2010

ENGINE: four-stroke; four in-line transverse cylinders inclined forwards through 20°; cylinder head in aluminium alloy; block in aluminium alloy with closed deck architecture and cast-in liners with ceramic composite bore plating; aluminium alloy pistons; forged steel con-rods; aluminium alloy crankcase; forged steel one-piece crankshaft on six main bearings. Displacement: 998 cc; bore and stroke: 76x55 mm; compression ratio: 13.1:1 maximum power: 186 hp at 12,900 rpm; maximum torque:11.4 kgm at 9,500 rpm. Four radial valves per cylinder inclined at 22° and directly actuated via bucket tappets by two overhead camshafts driven off the crankshaft by a central chain. Valve diameters: intake: 29 mm; exhaust: 25 mm. Tolerances: intake: 0.15-0.20; exhaust: 0.20-0.25. Valvegear diagram: intake aperture: 12° before TDC; intake closure: 42° after BDC; exhaust aperture: 30° before BDC; exhaust closure: 10° after TDC.
FUEL SYSTEM: Magneti-Marelli IAW 7BM sequentially phased multipoint integrated electronic fuel injection and ignition. Torque Shift System with variable geometry intake tracts. 46 mm throttle bodies.
IGNITION: electronic inductive discharge.
COOLING: liquid with separate oil cooler.
LUBRICATION: wet sump with lobed oil pump. Oil capacity and type: SAE 15w-50 with filter, 3.5 kg.
PRIMARY TRANSMISSION: straight cut gears, ratio: 50:79.
CLUTCH: hydraulically actuated, multiple plates in oil bath.
GEARBOX: extractable cassette-type with six speeds and constant mesh gears. Pedal actuation, with single lever on the left. Ratios: First = 13/38; second = 16/34; third = 18/32; fourth = 20/30; fifth = 22/29; sixth = 19/23.
SECONDARY TRANSMISSION: chain; ratio: 15:41.
ELECTRICAL SYSTEM: 12 V, 12 V/9Ah battery, 350W alternator at 5,000 rpm.
FRAME: combination of chrome-molybdenum steel tubes and aluminium alloy swinging arm pivot sections.
SUSPENSION: front: upside down 50 mm fork equipped with adjustable compression and rebound damping and spring preload; wheel travel: 120 mm. Rear: single-sided swinging arm in aluminium alloy with progressive leverage and a Sachs monoshock equipped with compression and rebound damping (high and low speed damping) and spring preload; wheel travel 120 mm.
WHEELS AND TYRES: aluminium alloy rims; front: 3.50x17"; rear: 6.00x17". Tyres: front: 120/70-ZR 17" M/C; rear: 190/55-ZR 17" M/C.
BRAKES: front: 320 mm dual floating discs, monobloc radial caliper with four pistons; rear: 210 mm single disc, caliper with four pistons.
DIMENSIONS AND WEIGHT: wheelbase: 1,414 mm; length: 2,026 mm; width: 820 mm; saddle height: 805 mm; minimum ground clearance: 135 mm; trail: 101:5 mm; declared dry weight: 192,5 kg.
DECLARED PERFORMANCE: maximum speed: 305 kph.

F4 RR CORSACORTA

ENGINE: four-stroke; four in-line transverse cylinders inclined forwards through 20°; cylinder head in aluminium alloy; block in aluminium alloy with closed deck architecture and cast-in liners with nickel-carborundum bore plating; aluminium alloy pistons; forged steel con-rods; aluminium alloy crankcase; forged steel one-piece crankshaft on six main bearings. Displacement: 998 cc (bore and stroke 79x50,9 mm), compression ratio: 13,4:1, maximum power: 201 hp at 13,400 rpm, maximum torque: 11.4 kgm at 9,200 rpm. Four valves per cylinder inclined at 22° and directly actuated via bucket tappets by two overhead camshafts driven off the crankshaft by a central chain. Valve diameters: intake: 31.8 mm; exhaust: 26 mm.
FUEL SYSTEM: Magneti Marelli IAW 7BM multipoint integrated electronic fuel injection and ignition. Mikuni throttle bodies. Fuel tank: 17 lt.
IGNITION: electronic inductive discharge.
COOLING: liquid and oil with separate radiators.
LUBRICATION: wet sump.
PRIMARY TRANSMISSION: straight-cut gears.
CLUTCH: multiple plates in oil bath with slipper system.
GEARBOX: extractable cassette-type with six speeds and constant mesh gears. Pedal actuation, on the left. Ratios: First = 14/37, second = 16/33, third = 18/31, fourth = 20/30, fifth = 22/29, sixth = 21/25.
SECONDARY TRANSMISSION: chain, ratio 15/41.
ELECTRICAL SYSTEM: 12 V, battery 12 V/9 A, alternator 350W at 5000 rpm.
FRAME: combination of chrome-molybdenum steel tubes and aluminium alloy swinging arm pivot sections.
SUSPENSION: fully adjustable Öhlins front fork, wheel travel: 120 mm. Progressive leverage rear, with fully adjustable Öhlins damper, wheel travel: 120 mm.
WHEELS AND TYRES: forged aluminium rims, front 3,50x17" and rear 6,00x17". Tyres: front 120/70-ZR17M/C, rear 190/55-ZR17M/C.
BRAKES: front Brembo twin floating 320 mm discs with four-pot radial monobloc calliper; rear single 210 mm disc with four-pot calliper.
DIMENSIONS AND WEIGHT: wheelbase 1430 mm, length 2100 mm, width 750 mm; saddle height 830 mm; trail 100.4 mm, declared dry weight 192 kg.
DECLARED PERFORMANCE: maximum speed: 298 kph.

ADDRESS BOOK:
MUSEUM,
REGISTER, CLUBS AND COLLECTIONS

MV Agusta Motor spa
via G. Macchi 144, 21100 Schiranna (Varese)
tel. 0332 254111
www.mvagusta.it

CRC-Centro ricerche Cagiva
via Ovella 35, 47893 Borgo Maggiore (San Marino)
tel. 0549 903976

Agusta Museum Foundation
(Open on Sundays from 9.30 to 12.30
and from 14.00 to 18.00, on Tuesdays
and Wednesday from 14.00 to 18.00.
For groups of more than 10 people different times
and days may be booked by calling during
the normal opening hours).
via Giovanni Agusta 510, 21017 Cascina Costa
di Samarate (Varese)
tel. 0331 220545
fax 0331 222807
www.museoagusta.it
info@museoagusta.it

MV Agusta Virtual Museum
www.mvagusta.it/museovirtuale

**MV Agusta Historic Register (in association with
the Italian Motorcycling Federation)**
c/o ricamificio Dama
via Montesanto 5, 21017 Gallarate (Varese)
tel. 0331 795586
fax 0331 772525

Collezione Ubaldo Elli
(visits by appointment)
via Palermo 36, 21052 Busto Arsizio (Varese)
tel. 0331 639441
serena.elle@elly.it

**Elaborazioni MV Agusta
di Arturo e Giovanni Magni**
www.magni.it
(with pages dedicated to the Factory Club
MV Agusta, the Moto Club Internazionale
MV Agusta, the Agusta Museum
and the MV Agusta Historic Register).

Classic MV Agusta-The bike Museum
www.thebikemuseum.com

MV Agusta Club America
box 185, Wiscasset, Maine 04578, USA

Moto Club Internazionale MV Agusta
c/o Bar Ristorante da Mario
via Cascina Costa 2, 21017 Samarate (Varese)
tel. 0331 220030

MV Agusta Factory Club, Italia
www.mvagusta.it/it/factory-club/factory-club

MV Agusta Forum
(in English)
www.mvagusta.net

MV Agusta Club Deutschland e.V.
Dieselstraße 123, 47608 Geldern, DE
www.mv-agusta-club.de

MV Agusta Club France
www.mvagustaclubdefrance.com

MV Agusta Club Nederland
M. Hobbemastraat 23, 2902 GL Capelle aan de Ysel, NL

MV Agusta Club Oesterreich
www.boku.ac.at/chemie/oc/staff/ah/mvagusta.html

MV Agusta Club Schweiz
Zwinglistrasse 8, 4127 Birsfelden, CH
www.mv-agusta-club-schweiz.ch

MV Agusta Online
(in German and English)
www.mvagusta-online.de

MV Agusta Owners Club Benelux
www.mvocb.nl

MV Agusta Swiss Racing Team
Baselstrasse 55, 4147 Aesch, CH
www.mv-agusta-swiss-racing-team.ch

MV Agusta Owners Club GB Limited
7 West Drive, Doveridge, Ashbourne,
Derbyshire DE6 5NG, UK
www.mvownersclub.co.uk

INDEX OF NAMES

INDEX OF BRANDS AND MODELS

BIBLIOGRAPHY

MV comes of age, Motorcycles Sport ed. (1970-1971)

Gruppo lavoratori anziani MV Agusta,
Guida al Museo della tecnica e del lavoro MV Agusta,
Agusta ed. (1977)

R. Bacon, *Foreign racing motorcycles*,
Haynes ed. (1979)

P. Carrick, *The story of MV Agusta motorcycles*,
Stephens ed. (1979)

Champion of champions, Orbis ed. (1979)

G. Borgeson, *The classic twin-cam engine*,
Dalton Watson ed. (1981)

J. Clew, *MV Agusta 750 S America and other 750/850
fours*, Haynes ed. (1983)

E. Ferdinandsson, *MV Agusta Italy 4/4 dohc history
1945-1979*, Ferdinandsson ed. (1984)

C. Spahn, *MV Agusta: technik und geschichte der renn
motorräder*, Serag ed. (1986)

M. Walker, *MV Agusta, all production road
and racing Motorcycles*, Osprey ed. (1987)

M. Colombo e R. Patrignani, *Moto MV Agusta*,
Giorgio Nada ed. (1987-2006)

S. Colombo, *Gilera quattro*,
Automototecnica ed. (1994)

E. Restelli, *Le moto della provincia di Varese*,
L.V.G. ed. (1997)

G. Sarti, *Bimota-25 anni di eccellenza*,
Giorgio Nada ed. (1999)

M. Walker, *MV Agusta fours-The complete Story*,
The Crowood Press ed. (2000)

F. Spairano, *Etica e management*,
Franco Angeli ed. (2001)

E. Restelli, *Le motociclette MV Agusta*,
GLA Agusta ed. (2002)

Cycle
Cycle World
La Gazzetta dello Sport
Il Pilota Moto
In Moto
La Manovella
La Moto
Legend Bike
Milano Finanza
Motociclismo
Motociclismo d'Epoca
Motor Cycle News
Motor Cycle Sport
Motorcyclist
Motorrad Classic
Motosport
Motosprint
Moto Storiche e d'Epoca
Moto Tecnica
The Motor Cycle
Two Wheels

AUTHOR'S ACKNOWLEDGEMENTS

It would not have been possible to produce this book without the help of many friends, some of whom are no longer with us today. Thanks to all of them.

Giacomo Agostini
Martino Bianchi
Paolo Bianchi
Giuseppe Bocchi
Gianfranco Bonera
Luigi Botta
Ferdinando Cassese
Claudio Castiglioni
Giovanni Castiglioni
Massimo Clarke
Ginetto Clerici
Gigi De Martini
Enrico D'Onofrio
Ubaldo Elli
Piero Ferrari
Roberto Godone
Andrea Goggi
Fortunato Libanori

Arturo Magni
Giovanni Magni
Mauro Marelli
Umberto Masetti
Ruggero Mazza
Andrea Mazzali
Angelo Menani
Francesco Milo
Peppino Minervi
Giuseppe Morri
Adrian Morton
Moto Club Internazionale
 MV Agusta
Museo Agusta
Fabio Orlandi
Gian Pio Ottone
Alberto Pagani
Nello Pagani

Roberto Patrignani
Carlo Perelli
Giovanni Petronio
Phil Read
Registro storico MV Agusta
Carlo Remor
Alessia Riboni
Franco e Mario Rossi
Mario Rossi
Giuliano e Roberto Segoni
Gigi Soldano
Andrea Tamburini
Massimo Tamburini
Prisca Taruffi
Emanuele Toccaceli
Daniele Torresan
Carlo Ubbiali
Sansai Zappini

PICTURE CREDITS

ALKA DESIGN (COURTESY) 225r
ARCHIVIO GIORGIO NADA 27ul, 27cl, 29dl, 29ur, 31ur, 31cr, 41dr, 53u, 57ul, 59ul, 59ur, 59d, 63u, 69dl, 71u, 71dr, 111(2,3), 226l, 226c
MASSIMO CLARKE 57dl
COLLEZIONE ELLI (COURTESY) 45ul, 45uc, 45ur
© **FARABOLAFOTO** 65
FEBUR (COURTESY) 224
ARCHIVIO FERRARI ENGINEERING (COURTESY) 87 (1-3), 91(1,2,4)
FONDAZIONE MUSEO AGUSTA (COURTESY) 21, 23ul, 23ur, 23d, 27dl, 27r, 29ul, 29cl, 29dr, 31ul, 31dl, 31dr, 33ul, 33cl, 33ur, 33dr, 34l, 34ur, 34cr, 37u, 37dl, 37dc, 37dr, 39ul, 39dl, 39ur, 39dr, 41ul, 41dl, 41ur, 41cr, 43ul, 43ur, 43d, 45cl, 45cr, 45dl, 45dc, 45dr, 48u, 48dl, 51c, 51ur, 53cr, 55, 56, 57r, 63dl, 67, 69ul, 69ur, 69dr, 71dl, 73u, 73dl, 73dc, 73dr,

75dl, 226d, 227l
FOTO GIOVARA, GALLARATE 33dl
OTTO GRIZZI 61d, 63dr, 75u, 75dr, 79, 99(2)
IOANNONI CORSE (COURTESY) 225l
GIOVANNI PETRONIO 110, 112-113, 128u, 128d, 186l, 187, 188-193(1-32), 227c
FRATELLI ROSSI (COURTESY) 77dl, 77dr
FRATELLI SEGONI (COURTESY) 77ur
GIGI SOLDANO 204, 206-207, 208-209, 210(1-4), 211, 212-213, 213ur, 214-215
MAGNI (COURTESY) 77ul, 77uc, 77cr
MOTOCORSE (COURTESY) 225c
MV AGUSTA MOTOR S.P.A. E CRC (COURTESY) 2, 5, 6, 8 12-13, 14, 16-17, 46, 47, 48dr, 83, 85(1-4), 87(4) 89(1-3), 91(3), 93, 95 (1-7), 97 (1-7), 98, 99(1,3-5), 101, 103, 105 (1-6), 107 (1-5), 109, 111(4), 115(1-3), 117(1-3), 119(1-5), 120-121(1-5), 123,

125, 127(1-3), 129ul, 129cl, 129dl, 129ur, 129dr, 131(1-3), 133, 135(1-4), 137(1-4), 139(1-5), 141(1-3), 143(1-4), 145, 146u, 146d, 147(1-9), 149(1-3), 151(1-5), 153(1-7), 155(1-4), 157(1-5), 159(1-9), 161(1-3), 163, 164u, 164d, 165(1-7), 167(1-5), 169(1-8), 171(1-9), 173(1-7), 175(1-6), 176-177(1-8), 178-179, 181(1-7), 183(1-9), 184u, 184d, 185(1-7), 186r, 194, 195, 197 (1-3), 199 (1-4), 201 (1-7), 203, 216, 217, 218, 221u, 221dc, 221dr, 223u, 223dc, 223dr, 227r, 228l, 228c, 228r, 229l, 229c, 229r, 230l, 230c, 230r, 231l, 231c, 231r, 232l, 232c, 233, 234
OLYCOM: © **PUBLIFOTO** 25c, 25ur, 35, 61ul, 61ur
RENOVATIO GARAGE (COURTESY) 225u
CESARE RESTA 53dl, 53dr
SANSAI ZAPPINI 18-19, 80-81, 129cl, 129cr, 213cr, 213dr